RETURN TO JAPAN

By Elizabeth Gray Vining:

RETURN TO JAPAN
THE VIRGINIA EXILES
WINDOWS FOR THE CROWN PRINCE
FRIEND OF LIFE:
THE BIOGRAPHY OF RUFUS M. JONES

RETURN
TO
JAPAN

BY

ELIZABETH GRAY VINING

J. B. LIPPINCOTT COMPANY

PHILADELPHIA AND NEW YORK

The poem on page 145 is reprinted by kind permission of William S. Lord, executor of the estate of Curtis Hidden Page.

To

MY FRIENDS

SHINZO AND TOMI KOIZUMI

CONTENTS

CONTENTS

RETURN TO JAPAN

1

The Way Back

AFTER seven years I was on my way back to Japan, where from 1946 to 1950 I had served as tutor to the Crown Prince. Near me in the big plane cleaving its way through the dark between San Francisco and Honolulu slept some of the major figures of modern American letters: John Steinbeck, John Dos Passos, John Hersey, Elmer Rice. John Brooks and Lewis Galantiere were on board too, and Casimir Wierzynski, an exiled Polish novelist. We were all on our way to Tokyo to the Congress of the International P.E.N.

This was not the way I had expected to return to Japan, but then little that I have ever done in connection with that country has followed any foreseeable pattern. When I left Tokyo on the first of December, 1950, many of my friends had said to me, "You must come back for the Crown Prince's wedding." The Crown Prince, however, was now twenty-three and in spite of newspaper rumors and speculations, no wedding was in sight. When the opportunity came to attend the P.E.N. congress in Tokyo during the first week of September, 1957, and to stay on afterwards to renew my friendships in Japan, I accepted it eagerly.

The P.E.N. club was started three years after the First World War by John Galsworthy, at the instigation of a Cornish writer, Catherine Dawson Scott, who had it firmly in her mind that if the writers of the world could meet for the friendly exchange of ideas, they might be a force for peace. Galsworthy enlisted the help of Bernard Shaw and of Anatole France, and the first international congress was held in London in 1923. The initials of its name stand for poet (also playwright), essayist (and editor) and novelist. There are now fifty-four centers all over the world. The twenty-ninth congress in 1957 was the first to be held in the Orient and for that reason seemed to be a particularly significant one.

During the past seven years I had written three books, had traveled widely in the United States and made a brief excursion into Canada, had been twice to Europe. I had bought a little house, more than a century old, in a suburb of Philadelphia, and to it had come many of the Japanese friends to whom I had said good-by so sorrowfully in 1950, wondering if I should ever see them again. Even the Crown Prince himself had turned up on my doorstep! In 1953, on his way home from the coronation of Queen Elizabeth II, he had spent three days with my sister and me in Mt. Airy. Through letters and Christmas cards, messages and gifts, I had been in close touch with those of my friends who had not left Japan during these years. Now as I shot through the night in the throbbing plane, I had a sense of homecoming. My mind went back to a vivid moment in which one of those rare, fleeting, yet lasting experiences of the mind and heart had taken place.

One sultry July day in 1948, when I had been in Japan nearly two years, I was on my way to Koganei, where the Crown Prince then had his house. It was about a forty-minute drive from my home and the last third of the way lay along the Omeikaido, a famous old road going out of Tokyo to the northeast. For a few lovely miles it passed between rows of great trees that met overhead, through farming villages untouched by the spreading deadly smear of the city.

Always, before that moment, looking at the Japanese land-

scape, appreciating its beauty, interested in what it told me
about the Japanese people, I had been a stranger, seeing it from
without. That day, that moment, suddenly, as if a glass door
had slid open before me, I entered wholly into this land and I
took it into my heart. Rolling quietly along the dusty, shady
road in the brooding summer heat, I heard skylarks overhead,
saw splotches of bright sun on the brown road, bamboo trees decorated with poems and bright paper streamers for the Star Festival, the ice-candy man with his blue wooden box and bell, women
with big straw hats and baggy cotton trousers picking tea; little
houses open all the way through, so that beyond a pool of dim
indoor light I saw sun-baked yards and glossy-leaved camellia
bushes; half-naked children playing at the side of the road; grain
drying on straw mats; girls in dark blue uniforms fanning themselves as they came from school. These were the same things I
passed, going and coming, three times a week, but now I felt and
saw them freshly, yet with a deep feeling of recognition. From
that moment I lived differently in Japan, a sojourner but no
longer a stranger.

The congress had already started when I actually reached
Tokyo on Sunday evening, September first. My illustrious fellow
travelers were at the opening reception given by the Japanese
Center at Chinzanso, a large and beautiful garden. I had stayed
over in Honolulu for twenty-four hours to rest and catch my
breath.

So it was that when I emerged into the warm moist night air
at Haneda Airport, only old and dear friends were there to greet
me. The first person whom I saw, labeled with a round badge
which admitted her beyond the barrier, was Tané Takahashi, who
had been my secretary and interpreter and much loved "little
sister" during my years in Japan. She had spent a good part of
the intervening time in Philadelphia, acquiring a degree in library
science at Drexel Institute and working in the Bryn Mawr College library; new she was acting librarian of the new Interna-

tional Christian University in the outskirts of Tokyo. In the excitement and confusion of arrival she was like a little shining pool of happiness and serenity.

Among the reporters and photographers who ran along beside us with their flash bulbs and questions—"What are your impressions of Tokyo since your return?" "Why do you think English is so difficult a language for the Japanese?"—was one of my former students, a boy in the Crown Prince's class, who was now a proud member of Kyodo, the Associated Press of Japan. A few days later he would come to interview me at the Imperial Hotel. "Now I am a reporter," he would say, with an engaging smile. "Excuse me to ask you rude questions." And, when the interview was over, "Now I am your student again."

After the formalities of customs I could meet those others who were waiting on the floor above, Dr. Shinzo Koizumi, the Crown Prince's chief councilor, with whom, or rather under whom I had worked so happily, and his flower-like wife; Mr. Katsunoshin Yamanashi, who had been my earliest guide and adviser in Japan; Michiko Fusejima and Masako Inoue, who had been part of my household; Mr. Jutatsu Kuroki, one of the Crown Prince's chamberlains, who came to represent him, and several more of my Peers' School students.

Throughout the ride from Haneda to the Imperial Hotel, the changes in Japan kept pressing in on me. Everything I saw, from the handsome new airport to the street in front of the hotel torn up for the new subway, showed me that Tokyo was expanding and prospering. I had left a country still occupied and only just beginning to pick itself up after devastating defeat. What had been built, up to the end of 1950, had been built in wood, occasionally plastered over to look like concrete. There had been a few bright new taxis for Western visitors, but shabby, wood-burning cabs still snorted and smoked through the streets. Restaurants had been few, expensive and poor. The stores had just begun to sell yard goods and leather shoes to Japanese. Foreigners did most of their shopping in curio shops and mail-order catalogues.

Now I saw new concrete buildings on every side; the streets were jammed with cars and thousands of taxis darted with hooting horns and screeching brakes through the moving maze. As I was to learn during the days that followed, there were countless attractive restaurants with every kind of cuisine, French, Chinese, Hungarian, Italian, coffee shops where you could sit all afternoon over a cup of excellent coffee, listening to music either live or recorded, and in the department stores enchanting things from all over the world were to be bought. There were new theaters handsomer and more modern than any that I knew at home. People on the streets were well dressed and well shod; they looked cheerful and purposeful, as if once more they were aware of having a future. The greatest difference that I saw, and the greatest relief, was the disappearance of Occupation personnel. Though it was, taken as a whole, probably the most benign occupation in history, it had the defects inherent in military occupations. And even as an American in Japan I had felt oppressed by the presence of soldiers barring the way to all the most desirable facilities.

The congress officially opened on Monday morning with a ceremony and speeches. Buses took us from our various hotels to the Sankei Kaikan, a new building amply provided with the most modern of lecture halls, conference rooms and lounges. On the stage were flags of the twenty-seven countries represented and the most interesting personalities of the week began to emerge.

Yasunari Kawabata, the president of the Japanese Center, was easily the most colorful and appealing figure there. A wisp of a man in his late fifties, he had a great shock of gray hair, enormous eyes, a big sensitive mouth and pointed chin. He was rumored to be extremely shy, and the effect of his personality was somewhat that of a deer emerging tentatively from deep woods, ready to disappear in a single bound at a sudden noise or movement, but he conducted meetings and made speeches with skill and ease and I soon decided that his shyness was only part of his legend. Two of his novels, *Snow Country* and *The Thousand Cranes*, have been translated into English. They are strange, beautiful, sensitive—and very interesting—books. André Chamson, novelist, and curator of the Musée du Petit Palais, was the president of the International P.E.N. and the leader of the French delegation, which, with forty members, was the largest one there. They had flown all together from Paris in a chartered plane. John Steinbeck, of all the writers present, aroused the most general excitement. As a famous writer and as a personality he stood out. If Mr. Kawabata was a deer, Mr. Steinbeck was a grizzly bear, soft-hearted but powerful and possibly dangerous. At the end of the opening ceremony, after several addresses had pushed the hour close to lunchtime, he delivered a twelve-line speech, modest, simple and sincere. One heard it praised afterward on every side. It was unfortunately his last appearance at the congress, for the next day he came down with Asian flu, and was not seen again until, white and shaky, he was about to depart for home.

The pattern for the next five days was now set. Every morning and every afternoon a literary session was held in the big conference room of the Sankei Hall, where earphones at every seat and a battery of interpreters' boxes high on one wall made it possible to conduct the proceedings simultaneously in English, French and Japanese. At each session from five to fifteen people spoke on the general theme of "The Literatures of the East and West and Their Reciprocal Influence."

It was my first P.E.N. congress, indeed, my first international conference of any kind. I found in it a surge of understanding and friendship across national boundaries and even a unity of spirit not perfunctory but fresh and urgent. To the poet, Stephen Spender, however (another outstanding figure, with his mop of yellow hair and tall good looks, his gift for vigorous and stimulating speech), who was a veteran in such conferences and who has satirized them in his novelette, *Engaged in Writing*, the talk of unity was "soup." Our duty as writers, he insisted, was to see differences rather than likenesses. "Artists are sensuous beings who should be conscious of the fact that although belonging to one humanity they are distinct."

The most courageous words spoken at the gatherings were those of the Polish poet, Antoni Slominski. When he talked of human brotherhood it was not "soup"; he coupled it with the necessity for freedom, and the danger to him that one saw shadowing his words gave them sharp substance. Tall, thin, gray, infinitely sad, he said,

"The Communism of Stalin created many myths. Recent times have seen life itself and personal freedom dependent on the sentence of a powerful deity and on the whim of a galaxy of vindictive demons. We have no certainty that that era will not be repeated. How, then, shall we give battle to such resurgent demons? Apt here is the well-known answer of Confucius to disciples who questioned him concerning the role of deities and demons: 'Have as little to do with them as possible. First, study how you may live with your fellow men in peace, justice and love.' When asked what he would do first for the people, he replied, 'Feed and enrich them.' 'What next?' He replied, 'Educate them.' "

Perhaps the most moving thing said was said by the Chinese writer from Hong Kong, Shui Chieng-Tung, a novelist, short-story writer and teacher; a statement which seemed to me to arise out of the spirit of unity and understanding which I felt to be strongly present in the conference. After speaking of the debt which Chinese writers owed to the writers of Japan for handing Western literature on to them, he pointed out that Japan had also cherished and preserved the ancient Chinese literature. "The day will come," he said, "when Chinese writers will feel the need to get back some of their old literary legacy; they will have no alternative but to do so through the writers of Japan. War and politics must not blind us to this truth: Japan has always been the faithful torch-bearer, caretaker and true lover of Chinese literature. I am grateful. I am also grateful to the present P.E.N. congress for making me realize this fact, and I speak it as a truth in the most appropriate moment, in a most appropriate place, before a most appropriate audience."

It was frequently said—and often deplored—that the influences were scarcely "reciprocal," that the literature of the West had had far more effect on that of the East than vice versa. Along with this went a discussion of the character of East and West and the differences between them. The writers of Asia were more interested in this aspect of the subject and more articulate about it. The drift of their opinion was that the old categories of material West and spiritual East no longer hold true, that there has been a passing back and forth of technology and philosophy that has brought the two together in a new way.

"Eastern literature today is superficially more interested in material values than in the spiritual," said Mr. Srinivasa Iyenagar, an Indian professor and critic, "while some Westerners at least—Eliot, Faulkner, Mauriac, to give a few names—are more keenly conscious of the spiritual malady that is at the heart of human ills."

Mr. Alisjahbana, an Indonesian with a round and merry face, a pioneer of modern Indonesian literature, a philosopher and a member of Parliament, who looked like the pictures of the winds with puffed-out cheeks on seventeenth-century maps, went further: "The gap or the cleavage between East and West goes through every country in the world, even through every one of us."

Between literary sessions, at lunch, at dinner, in the evening, we were gloriously entertained by our hosts. Japanese hospitality is compounded of infinite care and exuberant energy, of imagination, of unbounded generosity, and of gaiety. The foreign minister gave a reception, the minister of education gave a luncheon, there was a special performance of a Noh play, the best seats in the house were reserved for us for the regular evening performance of Kabuki, the governor of Tokyo gave a buffet supper and entertainment in beautiful Kiyozumi Park.

After a lavish meal of lobster, cold chicken and salads, we sat in the garden beside a pond and watched Japanese dances, both formal, classic dances with fans and parasols and stylized movements of the hands, and gay earthy lively folk dances. After the dark closed in, there was a brilliant display of fireworks, set pieces elaborate and ingenious, showers of sparkles, golden rain, fountains of dazzling color, all reflected in the still water. Between numbers we walked along winding paths under twisted pine trees and stopped at little booths set up as if it were a country fair, where all kinds of odd and delicious things to eat were offered to us.

The last evening the Japanese Center gave a formal farewell banquet. It must all have been extremely expensive, and writers as a group are not affluent. I was interested, and touched, to learn later where the money came from not only for the parties, but for the buses, the use of the hall, the translaters, typists, printed reports and all the rest. The government contributed, and the banks and business houses. When that still was not enough, Mr. Kawabata went on the air and appealed to the people, and the people—day laborers, school children, patients in tuberculosis sanatoriums,—responded. It is not difficult to get money in the United States to help people suffering from floods, earthquakes, fires, or other disasters, but how much response would you get from school children and truck drivers if you asked for money to entertain a crowd of writers?

On Saturday morning those who had not been in Japan before went on to Kyoto and Nara for two more days of sightseeing and banquets; the rest scattered. I stayed on in Tokyo. The Imperial Family had returned the day before from holidays in Nasu and

Karuizawa; I would go to the Crown Prince's house and to the Palace, would meet again former students and friends, would travel in western Honshu, seeing Japan this time not as an employee of the Imperial Household, nor yet quite as a tourist, but as a visitor. Eighteen months later I was to come again to Japan for the Crown Prince's wedding.

Of these two visits and of memories which they awoke of my earlier four years there, is this book made.

2

The Crown Prince Grown Up

ALL through the week of the congress a typhoon threatened and the air was heavy, wet and warm. Now and then a sultry wind blew furiously or a bucket of hot water poured down abruptly from the sky, to rise again in the form of steam. By Saturday evening the typhoon was reported to have "gone round," but clouds still blanketed the city.

The bellboy who came to tell me that my car had come was bright with interest, and the doorman opened the door for me as if he knew—and he probably did—where I was going. The car was a big black Mercedes-Benz, so new that it still smelled new, and the driver, Sato San, was one of the Imperial Household's best and most dependable chauffeurs. Mr. Usami, the grand steward, had put car and driver at my disposal for as long as I should be in Tokyo.

It was perhaps a fifteen-minute drive to Tokiwamatsu, the section of the city where the Crown Prince lived. In the dark the streets all looked alike, until suddenly we made a turn that was familiar, off a main road into a side lane where black trees rose above high walls. Sato San switched on the light inside the car and two policemen at a gate sprang to attention and saluted. We circled round a paved courtyard and came under a porte-cochere from the left-hand side.

The big door stood open, and smiling on the steps were two

menservants who had been in the Crown Prince's household ever
since I had first known it, Suzuki San, small, active and elderly,
with bright eyes and a gray moustache, and Oshitani San, who in
spite of his receding hairline still looked young and slightly
chubby. We greeted one another warmly, and I noticed in passing that they wore handsome new livery, another sign of prosperity, for in the days after the war even the Imperial Household
had been hard put to it to get clothes and shoes for its employees.

Around the side of the standing gold screen that faced the
door came Mr. Toda to welcome me. He was one of the Crown
Prince's chamberlains whom I knew best; he and Mr. Kuroki
had been with the Prince in the United States. He is a tall, fine-
looking man, no longer boyish, as he was when I first knew him.
He would be, the Crown Prince told me once, the feudal lord
of Matsumoto, if feudal lords still existed. He led me up the wide
staircase to the sitting room where the Crown Prince was waiting, and after announcing me he withdrew.

The Prince, slim and handsome in white dinner jacket, smiling
gravely, shook hands with me, said he was glad to see me and
offered me a chair. I had been invited to come early, so that we
might have a little time alone together before the rest of the
guests arrived, and I was grateful, for after four years of separation a certain stiffness creeps into first meetings and it takes a
little while to limber up. The last time I had seen him was in
1953, when I said good-by to him in the Boston airport. After his
visit to Philadelphia I had traveled for a week with him and his
suite to New York and Boston. As we now exchanged the usual
conventional questions and observations about our summers and
our travels, and he opened the little gift I had brought him, I
looked to see what changes the years had wrought.

He was more mature, I thought, more at ease, but otherwise I
could see no difference in him. His glance was as direct as ever,
his manner as simple and natural, his smile brought the same
sudden light into his face. One of his classmates at the Peers'

School had written a much-discussed novel about him called *The Lonely Man,* and I thought of that now and wondered. The Crown Prince as a young boy had indeed seemed lonely to me, living as he did in a house of his own, separated from his family and even from his brother who was only two years his junior, and seeing his classmates seldom outside of school hours. As he grew older, however, and could make more of his own decisions, he saw his friends more freely. His summer vacations in Karuizawa were, I knew, times when he drove his own car, played in tennis tournaments, visited his friends' homes and gave parties at his own. But there was, of course, an isolation inherent in his position, and whether he realized it or not, it must have weighed on his spirits. Only a wife, I thought, who was truly a companion, could share and lift that burden of responsibility which the Crown Prince carried and which, except at times when he completely lost himslf in some absorbing interest, sport, or friendly exchange, made him a little more sober, a little less light-hearted than the average young man of his age. A group of his advisers had been working for several years upon the search for a suitable wife for him, but so far nothing had come of their labors. That he had within the last month met and played tennis with Michiko Shoda had been noted only by himself and no doubt Miss Shoda.

In a short time the court photographer came in to take pictures of our first meeting for the newspapers and then we went downstairs to dinner. The other guests meanwhile had assembled in the drawing room below. They were those whom I knew best about the Court: Mr. Takeshi Usami, the present grand steward, Mr. Michiji Tajima, who was grand steward when I was there; Mr. Takanobu Mitani, the Emperor's grand chamberlain, Dr. Yoshishige Abe, who was head of the Peers' School or Gakushuin, as it is now called, Mr. Yamanashi, Dr. Koizumi, and their wives, and Mrs. Matsudaira, who was on the Crown Prince's council and who gave me much help and support when I first came to Japan. "Just be yourself," she used to say when I asked her about court etiquette, and, "Well, never mind!" when I worried about some hurdle that loomed ahead.

After orange juice or sherry in the drawing room we went into the big dining room where the long table was beautifully and formally set. The Crown Prince sat in the middle of the table with Mrs. Matsudaira across from him. I was on his right and Dr. Koizumi next to me.

As the delicious courses came on, I was touched to see that Nemoto San, the Crown Prince's chef, had remembered the things I liked best. He had reason to know what they were, for in the old days, when the Crown Prince was away or staying in the school dormitory, I used to be able to borrow his chef occasionally for a special dinner party. He had a particularly delicious way of cooking chicken in wine, and he made a steamed fruit pudding that was lighter than air.

The conversation flickered in a lively way over the P.E.N. meetings and personalities, modern Japanese novels, changes in the Japanese language (Prince Akihito takes a knowledgeable interest in his language and its history), Kabuki, *Around the World in Eighty Days,* which was then packing full the newest and biggest movie theater in Tokyo, skiing, tennis in Karuizawa, and so on. I saw the Crown Prince taking part easily, directing remarks to people who might otherwise have remained too long silent, introducing new topics when the old ones flagged, and my mind went back to the first dinner party he had given to foreign guests. He was just sixteen and the guests of honor were Edmund Blunden, poet and cultural adviser in the British Embassy, and his wife, who were about to leave Japan after two years' service there. Dr. Koizumi and I had talked the party over in advance with the young host, and rehearsed him in his responsibilities; we held ourselves ready on the evening to fill any gaps and supply any help that might be needed, and we exchanged jubilant congratulations afterwards when everything had gone off beautifully and our Prince had passed his first social test with honors. He had come a long way since then.

Early the next week I saw him again, this time with his family, when the Emperor and Empress invited me to dinner at the Palace. All of the Imperial children were there, and I had some talk with them as we waited in the big drawing room in the Imperial Household Building for Their Majesties to appear. Mr. and Mrs. Higashikuni (Princess Shigeko) and Mrs. Takatsukasa (Princess Kazuko) came in together. Mr. Takatsukasa was away on business connected with the Railroad Museum, of which he is a curator. Princess Atsuko, now Mrs. Ikeda, had come up from her home in Okayama for the anniversary of their grandmother's death the day before. A schoolgirl when I had last seen her, she was now a very attractive young matron living a life as different as could be imagined from the formal and restricted existence behind the moat in which she had grown up. Prince Masahito was in his final year at Gakushuin University, where he was specializing in chemistry. Rather delicate as a child, he was now sturdy and strong; he had an earnest, open and cordial manner. Princess Takako, the baby of the family, was at eighteen the tallest of them all, slender and lovely in a full-skirted blue taffeta evening dress. She had graduated from the Peeresses' School (Joshi Gakushuin) the spring before and resisting attempts to send her to a girls' finishing school she had entered the freshman class of coeducational Gakushuin University to take the English literature course. They all turned toward the Crown Prince, as if he were the leader and favorite among them.

While we stood chattering, Their Majesties came into the room unnoticed. Suddenly they were there. The Emperor welcomed me kindly, the Empress, with whom I had already had an audience three days before, smilingly. Tonight she was wearing a kimono patterned with wild flowers of Nasu, bellflowers, lilies, bush-clover, and I was told that she had painted it herself. Mr. Mitani, Mrs. Takaki, the Empress's interpreter and my old friend, and

Mrs. Hoshina, the chief lady-in-waiting, completed the party.

Once again I felt, as so often before, a sense of amazement at being so informally and naturally with this family. Beyond the formal—and literally palatial—room, beyond the wall and the moat, was Tokyo, to most of whose citizens the Imperial Family were almost as much of a mystery as they were to my own fellow countrymen eight thousand miles away. Yet behind the barriers, physical, traditional and psychological, were warm, natural and lovable people, a united family who took delight in being together. I felt again that my own presence was a welcome excuse for a gathering that could be only occasional in the rigid structure of their lives.

After dinner Mr. Mitani and the two ladies-in-waiting withdrew to one side of the room, leaving the rest of us together in a circle to talk in a haphazard but comfortable mixture of Japanese and English. The Empress motioned me to sit beside her on the sofa, and with much laughter and many appeals to the Crown Prince for assistance with English words, we all exchanged news of the past seven years, while the Emperor sat a little apart, as was his wont, and beamed benevolently upon the scene.

Before I left Japan, five weeks later, Their Majesties gave another party for me, this time an informal one at the Kaintei, the little pavilion deep within the Palace grounds which they used for their family gatherings. My friend Esther Rhoads, the representative of the American Friends Service Committee in Japan, who had succeeded me in teaching English to the Crown Prince for several years and who was still giving an English lesson once a week to the Empress, was also invited, and we were warned to wear "rough" clothes, for it would be a kind of picnic and part of the dinner would be cooked out of doors. Feeling that an imperial "cook-out" would still retain elements of formality, we wore silk daytime dresses and street pumps.

I have always loved going to Kaintei at night. As "my" Mercedes-Benz approached the big gate, Sakashita Mon, Sato San signaled by switching the headlights on and off; the high wooden doors swung open and policemen saluted. At intervals along the driveway within the walls, policemen waved us on with lighted paper lanterns. We turned off the main road, which went from Sakashita Mon through to Inui Mon, on the far side of the 247-acre tract, on to a narrower one along a high wall that enclosed the Fukiage garden, where there were, I knew, trees and paths, a waterfall and a tea house. Again we turned, between the pillars of another gateway, and a moment later drew up before the Kaintei. We found Mr. Mitani and Mrs. Takaki already there.

A few minutes later the Imperial Family arrived, the Empress wearing a blue kimono flecked with gold, and a pale obi. It was a gay and lively evening, with many small jokes and much laughter as we moved from the dining room out onto the terrace and back again. The cook-out part of the meal was a "Jenghis Khan" held in the open air.

This is a Mongolian way of cooking lamb reputed to have been brought by Jenghis Khan to Korea in the thirteenth century and from Korea to Japan. A charcoal fire is built in a special kind of grill, over which small pieces of tender lamb which have been dipped in a complicated and delicious sauce are broiled by the diners themselves. The sauce is compounded of soya sauce, lemon, ginger, curry, nuts, and another ingredient which I have forgotten. Each of us had chopsticks and a saucer and we went ahead on our own, though two white-coated chefs with tall hats were there to assist the process. Just beyond the terrace was a little pond where the wind rustled the reeds and a small old stone lantern was reflected in the dark water; overhead were tall black trees and the star-strewn sky.

We returned to the dining room for the rest of the meal, and in the drawing room afterwards we had tea and cakes. At a signal Mrs. Takaki and Mrs. Hoshina arose like dancers and came back with lacquer trays of gifts. Imperial gifts are always presented open on trays, are admired and thanked for, and then taken away to be wrapped up and put in one's car.

Her Majesty had herself painted for us white scarves with the wild flowers of Nasu, blue bellflowers for me, wild pinks for Esther Rhoads, and violets for me to take to my sister, Violet. There was also a dress length of printed silk chiffon for me, and other lovely farewell gifts from the young people. Princess Takako had painted roses and violets on white china coffee cups that were big enough for a really satisfying cup of morning coffee.

When the chamberlain and ladies-in-waiting had gone to see these things suitably wrapped, the Emperor was ready to say good-by—and no one was at hand to interpret. All heads were turned expectantly toward the Crown Prince. He laughed and said teasingly to his younger sister, "You're the English major! Here's your chance." To which she replied spiritedly that he had been abroad and his English was better. Everybody laughed.

The Crown Prince then, seriously and with dignity, acted as his father's interpreter, standing a little to one side, translating first from Japanese into English and then from English into Japanese. He made only one departure from strict accuracy, perhaps out of boyish diffidence. He delivered as "I wish you a good trip" what in the Emperor's words had been, "I pray for your safe return home."

Though I have seen the Crown Prince often alone in his lessons, in school with the other boys, and with his family, I have had very few opportunities to see him in public, when he appears before his people in his role of Crown Prince. For that reason I was especially pleased when Dr. Koizumi suggested that I accompany him to a rally of Four-H clubs at which Prince Akihito would appear.

It was a beautiful day in late September. Fuji had retired in a blue haze, but the ranges of the Hakone mountains to the west and the Chichibus to the northeast were clear against the sky. When Dr. Koizumi and I reached the prefectural building in a small village in Saitama, the large hall was already filled with farm boys and girls from all over Japan, and the program which was going forward on the platform had reached item five. Our arrival to take the front seats reserved for us was obviously regarded as a sign that the Crown Prince, who had spent the morning inspecting a tea plantation and a stock-farm, would be coming any moment.

A sudden tremor ran through the room, heads were turned, breaths were caught, and on a wave of excitement everybody stood up. A gleaming black limousine with the Imperial chrysanthemum on the side and a flag up front wheeled up to the door of the hall, and the Prince, looking very trim in his cream-colored summer suit, got out followed by the governor of the prefecture. The Prince stopped to shake hands with me on his way to the place saved for him.

The program then continued. Two fresh-faced young girls in *mompei* (the baggy cotton trousers worn by farm women) with clean cotton towels tied around their heads, demonstrated how to grow mushrooms on logs, and a boy discoursed learnedly, with charts, on kidney disease in chickens. The Crown Prince listened attentively with an air of interest. He was next conducted (with a long trail of officials and visitors following him) to an adjoining building, where he made the round of exhibits and charts. I noticed that he had learned not only to look but to ask questions and make comments.

After that we all adjourned to a nearby field, where several hundred boys and girls waited to perform calisthenics for him. He stood behind a small table and the governor took up a respectful position behind him. I was pleased to see how naturally Prince Akihito turned to speak to the governor and brought him up to stand beside him. From time to time as the young people spread over the field like dots on a chart bent and rose and wheeled, the Prince and the governor exchanged comments.

I have often thought that people appear to their best advantage when they are absorbed in doing their own jobs and doing them well. A young mother spooning cereal into a bird-mouthed toddler, a captain on the bridge of a ship, a scientist in his laboratory, all have an especial appeal in direct proportion to the degree of their self-forgetfulness. The Crown Prince of Japan giving his entire attention to a routine royal chore was no exception.

In all, during those six weeks in 1957, I was with the Crown Prince eight times. The last time, which was the final one of the four parties that he himself gave for me, was the happiest of them all. It was the one which he had arranged and planned in detail himself, and into which he entered most completely.

Dressed in "sport-wearing," as we had been advised, we went to the Imperial villa at Hayama on Sagami Bay on a sunny October morning two days before I was to leave: Esther Rhoads, Dr. Koizumi and I. The other two guests, classmates of the Prince's, were already there.

When we emerged from the grove of pines that veils the villa from the shore and went out on a little rocky point, two boats were waiting, a largish police launch and the Crown Prince's own small boat, which was new, built especially for an outboard motor imported from the United States. A little cluster of passers-by had gathered to watch our departure, and there was the usual milling about of hosts, guests, chamberlains, bodyguards and Palace servants before such an expedition. Prince Akihito installed me in the bow of his boat, on a gay embroidered silk cushion, and then sat down beside me. There was a boatman in the stern, and a chamberlain stepped forward to fill the last place. The Crown Prince waved him back and called his brother, who hopped in nimbly. The boatman started the motor and we were off with a wide swing and a circling wake. The fourteen others piled into the police boat and set out apace after us.

The light mist with which the day had begun disappeared as the patches of blue sky spread and merged. Fuji floated faintly above the Hakone mountains across the bay and on the jagged little hills along the near shore dark pines, golden ricefields and half-concealed temple roofs showed clearly. Fishing boats scattered over the water went on with their business and here and there we saw a fish's scales flash briefly in the sunlight as somebody made a catch. We followed the coastline past Zushi and Morito. Kamakura, strategic spot in the days of civil war long ago, came into sight on its long point, cut off from the land behind by cliffs and mountains. We reached the bare little rocky island of Najima in about twenty minutes. This was one of the places where the Emperor goes to collect specimens, but all we saw scuttling away from our feet as we climbed on shore were some hermit crabs.

There was nothing on the island but a large red torii—the two upright posts with a cross-piece characteristic of entrances to Shinto shrines. Where was the shrine to which this torii belonged? When the rest of the party joined us various theories were offered: that the shrine was in Morito across the water; that the whole island itself was a shrine; that the shrine was in the sea. The Crown Prince realistically remarked that the torii was probably only an advertisement to attract visitors to the island. It made a satisfactory frame for a photograph, however, and many a snapshot was taken, while the menservants spread straw mats on a flat place and put out the lunch boxes.

At each place were two plastic boxes containing chicken galantine, glazed ham, cold salmon in a sort of white aspic, decorated with a tiny fish cut from a carrot, and slices of roast beef sealed in a gelatine of its own juice, potato salad, little rolls, and big green grapes. On top of the boxes, protecting them from the sun, were big linen napkins and heavy silver knives and forks. From thermos bottles came fruit juice and cold tea to drink.

The lighthearted talk as we sat on the mats in the sun and light breeze, three older people and four young men, with Mr. Uryu, the vice-grand steward, midway between, dealt in both

Japanese and English with reminiscences of schooldays and more recent experiences, touched on flying saucers, classmates abroad, fishing, and ways of smoking salmon.

After lunch we explored the island, which was in two parts linked by a stone bridge. The highest rocks took a bit of scrambling and both princes were very gallant with helping hands.

Returning to the mainland and the villa, the Crown Prince ran his new boat himself, missing some submerged rocks with skill and pulling up to the landing in fine style. Those minutes in the boat were for me pure bliss: the fresh salt air in my face, the sun on my head, the sea and the mountains all around, and the joy of being with this boy whom I loved, seeing him happy with his new boat, his friends, and the untrammeled day.

3

The Empress Dowager

THERE is one inevitable sadness in returning to a country after an absence of seven years. Some of one's friends are no longer there to greet one. When I went back to Japan in 1957 I could not see again Prince Chichibu, the Emperor's younger brother, who with his lovely wife had been so kind and charming to me in Gotemba, Miss Michi Kawai, Bryn Mawr graduate and founder of Keisen Girls' School, Mrs. Motoko Hani, of "Freedom School," Mr. Koichi Nomura, the Crown Prince's gentle grand chamberlain, or the Empress Dowager, his grandmother.

Though she had "retired" from the world after the death of the Emperor Taisho in 1925, she had been still an impressive and influential figure in Japanese life during my four years there. Often she was called by Westerners the Queen Mary of Japan. Small, erect and immensely dignified, she wore always a black silk dress, floor length, made in the style of the Nineties, with a V-neck and a black lace inset and high collar, a diamond and platinum brooch or a rope of pearls, a small black toque, if she was out, and white kid gloves, at home or abroad. A person of warmth and humor, she had a keen mind and many interests; she was equally famous for being a lively talker and a good listener. Never informal, she still knew how to put people at their ease, and she never allowed herself to be hampered by the arrangements of her chamberlains and ladies-in-waiting; it was she, not they, who determined the length of any audience. She took a great interest in sericulture, traveling over Japan to visit research projects and filatures, and she had many charities which she encouraged and supported. The one for which she was best known was the welfare fund for lepers which she had herself established and to which she contributed generously, curtailing her own expenses in order to do so. It might have been written of her, as Lady Murasaki wrote of an imagined eleventh-century empress: "She was devout but unlike many religious persons she did not display her piety by impressive benefactions paid for out of funds which other people had collected. Her charities (and they were considerable) were made at the expense of her own exchequer." Between her and her grandson there was a close bond of affection and understanding. The Crown Prince often went to see her; she took a great interest in all his activities and he confided in her freely, as boys will in a grandmother with whom they are in rapport.

Born in 1884, the daughter of Viscount Michitake Kujo, of the Fujiwara family, she belonged to the court nobility but was not a princess "of the blood." Following the old practice, she was sent as a child to live away from her home, but with a difference: she was brought up on a farm, an experience which gave her a lifelong love of the country and an understanding of ordinary people unusual in one of her position. She was chosen as the bride of Crown Prince Yoshihito chiefly because of her brilliant mind and sterling character, though early photographs of her show her to have been pleasing in appearance too.

Her life with the Emperor Taisho, who was for many years an invalid, cannot have been an easy one, but she was a model of faithfulness to his memory, unfailing in the performance of all the ceremonies of respect and devotion. Her real joy must have been in her four sons and in the grandchildren. "She was a wise and thoughtful woman," Dr. Koizumi wrote me, "and a wonderful judge of men. It was natural that many of our leading personages, especially Count Makino and Baron Shidehara, had sought opportunities to talk with her." During the war, the Omiya Palace, where she lived, was bombed and she barely escaped with her life. The house built for her on its site afterwards was necessarily a small, rather makeshift affair.

Her name was Sadako, but I never heard it spoken in Japan. She was always referred to by her title, as indeed all members of the Imperial Family are. The names Hirohito, Nagako, Akihito, are used by foreigners but never by the Japanese. Even his own family does not call the Crown Prince by the name Akihito: to them he is Togu Sama, Eastern Prince. After her sudden death of heart failure in May, 1951, the Empress Dowager was given the posthumous name by which she is now known: Teimei.

The custom of giving a posthumous name dates from the eighth century and like many other customs in Japan is based on earlier Chinese practices. The Emperor himself selected the name, and a complex interrelationship of meanings and associations determined the choice of the two Chinese characters of which it is composed. Mr. Tajima, then grand steward, wrote and explained it to me.

Tei means chastity, which is defined as constancy to one person; it also means righteousness, *sei*. The character for *sei* can also be *sho*, as in Taisho, thus linking Sadako's new name with that of her husband. Through a quotation from the "Shi-fa" of Chou, which is a guide to the selection of posthumous names, *tei* or *sei* can also be linked to the *Sada* of Sadako. *Mei* means enlightenment. In the "Hsi-Tzu," which is ascribed to Confucius, it is written, "Nichigetsu no michi wa *teimei* nari," which means, "The path of the sun and the moon is that of righteousness and enlightenment." This name was bestowed on the Empress Dowager three weeks after her death in a ceremony at the Omiya Palace, called "Rite of Informing her Spirit of the Posthumous Title."

I cherish the memory of my own meetings with the Empress Teimei, which were few but full of meaning for me. I went twice to her home to have tea with her, and both times were occasions of warm happiness and, I felt, real communication between us, even though we spoke through an interpreter. One always felt that she was giving her entire attention to the moment; there were none of the dreamy stares and vague remarks that often betray a hostess's wandering thoughts. She planned her tea parties carefully, choosing the cakes herself and the treasures which she brought out to show. And what was a great joy, of course, to me, she really wanted to talk about her grandson, to ask questions and make comments and suggestions. Besides the other times when I met her more briefly—mostly school programs in which her grandchildren were involved—she sent me messages from time to time, and once when the Crown Prince was coming to my house straight from hers, she sent me by him a fish, beautifully wrapped in ferns, in a bamboo basket. I have the basket still.

One of the things I wanted to do in 1957 was to visit her grave. I knew that she was buried at Tamagorio, the beautiful park in the western suburbs of Tokyo which is devoted to the Emperor Taisho's mausoleum. I had been there several times, casually, just because it was a lovely spot on the way to Fujimi, near Mt. Takao, where we liked to go for picnics and to get a spectacular view of Mt. Fuji. The last time had been on an October day, when the small pond at Tamagorio had reflected the scarlet and gold of maples and a sky of the same blue as the handful of gentians which the guard on duty picked in the woods and presented to me.

The visit on this September morning in 1957 was more formal. Tané and Dr. Koizumi accompanied me, and word of our coming was sent ahead. The day was cloudy and mist drifted through the avenue of tall keiyaki trees through which the car approached

the entrance to the park. We went first to the little office building
to the left of the gate where we were given tea.

The waiting room was like other Imperial waiting rooms I
had known, with chairs about a central table, which was covered
with a familiar silk brocade cloth, patterned with red, blue,
green and yellow squares, each with a modified fleur-de-lys in
the center. This same cloth appears in one of the eighty paintings of the life of the Emperor Meiji in the Meiji Picture Gallery;
the picture immediately preceding it in the series shows for the
first time the Empress Shoken and her ladies wearing Western
dress, and I suppose that the tablecloth with the fleur-de-lys
swept in on the same wave of Western influence as the Paris
gowns. At any rate, things change in the court, but not often,
and I have seen this tablecloth in the waiting rooms of Koganei,
the Imperial Household Building in Tokyo, the Shosoin office in
Nara, the Kyoto Palace, and the Empress Dowager's Omiya
Palace.

With a guard to lead the way, we started up the curving path
to the mausoleum. It was a wide avenue of carefully swept fine
white pebbles, winding between tall, symmetrical cryptomeria
trees. They had been ten-year-old saplings when they were
brought here thirty years before; now they looked timeless.
Walking between their silent columns, we rounded the last curve
and came into a wide plaza facing the hills where the graves were.

After bowing before the Emperor Taisho's tomb we went on
to the Empress Teimei's, which was like her husband's in every
way except that the hill on which it stood was lower and it was
placed lower on the hill, as if to emphasize the wife's lesser importance.

Under a large torii, stone steps mounted a beautifully planted
slope to a severely simple tomb in the shape of a low, round
mound covered with plates of granite, with a large Imperial
chrysanthemum, sixteen-petaled, on its face. Among the evergreens flowering shrubs and trees had been planted so that there

might be beauty in every season, cherry blossoms for April, maple leaves and white sasanqua for November. Now in September crepe myrtle was in bright bloom.

The barrier at the foot of the steps had been removed; in turn we climbed the stairs and standing on a straw mat which had been put there for us, we bowed before the tomb. There was no sound but the twittering of tits in the trees as we performed this little ceremony of remembrance, and in silence we returned to the car between the tall solemn cryptomerias.

I was thinking, as I walked along, about Japanese women. They have been trained from childhood to gentleness, self-effacement and obedience. Before 1947, when the new Constitution swept in and endowed them all at once with the vote, the right to hold property, to get divorces and other benefits, they had practically no legal existence apart from their husbands or fathers. Yet, even more than in matriarchal America, men in Japan are emotionally bound to their mothers, and a Japanese woman of real force of character makes her influence felt far beyond the walls of her home.

4

The Last Samurai

M**R.** YAMANASHI invited me to tea at the Sendai Dormitory, over which he and his wife had been in charge for the past six years.

Most Japanese colleges, especially in Tokyo—and more than half of the colleges and universities in Japan are in Tokyo—do not have campuses as we know them, with dormitories for resident students. The students live at home or with relatives, or they find lodging where they can. A rather small number of the whole stay in dormitories endowed or maintained by individuals or institutions other than the university.

The Sendai Dormitory had an interesting history. It was the descendant of a school which Count Daté, one of the greatest of the feudal lords, established in 1736 to teach Chinese literature and Confucianism. Nearly a century later, seeing the inevitable approach of the West, the authorities introduced the study of the Dutch language, under the impression that it was the universal language of commerce and Western culture. After 1868, when the government of the Restoration came in and the daimyos—feudal lords—yielded up their domains and their power, the school passed through successive changes, ending up in Tokyo as a dormitory for undergraduates from Sendai Prefecture who were studying at any of the universities in Tokyo. Destroyed by fire during World War II, it was rebuilt in 1951, and Mr. Yamanashi was asked to be the director.

"I am over full eighty," he wrote me in 1957, "and my wife is over seventy. To have a glimpse of such simple hard daily life will assist you, I dare say, to have an idea of what belief and conviction we are going on. An ancient ray of older Japan!"

Mr.—formerly Admiral—Katsunoshin Yamanashi belongs to the vanished caste of the samurai, those knightly followers of the daimyos who were forced to commute their hereditary rice allowance into cash when the feudal estates were broken up and who after the first shock went into government service, business or the professions. The samurai virtues of loyalty to the feudal lord, contempt for money, frugality, simplicity, stoicism and pride are still cherished as ideals among their descendants, but there can be few left today who have themselves lived out the philosophy of the samurai as Mr. Yamanashi has done.

He is one of my oldest and truest friends in Japan. He came to see me on my first day there in 1946; from the beginning he gave me support and understanding. Late winter afternoons when he used to come to my house—a small, dignified, erect figure wearing a fur-lined waistcoast—to find out how things were going and to stay for tea and a good talk about history, literature and, always, the Crown Prince, whom he adored, were "cementing" (as Quakers say) times, and since my return home I have looked forward to the days when I received from him a bulky letter, written in his clear, distinguished hand on many sheets of thin paper tied together at one corner with cotton thread.

Over the years through conversation and letters I have learned something about his life. He was born in Sendai, the largest city in northeast Honshu, in what had been the feudal domain of Count Daté. After early schooling there he went to Doshisha High School, in Kyoto, where he came under the influence of Dr. DeForest, the Congregational minister. There were, he told me once, three great influences in his life, the Confucian teaching of his boyhood, the Christianity of Dr. DeForest, and "patient long devotion to Zen Buddhism." After three years at Doshisha, longing to see the world and too poor to travel, he joined the navy.

His first foreign service took him to England, which he loved. The beauty of the countryside, the poetry and the people of England all went straight to his heart, where he has kept them ever since. After the Russo-Japanese War, he was made secretary to the navy minister, and from that time on his work was in offices and conferences rather than at sea.

He spent most of World War I in Russia, though he was in England at the time of the Battle of Jutland and in 1916 he came to the United States on the troopship *St. Paul.* He was in Washington in 1921 with the Japanese delegation to the Conference on the Limitation of Armaments, and went to the Christmas Eve service at the Congregational church. In 1928 he became vice-minister of the navy, but five years later, when the tide of thought and feeling had turned so drastically in Japan, he was forced to retire from the navy altogether on account of his liberal and pro-Anglo-American ideas.

He took up rose gardening, he told me, "after a rare public ordeal preceding my retirement." He would not under any circumstances mention money, but he had evidently had some anxious years. "Sorrows come not in single spies," he quoted. Then in 1939, a few months before the little Crown Prince started to primary school, he was appointed head of the Peers' School.

It was a position of honor and responsibility. In spite of the sorrow of the war, his care for the growing Crown Prince and the association with the older boys brought him deep satisfaction, and the integrity and power of his personality made a profound impression upon the students.

With the end of the war and the Allied occupation of Japan, he who had already been penalized by the Japanese for being too pro-American was now "purged" for having once been vice-minister of the Japanese navy. Before he withdrew from the Peers'

School, however, he had one more job to do: to make the arrangements for the coming of the Crown Prince's American tutor.

He has at different times told me something of what went on behind the scenes before I came, or as he put it, "destiny summoned with her silver wand."

"When the Emperor suggested an American tutor," he said, "we quite agreed in principle, but we saw that the practicalities would be very difficult. His Majesty, being "extremely firm and earnest," they (Mr. Yamanashi and the chamberlains) concurred. Dr. Stoddard, chairman of the American Education mission, sent two names, and the Education Section of G.H.Q. through whom the communication came, refused to indicate their preference in any way. "They were very sagacious and prudent," Mr. Yamanashi commented. The decision was made by consultation with a number of people close to the court, though I gather that the final word was Mr. Yamanashi's, and that after that it was taken to the Emperor, who gave his approval.

Having yielded on the issue of the tutor, Mr. Yamanashi spared no effort to make the Emperor's project a success. He found a pleasant and comfortable house for me—no easy task in ruined Tokyo with the Occupation also seeking suitable houses. It was the more difficult because he had determined that it must be near the Peers' School grounds and his own house there. He was afraid that there might be serious opposition on the part of hotheads to an American tutor so soon after the war, and in case my life should be in danger he wanted to be near enough to come to the rescue!

What was more important to me, he sought and found exactly the right person to be my secretary and interpreter and to live in the house with me, Tané Takahashi, a teacher at Keisen, a member of the Society of Friends, and a most lovable young woman. As I have written elsewhere, when I found that someone had taken the trouble to discover Tané for me, I knew that the

Japanese themselves wanted the experiment to work, and all my apprehensions slipped from my shoulders.

He planned for me, too, my first trip to Kyoto in November of 1946, which gave me a glimpse of an old and beautiful Japan untouched by the war, and again and again he arranged for me to meet people whom he thought I would enjoy or who could help me. The only time that I felt I could not accept a kindness that he wanted to arrange for me—but this was years later—he wrote me a letter understanding and respecting my point of view while reiterating his own, and entitled it, "Sweet and Pleasant Discord between the Most Devoted Friends."

When he undertook the work at the Sendai Dormitory, he wrote me, "New novel destiny is dawning before us and we shall do our best to adapt us for new position innocently and pleasantly as water fits for any vessel."

The dormitory was situated on the grounds of a mansion in Shingawa that had belonged to Count Daté. I had been there twice before the dormitory was built, once when the Empress's lady-in-waiting, Miss Daté, and her brother dressed up in their eleventh-century court robes so that a group of us could see them and take photographs, and once to a Jenghis-Khan party which they gave.

The mansion is now, I think, a hotel, and the dormitory stands near the entrance to the grounds, under the slope of a hill where trees and flowering shrubs from Sendai had been planted. The forty students who live there and attend various colleges are all from Sendai. There were four times as many applicants as there was room for, and the choice was made, Mr. Yamanashi told me, not on the basis of favoritism or connections, but by an examination which he himself composed and which was considered difficult. One year he gave the candidates part of a speech on freedom by Lincoln and had them write an essay on the subject. Another year they were to discuss a passage on Valley Forge and the meaning of the suffering there. He showed me the book from

which he had taken the passages: an American college textbook
of excerpts from writings on United States history; it was carefully covered with a brown paper case, and it was well worn.

Mrs. Yamanashi, gentle and retiring, is the daughter of one of
the earliest diplomats to go from Japan to Europe. Later her
father became governor of Kanagawa Prefecture and with his
wife "was one of the most advanced advocates of the Western
mode of life. But my wife," Mr. Yamanashi continued, "ever since
our marriage always remained as *femme domestique,* not against
her mood, as my official career had been austere and extremely
busy all the time. We have passed through all the sorrows and
reverses of human life, public and private, sometimes feeling one
trying hour to be worth one year's duration."

We had tea in the reception room of the dormitory, where
paintings of Sendai scenes hung on the walls. Among the guests
were the Yamanashis' granddaughter, who went to Friends Girls'
School, Esther Rhoads, and Admiral and Mrs. Zenshiro Hoshina.
Admiral Hoshina, once junior to Mr. Yamanashi in the navy, is
now a member of the Upper House of the Diet.

After tea I was taken on a tour of the dormitory. In the common room, which was also the dining room, several students in
dark trousers and white shirts were reading newspapers and
talking. Out of that room opened the kitchen, dark as most
Japanese kitchens are, with large gas burners, big iron kettles
for rice, with heavy wooden lids, a dark metal sink, and cupboards along the wall. The bath next to it was a big metal
cauldron, where three or four could stew at once, with plenty of
rinsing and splashing room outside. In an adjoining room stood
a bright new electric washing machine, a recent acquisition much
prized by the boys, who did their own laundry.

Upstairs were the twenty bedrooms, in size six mats each (i.e.
nine by twelve feet) all preternaturally neat for our inspection.
Clothes hung on hangers from hooks on the wall, books, shaving
gear and oddments filled high shelves; there were two desks in

each room. The beds, of course, consisted of quilts stowed away in the cupboards during the daytime. Though the rooms were strictly utilitarian, the wide windows looked out over the garden and the roofs of the city to Tokyo Bay beyond, a view lovely enough to be thoroughly distracting.

For their board and lodging and all expenses the students paid thirty-eight hundred yen a month—about ten dollars. They were hard-working boys, Mr. Yamanashi told me, serious and well behaved. The purpose of the dormitory was to encourage the students, first, to seek "the Word," second, to be Sendai people, and third, to be Japanese. But he did not lecture them or preach at them, but let them see how he lived his life. "Deliberation, tolerance and simplicity," he said, "are my guiding motto in attending them."

The Yamanashis themselves occupied a tiny two-room house attached by a covered passageway to the dormitory. The main room had a low square table in the center and books everywhere. Mr. Yamanashi at the time was very much interested in Pocahontas. "One would feel the American history of early age," he said, "to be somewhat lonesome and sterile without such romantic stories." He had read my novel of the American Revolution, *The Virginia Exiles,* most attentively, and his comments on it were some of the most interesting, as well as appreciative, that I received. He pointed out two passages in it that were very close, he said, to Zen Buddhism. One was the passage in which Caleb thinks of "a marriage in which there could be such complete union that one would not know where flesh stopped and spirit began, or even what was man and what was woman." The other was the words of the old Quaker saint, John Hunt: "I have heard with my inward ear and have seen with my inward eye." "But that," I answered, "is straight Quakerism!"

Every morning, he told me, he got up at half past five to work in the garden. This was not so much for the benefit of the garden —though it was in beautiful condition, with not a weed anywhere

—as for the benefit of the students, who might thus see in action his concept of values, and learn self-discipline through example rather than precept.

Since the day of that tea party, he has retired from the dormitory, and he and Mrs. Yamanashi have gone to live a less strenuous life in Yokohama, where no doubt he would say again, as he wrote me in 1950 from Katase, where he was then living, "Now advanced in ages, serene and content, we are satisfied with what we get, not seeking what we can't, are leading simple and peaceful life."

We Americans, like the Japanese, are sensitive to what the outside world is saying about us. Finding ourselves suddenly unpopular in countries where we feel we have been friendly and helpful we are apt to wring our hands and feel betrayed. When people ask me sometimes, Have we a friend left in Japan? I think of what Mr. Yamanashi wrote to me three or four years ago:

"In the last year or two I recognize some kind of apprehensions prevailing among your people about Japanese sentiments toward the United States, which appear not to be so friendly as in the days of occupation. My observation supported by many influential friends is this:

"Immediately after the tragic defeat U.S. appeared to be the greatest, warmest and kindest country to help the desperate situation of Japan. In fact there was no other who could or had the will to do. So that they [the Japanese people] followed, obeyed and were grateful without any reserve. No wonder U.S. was honored and thanked for as the true savior, G.H.Q. its angelic agent. But when time went on and they have recovered from desperate shock, gradually and quite naturally people have begun to examine and analyze the situation more coolly and critically. Like mathematical sine curve reaction coming after action has taken place. At the same time fresh curiosity and interest toward Soviet and Communist China have sprung up fanned by the persistent instigation of unfriendly clique. Yet noisy and blatant party are nowise always majority. Silent and serious thinking people never lose sight of sound political situation and we are all sure no matter how rapprochement with other countries may happen, it would never undermine firm inherent ties between your country and ours, having its deep foundation of vital national interests and common moral sense. Please do keep the present National Policy toward us without wavering or hesitation coming from the temporary passing phenomenon."

5

A Call from the Mikamis

WHEN I heard that the Mikamis had come I hurried downstairs eagerly to meet them. It was almost exactly seven years since we had last met, but when I saw them standing there in the hotel lobby, the father and the daughter, it seemed as if no more than seven days had passed over their heads.

We met this time without Tané, who was busy at her library, and we missed her at once. It was Tané who had brought us together, and Tané who bridged the gap between their reading knowledge of English and my almost non-existent Japanese. Now, with a small dictionary between us, with much effort and laughter, we renewed the friendship which had begun when Tané and I had visited them in Kyushu and which had been kept alive ever since by memories of that exhilarating visit and by intermittent correspondence.

Keiko Mikami, a beautiful girl in her twenties, ardent, vivid and gentle, had been one of Tané's pupils at Keisen School during the war. Her father, Hideyoshi, was a teacher and a writer, a thin, energetic man with deep-set eyes, a rather long nose, a moustache, and slender but determined chin, a man of original ideas and of a wide knowledge of art, literature and history. The mother, who was dead, had been an artist. Just before the end of the war, after her graduation from Keisen, the father and daughter had left Tokyo and had gone to Kyushu, the southern-most of the four islands, to teach in a small school in the tiny hamlet of Hachigamine, which was perched on a mountain fifty miles or more from the city of Hitoyoshi. In this remote spot, surrounded by woodcutters and charcoal burners, they had found an absorbing interest and deep happiness. They liked and admired the rugged, simple folk among whom they had come to live; the only teachers on their mountain, they created a school according to their own ideas and put their dearest theories into practice. The extraordinary natural beauty which lay at their doorstep, the simple yet comely home which they built, the freedom from conventionality they enjoyed and the friendship they won from the mountain people, all made their life there an idyll, especially against the contrast of Tokyo, beleaguered and destroyed. Letters and books kept them from intellectual isolation, and once a month they walked down the long mountain trail to Iino, a logging village, where they got a train to Hitoyoshi. There they spent a night in comfort and elegance at the Nabeya Inn and satisfied their need for conversation with their own kind. Keiko by the time she was twenty had written and published a book about their mountain school which had attracted a good deal of favorable attention.

They had invited us to visit them and their school in 1950, and in October Tané and I boarded a third-class train from Hakata. After we crossed the border into Kumamoto Ken, a prefectural official, Mr. Takagi, came on the train and informed us that he had been sent by the governor to escort us to Hitoyoshi, that a prefectural car had been sent ahead for our use there, and that a plain-clothes policeman, whom he introduced, would be with us everywhere for our protection. These attentions, which rather overwhelmed us, were due to the fact that this trip was a sort of farewell present to me from the Emperor and Empress, and the Imperial Household had alerted the local officials all along the route.

Up and up the train wound along the Kuma River, which rushed, twisting and foaming over rocks, between the steep flanks of sharp, pointed mountains. On the station platform at Hitoyoshi the Mikamis waited for us, with the stationmaster, dignified in navy blue uniform and white gloves, Mr. Tomita, the innkeeper, who was also chief of the Town Councilors, and sundry others.

After a sightseeing tour of the city and an excellent sukiyaki dinner, we sat late discussing plans for the following day, into which Mr. Mikami hoped to crowd all that he thought we ought to see. He had invited us to stay four days, but since this was impossible, he was fitting together, like pieces of a jig-saw puzzle, the things that he could not bear to have us miss. Afterwards I realized what a prodigious effort of planning and coordination it all took, the number of people who had to be asked to cooperate, and the complicated time schedule which must be met, but that evening I was aware only of the joy of anticipation, not of the work and strain that had preceded it. Even the service of "purification" performed when we visited the Aoi shrine by a tall priest in billowing white and pale blue robes and a high black lacquered silk headdress and which I was told was to ensure a safe journey the next day had seemed to me only a colorful experience, not a serious precaution.

We started off at seven the next morning, Tané and I and the Mikamis in the prefectural Buick, Mr. Takagi, our policeman and a town official following in a miniature green truck. We were going to drive to Iino over the Kirishima range of mountains since there was no morning train.

The city, old, busy, provincial and handsome, was soon out of sight as we climbed steadily up the mountain on a narrow, steep and winding dirt road, through thick forests which opened now and then on a tiny field fitted into the slope like a rock in a wall, or a sudden view of distant peaks. "That's my mountain over there," Keiko would say, and each time, as the road twisted, it seemed to be in a different place. Sometimes she said, "My mountain is hidden now." When we admired a view, she would exclaim, "Oh but the view from my mountain is still prettier!"

After an hour or so the road began to deteriorate. At intervals we had to stop to move boulders out of the way or fill in gaping holes with stones. Once we even borrowed a bundle of firewood from a farmer's roadside pile, when the supply of loose stones gave out. Presently the road was no more than a track and the rock outcroppings were so high and sharp that I was afraid of scraping a hole in the crankcase. Soon we had to get out and walk for quite long stretches where the road was so steep that the car could not pull a full load or so tilted toward a thousand-foot drop that the driver became nervous. And when a Japanese driver becomes nervous, then you know the situation is really acute!

When we came at length to the top of the Kakuta Pass, a vast new view opened out before us: a wide valley floor far below patterned with tiny fields and looped with the silver ribbon of the Sendai River. Far in the distance some roofs and a thread of smoke marked the village of Iino, our destination. So far, I thought, and the road so bad!

But we got there—and it was beautiful all the way—a little after ten. There we found waiting for us a "gasoline car," a tiny aluminum affair with a one-cylinder motor, made to run on narrow rails, into which five people could squeeze. The Forestry Division of the government had recently taken an interest in this region because lumber from here was being sent to Korea for reconstruction, and Iino had suddenly become the center of great activity. So when Mr. Mikami had appealed to them they had offered him the gasoline car and a man to run it. We climbed in, the motor was started, and with a roar we were off up the single-track railway, leaving behind the drivers of the Buick and the truck, Mr. Takagi, our policeman, and the Hitoyoshi official.

Now we were climbing Keiko's mountain, which was steep, thickly wooded, far away from farms and villages, away from even a bad road. Sometimes we saw the foot trail which the Mi-

kamis used on their monthly trips to the metropolis. Sometimes
we passed a lonely dwelling. The people who lived on the mountain were all woodcutters and charcoal burners. They raised a few
vegetables for their own use, they lived in the roughest and sim-
plest of houses, small wooden huts with thatched roofs and tat-
tered paper doors. Even the smallest of them, though, had its bath,
a crude iron tub in an open shed.

The young girls, Mr. Mikami told us, wanted to marry men
from the farms in the valley because the houses there were more
comfortable and food was more plentiful. The girls of the farms,
on the other hand, wanted to marry woodcutters, because on the
mountain family units are smaller, the young people go out to
new logging places where they build shacks of their own, at a
cost of 10,000 yen (less than $30) which the lumber company lends
them, and so they have greater freedom. The young men, apparently, from both valley and mountain want to marry girls unlike
their own sisters!

The religion of these people, Mr. Mikami continued, was primitive animism. Their god was the god of the mountain, who was
feared and propitiated. On the sixteenth of the month he was
thought to be counting his trees, and any one who cut down a
tree on that day was sure to have an accident. After they have
shot a wild boar—evidently their chief source of meat—they fire
off a blank cartridge, as thanks to the god of the mountain.

If there is a death, the neighbors make a rough coffin, and who-
ever knows the appropriate sutra (Buddhist scripture) recites it.
After the burial, they all go to the house of a neighbor and drink
shochu, a crude form of rice wine. They have no priest, either for
the ceremony or to help and comfort the family, but they help
one another generously, he said.

I asked about doctors. There was one in Iino, who could be
reached for serious cases. There was no midwife on the mountain.
The women helped each other, and in the five and a half years
the Mikamis were there they had known of no woman's death in

childbirth. Only one child had been lost, a baby born dead to a mother who had exhausted herself trying to walk to her parents' home in order to conform to the custom of having one's first baby under one's own mother's care.

As we talked we mounted steadily beside a clear brook. Michaelmas daisies bloomed along the track, as well as gentians, a little white flower rather like a windflower, called *umebachiso,* and some yellow flowers. The first sasanquas, too, were starry white among their glossy leaves.

I wondered what we would do if we met a train coming down, and soon I found out. Five flatcars loaded with long logs suddenly loomed up in front of us, preceded by a small engine. We got out of our gasoline car. The lumbermen jumped off their logs, which they had been riding, and casually lifted our little car off the track altogether and set it down. After the lumber train had moved past, they put our car back again on the tracks. The logs, whole trunks of fir trees, were destined for Korea.

Higher up on the mountain we passed a little cluster of houses where there was a tiny store and a telephone. Here the people had come out to meet us, mountain people, shabbily dressed, friendly, and at ease. Among them stood out a young woman in city clothes, with a small girl whom she kept close beside her, away from the other babies; she was the wife of the blue-suited young man who was running our gasoline car, whom the lumber company had sent to work on its expanded operations, and she seemed out of place and lonely in this remote outpost.

We came at length to Hachigamine, and climbed a narrow path up to the school, called Getsumei or "Moonlight" School.

The children were there, all sixty of them, in the playground waiting for us, fresh-faced, friendly, smiling, natural. Games had been planned, and they went into them with zest. Japanese schools have invented a great variety of relay races, and now I saw one of the most diverting. Two small boys with flags held in their teeth raced the length of the playground, shinnied up bamboo

poles and planted the flags at the top, scuttled back to touch the
next boys, who climbed the poles and removed the flags, and so
on until one side finished first.

Meanwhile word had gone out of our arrival and the village
elders came to greet us. The woman who was the head of the
Women's Association was so neat and well groomed and attractive
in her dark kimono that it was hard to believe that she had come
out of one of the primitive little cabins that we had passed. The
village head was an old man, with keen, hooded eyes, a long face
deeply lined and weatherbeaten. The son of the daimyo's falconer,
he had a rank and standing above the other woodsmen. The
daimyos resigned their power at the Restoration in 1868, when
the Shogun was deposed and the Emperor regained his old status.
Here in Kyushu I found people still very much aware of their
former feudal lords.

The house in which the Mikamis lived was perched on ground
higher than the school itself, and there we were welcomed by Mrs.
Mikami, Keiko's grandmother. It was a little wooden house with
a glorious view, built on the same plan as all Japanese houses,
with sliding doors that opened up and made two small rooms into
one large one at need. Oil paintings by Keiko's artist mother, the
ornament in the alcove called the *tokonoma* and the books in
evidence showed the interests of the family. Here we rested for a
little while and drank ceremonial tea prepared and served by Mrs.
Mikami, before we went down to the school for the tree-planting.

It had been planned ahead of time that I was to plant a tree
in the corner of the terrace in honor of the occasion, and both the
children and their parents had taken part in the selection of it.
The Mikamis had suggested a fir tree, but the parents preferred
a keiyaki, which is something like a beech; it was, they said, more
omedetai, more congratulatory, since the keiyaki stands for long
life. The children had examined the little sapling carefully to
make sure that it was "noble," that is, beautiful and strong, so
that it would grow well. The hole had been dug and one of the

parents was there to see that the tree went in properly, with the roots spread out. I was allowed to put in the last earth with the traditional hoe-like spade.

There is something very satisfactory about planting a tree, and especially so here among these people who live by trees and revere them. Since that day I have had messages from time to time that "my" tree was growing well, and once a snapshot of it came.

The school itself had been built since the war, when the new education law raised the years of compulsory education from six to nine. It was a one-story frame building painted yellow with two rooms, one for the primary school, which Keiko taught, and the other for the junior high school, which was Mr. Mikami's province. Inside, the desks were grouped by classes around tables, and on the walls the charts and decorations made by the pupils showed the type of work done: the activities of the student government association, the flowers of the region, its native animals, which included wild boar and monkeys, the cloud formations.

Our time there being limited by the train which we had to catch at Iino, there was no chance to see a class in action, but refreshment was provided before we left in the form of *oshiruko*, a cold soup made of sweet beans, very thick, very sweet, very *omedetai*. This was served to us by two of the oldest girls in the school, who were dressed in their best clothes: white blouses, dark skirts, white sneakers. Keiko told us that when the children help their parents in woodcutting, they are given money for it and expected to buy their own things out of it—a practice more advanced and modern than that of most Tokyo families, but one that has been common in the mountain regions for some years. The new sneakers which these girls wore probably represented long and careful saving.

The farming people whom I had known in the summers in Nagano Ken had seemed to me freer, more independent, less socially timid than city people; the women had more control over family finances and more part in family decisions; they spoke up much more openly about their lives, their dissatisfactions and their ideas. In this very brief encounter with the people of the forest, it seemed to me that again I saw a sturdy and untrammeled life, and a people ready for civic and political responsibility because they had long been making their own decisions. The children, who had had the benefit of the Mikamis' teaching and contact with their personalities and way of life, were altogether natural and charming, without any of the farouche shyness that country children often display.

The *oshiruko*, the thanks and the farewells took longer than had been anticipated, and the young man in the light blue suit looked anxiously at his watch as he urged us into the little car and started down the mountain.

Gravity and gasoline cooperating, we hurtled at a fearful speed down the steep incline, jerking so violently on the curves that I thought we might fly off into space any moment. Somewhere along the way we had a glimpse—possible only on a day as clear as this one was—of Sakurajima, the volcano on the tip of Kyushu, and Takachihonomine, the mountain onto which the grandson of Amaraterasu no Omikami, Jimmu Tenno, descended to found the Imperial line, reportedly in 550 B.C., but just where we had this fine view I cannot say. Tané and I held fast to each other as we appeared to be about to take off into the blue sky above a wide ravine, and afterward she told me that she could *see* the headlines about the sad end of the Crown Prince's tutor and wondered how many people would have to commit suicide because of it! As for me, I was in a state of delight. If I had been consulted about the excursion ahead of time, I should have conscientiously vetoed it, but I had no responsibility in the matter whatsoever. I was in the hands of the Lord and Mr. Mikami and the man in the light blue suit. For four years I had been discretion itself, but now I was getting a day off!

We had covered a good deal of the way in a very short time when we saw ahead of us a flatcar and men loading it with logs.

This time it was only one car. The lumbermen took the logs off when they saw us coming, tipped the car off the tracks, and we zipped by. When I looked back they were patiently putting the logs back again.

It was practically one o'clock when we reached the bottom of the mountain. A lumber truck was waiting for us. Tané and I scrambled up onto the high front seat beside the bare-chested driver, the Mikamis and those other companions who had been waiting impatiently for our return—Mr. Takagi, our policeman, and the Hitoyoshi official—stood up in the back of the truck. A lean face with handlebar moustaches peered in at us, said, "O.K." and we careened off across the lumberyard, in and out of lanes, to the railroad station, where the stationmaster was holding the train for us. One last run, and we were in. The two cars in which we had come, the prefectural Buick and the town truck, had long ago gone back in order to be at Hitoyoshi station to meet us.

The train was full of children going home from school, who looked at us with the greatest interest. *"Kotaishi Sama no sensei"* ran in excited whispers from seat to seat—"The Crown Prince's teacher." One small girl got off at the next station, where she met friends and we could see her obviously telling them, with all a small girl's *empressement,* about the rare sight she had seen. She demonstrated to them how I had waved good-by at Iino station. The train did a switchback, and when we started once more on a higher level, there was a whole row of little girls waving wildly to me as we went past.

At Hitoyoshi, because we still had a full program of sightseeing ahead of us, we ate our box lunches in the stationmaster's office, with the refreshing hot tea which always appears wherever you are in Japan, and then re-entered the waiting automobiles. I thought the drivers, who had been twice over the Kakuta Pass, looked a bit pallid, but nobody flagged.

We covered a great deal of beautiful countryside, and we saw many interesting things, but except for Suyemura village and John

Embree's house there, and for the school of which the Mikamis' school at Hachigamine was, to speak, a mission or dependent school, I cannot now remember what they were. Indeed, at the time, I was in somewhat of a daze, and it took all the resolution I had to climb out of the car at the school, respond to the cordial welcome of all the important people who had gathered there for us, hear a child play a Beethoven concerto, and receive an armful of flowers from another child.

At dusk, still far from Hitoyoshi and once more behind schedule, we stopped on a lonely road and all piled out of the car. For some time, silent now, we walked along a path through the ricefields, through the winding lanes of a little village, and along a railroad track until we came to a broad pebbly beach beside the Kuma River. Here a boat with three boatmen was waiting to take us downstream to Hitoyoshi.

The boat was the same kind that the Lord Sagara, the daimyo of Hitoyoshi, used to ride in, they told me, and he too used to leave from this spot. It was a long, narrow boat, unpainted, with a high, pointed prow. In the bottom was clean straw matting, and we took off our shoes as we got in. There were flat cushions to sit on.

Two boatmen manned the tall stern oar, and the one in the bow used a long pole, much as a pole is used in punting. When we came to the rapids, he put aside the pole and used a big paddle for steering.

The river was beautiful as the dark closed in and the moon rose. In one of the banks, Mr. Mikami said, pointing, there was a cave with prehistoric wall paintings. The sound of the water, the smooth motion of the boat, the quiet voices, lowered in deference to the peaceful scene, caused my fatigue to slide off my shoulders like an unneeded garment.

We came to the first of three stretches of rapids. The water rushed by very fast, splashing and churning; the bottom of the boat grated on stones, and big rocks loomed up and slipped away.

After the first passage someone said, "If you get through that safely, you're all right." As we approached the second, the Hitoyoshi official crept forward with a flashlight to make a light for the boatmen—"*abunai kara*," he said, "because it's dangerous"—and after the third stretch, the boatman got out his big handkerchief and mopped his forehead. I wondered, since they had told me that he was the best boatman on the river and had been on it for fifty years, why he should seem so relieved, but I did not know the reason till later.

As we drifted smoothly past the hill called the Sleeping Buddha, a *chidori* or plover sang for us, a lovely thrushlike note. A shaft of emotion went through the boat; to have at once the river, the moonlight, the hill where the daimyo's castle used to be, and the song of the night-singing plover! There is a popular song in Japan, "Moonlight over the Ruined Castle," and whenever I hear it I am transported back to that perfect moment on the Kuma River.

When we pulled up at the landing place in front of our inn, three maids with paper lanterns were out watching anxiously for us, and Mr. Tomita, the innkeeper, was pacing up and down praying to the Sleeping Buddha for our safety. It was then that they told me that no one had ever shot the rapids after dark before! But as Mr. Mikami later wrote to me, "If there are no thrill, one cannot immerse in the bosom of nature."

He confessed to me too, as we sat at dinner, going over the highlights of the day and savoring each one again, that the prefectural office and the police had opposed his plans "severely," both the drive over the pass and the boat ride, but that he had insisted on going through with it. A man of vision and of will, Mr. Mikami—and also of luck. But then, don't vision and will together make luck? He had been so much worried himself, the night before, that he could not sleep, and so he had got up and walked up and down the hall in the inn—where he had met the old cook, fully dressed, engaged in guarding my door.

Because of me, two people had had a sleepless night, the prefectural car and its driver had suffered goodness knows what strain crossing the pass twice over those ghastly roads, three conscientious officials had had a long day struggling to ward off disaster in a program of which they had disapproved, a young man had risked his life hurling a tiny car at great speed down a precipitous mountainside, a train had been delayed (a serious matter in Japan), a boatman had shot the rapids in the dark for the first time in his fifty-year experience, four people had had an anxious time of waiting—but I had had a glorious day.

It was good indeed to see the Mikamis again.

They were in Tokyo now, having reluctantly left their beloved school two or three years before. Mr. Mikami's health was not robust, and Keiko had taken all of the college courses that she could take by correspondence and was finishing the requirements for her degree at Keio University. She had published her fourth book and was at work on a novel, and was keeping house for her father besides. Her life was busy and full.

After lunch we went up to my room, where I showed them the dish-garden which the Empress had sent me, in which gentians and other wild flowers from Nasu were growing as if they were still in their own woods.

It was an old custom, Keiko told me, when friends were going on a journey, to perform a scene from a Noh play for them. As I was to travel in Japan, to say nothing of the long trip back to the United States, she and her father would now do for me a scene from the play, *Kurama-tengu.*

A son of the Minamoto clan, after their defeat by the Heike, lived disguised as a page boy in the Kurama temple, high in the mountains. Lonely and beauty-loving, he was mocked at by his fellow pages, and comforted by a *tengu,* a mountain goblin, who taught him the secrets of strategy and fencing. Twenty years later, as Yoshitsune, Japan's great hero, the one-time page fought and destroyed the Heike. A short song from this play is frequently chosen when lovers of Noh sing for their friends, as we might sing an aria or a chorus from an opera.

Mr. Mikami borrowed back the big Noh-dancer's fan which he had brought me as a gift, and without self-consciousness, in his blue business suit, unfurling and wielding the fan, he began in the conventional Western style hotel room the slow stately dance of the Noh. Keiko, sitting on a stiff chair, sang the *ko-uta*, the little song. Her voice, which is normally light and feminine, became round and hollow, with the strange resonances and cadences that go with that ancient art.

> When cherry-blossoms on my mountain bloom,
> I'll send a message to you.
>
> Oh, now the message comes, and I rejoice.
> Let us go at once to see the flowers.
> Saddle my horse!

The words in English give no idea of the play of meaning and pattern of echoing sounds of the Japanese. I was going to travel in the Kansai district and to see facets of Japanese life that I had not seen before, but never would I taste more of the inimitable flavor of Japan than at that moment, when father and daughter danced and sang for my journey.

6

Tourist in Kansai

I SELDOM have the chance to be a tourist and go sightseeing in Japan—though I have had so many opportunities to see treasures and enjoy experiences that no tourist can compass—but on the first of October I set forth with Tané for a week of doing the things a tourist does, or can do, in the Kansai district.

We took the day train to Kyoto, for I would never willingly go by night and so miss the gloriously beautiful ride along the seacoast presided over first by majestic Fuji and later by the serried peaks of the Japan Alps. We had engaged seats in the observation car of the Tsubame (swallow). Immediately after the war this train had been renamed Heiwa (peace) but when peace proved to be so slow in coming the realistic Japanese decided that this was no name for an express train and returned to the earlier and swifter Swallow.

Our seats, which were capacious overstuffed chairs, wore immaculate white linen slipcovers and in the corner of the car was a large blue vase filled with chrysanthemums. Green tea was brought to us by a white-jacketed "boy san" soon after we left Tokyo and again before we arrived in Kyoto.

It was a fresh sunny morning after an almost wholly rainy month. Fuji, blue to the top except for a few white streaks, came in and out of her clouds; white herons rose flapping from the ricefields; and armies of newly erected billboards that had not been there before spoiled some of the loveliest scenes as they do at home. Mid-morning two neat little girls in green cotton uniforms came to bring us menus and get our order for lunch. Shortly before noon they brought us hot wet towels for our hands, and when our table was ready they came again to lead us to the dining car, opening all the heavy doors for us between. We had an excellent meal—fried chicken, three vegetables, rolls and butter, caramel custard and coffee, all for the equivalent of a dollar, including service charge.

In Kyoto we went to the Tawaraya Inn, where I always stay, and that night as I drifted off to sleep I heard two sounds that mean Japan to me, which have now disappeared from Tokyo: the melancholy flute of the Chinese noodle man and the clip-clop of wooden clogs on the street.

The next morning we went off to see the Katsura Detached Palace, which I had seen twice before but not, until today, in sunshine. Built in the seventeenth century, the garden designed by Kobori Enshu, the great landscape architect of seventeenth-century Japan, it was a sort of pleasance for an Imperial prince, a week-end cottage, a Petit Trianon. He and his successors came here with their courtiers and ladies to watch polo and football games, row across the tiny lake and picnic on an island, attend rituals in the miniature temple or tea ceremonies in the small, exquisite tea-house, or write poems in the "flower-praising house."

The Katsura Palace belongs to the state now and is open by appointment to tourists, who are escorted through it on guided tours at stated times. Thanks to a telephone call from the Kyoto Palace we were taken through it by ourselves, with time to linger and admire where we liked and to roam on stocking feet through the jewel-like little palace, asking questions and getting detailed answers.

At intervals along the winding paths are old stone lanterns, small and low, to light the way for the feet. One is called the firefly lantern because when lit it presented its reflection to people in the moon-viewing house across the lake so that it looked like fireflies in the water.

Inside the palace, every room had a different outlook—a water view, a formal garden view, a lonely mountain view, a view of the polo field. Every detail in the bare, simple rooms, was consciously designed for beauty: the thickening of a shelf on the underside to give space and perspective to the room, the metalware on the sliding doors, the small ornaments over bolts and nails. Looking at these few rooms, the beauty of which lay in their perfect proportions, the view from their windows, the national treasures of art so small and subtle that you might easily overlook them—a sliding door painted with a crow on a dead tree, a huddle of pheasants in the snow—and the ten-acre garden of stone and water, trees and moss, that by the skill of its design seemed so much larger, I thought of Knole in Kent and marveled at the contrast. That great pile of Tudor brick and stone, with its seven acres of roofs, twelve courts, fifty-two staircases, and three hundred and sixty-five rooms, crowded with beautiful and historic furniture, hangings, rugs, china, silver, glass and paintings, its hundreds of acres of gardens and parks and miles of driveways, had not been built for royalty, though kings had visited it, but for a subject. Then I looked at Prince Tomohito's ample bathroom and deep tub and remembered the minuscule silver ewer and basin provided for the ablutions of James I when he stayed at Knole.

The first time that I had been in Kyoto I was not taken to see the stone garden at Ryuanji—and with good reason. Those who planned my trip knew, if I did not, that I was not ready for it. A garden consisting of nothing but sand and a few piles of rocks is merely baffling to the average Westerner fresh from the United States or Europe. Now, eleven years and many experiences later, I wanted at last to see Ryuanji.

We drove a little way out of Kyoto into a rural countryside, where the mountains of Higashiyama and Arashiyama rose into the sky above ricefields. Entering the temple grounds, whose great trees swept long shadows over a pond with pink water lilies, we passed a simple, rustic garden and approached the temple itself, which had an ancient and somewhat shabby look. In a dim, incense-smelling hall we paid a small fee and were told which way to go.

Suddenly the garden burst upon us. Enclosed by a tawny plastered wall roofed with black tiles, a rectangle a little larger than a tennis court, of pure white sand and five clusters of rocks of different sizes and shapes, with a little green at their base and the sand raked in circles around them: this was all. All—and everything, for the effect was immediate, authentic, awing. It was modern and it was timeless. It was an abstract and yet an abstract intense with meaning. The rocks were very rock, all rock everywhere, the suchness of rock itself. Their shapes and sizes, their relationship to each other and to the space of the sand enclosed by the tawny walls were right and inevitable.

After a large class of high school boys on an educational excursion had photographed it and taken themselves noisily away, we had a few minutes before the next incursion, to look quietly at this centuries-old creation of the human spirit and wonder how it happened. How, so long ago, did a Buddhist priest achieve so original and sophisticated a work of art, and, even stranger, how was it that here in a rural temple people knew it at once for a masterpiece and preserved it through the years?

According to the guidebook, the garden was laid out by Soami, a Zen Buddhist of the early fourteenth century and is entirely Zen in intention and feeling. This was interesting, as far as it went. Later, in a fascinating book, *Architectural Beauty in Japan* published by the Kokusai Bunka Shinkokai, I learned that the garden as designed by Soami had contained a glorious cherry tree, which was its real focus and that the rocks had in the beginning been only secondary. After many years the cherry tree died. The abbot of the temple decided not to replace it, recognizing the sufficiency and perfection of the rocks and space alone. So, as I suspect is oftener the case than we realize, this perfect work of art was not Soami's alone, but partly the product also of time and chance and some forgotten man, obscure but perceptive and courageous. As to the miracle of taste of the ordinary people who recognized and valued this rare garden through the years, perhaps that too owes something to chance and to the innate conservatism that likes to keep things as they are.

I had hoped to see Mr. Kanjiro Kawai again on this visit to Kyoto, but as he was out of town I had to content myself with remembering my meeting with him in 1950. With Mr. Hamada of Mashiko and two or three others, he is one of the great modern potters who have drawn such artists as Bernard Leach of England to Japan and whose work has been bought by art museums all over the world.

Professor Bunshiro Jugaku of Kanto Gakuin University, lecturer on English literature, authority on Blake (his bibliography of Blake, covering many languages, is probably the most complete and scholarly one that has yet been done) student of Zen and expert on handmade paper, took us, my sister and Tané and me, to Mr. Kawai's atelier. On the way up a narrow street we squeezed with difficulty past a pile of logs against a fence—fuel, Mr. Jugaku said, for Shimizu Rokubei's kiln. A little farther on we came to Mr. Kawai's narrow, unpretentious entrance. Once inside we found ourselves in a living folk-art museum.

Everything in that house was handmade, solid and beautiful. Most Japanese houses give an effect of fragility—and indeed that is part of their charm—but this one seemed rooted in the earth, strong and permanent. We sat in solid wooden chairs hewn out of trunks of trees and polished through years of use, which had once been mortars for pounding rice in Okinawa. The woodwork everywhere, the stairs to the second floor, the thick beams

of the ceiling, was heavy, dark and shining. The low table where
we sat for tea was broad and substantial; the handmade pottery,
the pieces of hand-blocked linen, the iron kettle, some small
stone figures: all were strong and solid.

Mr. Kawai himself was a slight, gray-haired man of sixty,
wearing the hand-woven kimono and *mompei* of the modern folk
artist. His face, sensitive and mobile, fairly radiated light, and
behind his half-spectacles, his eyes were keen and happy. While
we talked, his wife, a sweet-looking woman, motherly and comfortable, younger than he, prepared ceremonial tea for us and a
tiny granddaughter in a red kimono peeped around the edge of
the door. Mrs. Kawai performed the tea ceremony with concentration but without the mincing attention to detail and exact
movement which its devotees often display: she had mastered
the art and was using it, not ministering to it.

I asked about one of the stone figures and was told that it was
a modern copy of a wooden one made about a hundred and fifty
years ago by Mokujiki Shonin, a wandering priest who at the
age of sixty-four resolved to carve a thousand wooden figures of
the Buddha—and then proceeded to do so. He was untaught and
he did it purely for the love of it, scattering his works freely over
the temples of the land, signing and apparently numbering each
one. When he finished the thousandth at the age of ninety, he
began on some of the Shinto gods—no bigot, he. Mr. Kawai
owned three of the original figures; all had smiling faces with
cushion-y cheeks and triangular mouths; they were honest and
free and primitive. It was Mr. Sotestu Yanagi, of the Folk Art
Museum in Tokyo, which is the headquarters of the folk-art
movement, who discovered this artist, said Mr. Kawai, and has
written several books about him.

Mr. Kawai used Mokujiki Shonin and his thousand Buddhas
as a text for his own ideas on genius, which, he said, is universal
and needs only an unobstructed channel through which to flow.
With his own work, which, I knew, had passed through a number

of different phases, so that one can date a vase by its color, shape and glaze, he had had at first to think deeply and suffer to produce something: now he was able to make himself a channel and to let the work produce itself through him. His hands, shaping the clay, obeyed not the conscious motions of his mind but some deeper force that was not personal to him. Poetry too, he said, came in the same way, and he gave me a copy of one of his volumes of poems, beautifully printed on handsome paper. Not for the first time in Japan I felt acutely the limitations of my illiteracy.

His kiln was in the back yard of his house, and his workshop and wheel. The wheel has no electric motor. He laughed at the idea. He does not even use anything so mechanized as a foot-pedal. He kicks it with his feet until it turns swiftly and then uses the momentum as long as it lasts. A now well-known American potter came to Kyoto some years ago to study under Mr. Kawai; every morning he walked down the hill from the luxurious Miyako Hotel where he stayed, to work under Mr. Kawai's direction, but he never mastered the art of kicking the wheel. Mr. Kawai and his nephew kept it going for him. "When he came," said the potter with a delighted laugh, "we became electric motors!"

I have two pieces of pottery made by Kanjiro Kawai which I cherish: one of his early vases, round and swelling at the base with a tall narrow neck, brown glazed with a cream-colored design, beautiful but more formal than his later work; and a hexagonal jar with a lid, oyster-colored with a free decoration in rose and green, which he gave to me that day.

All of the folk artists and experts on folk art know one another. Because of what I had been told by Mr. Yanagi and Mr. Kawai of Mr. Tonomura of Kurashiki, I went to see the Folk Art Museum there while we were in Okayama. In the afternoon we were to visit Mrs. Ikeda; in the morning we set out in a local bus, and rattled and bounced the ten miles or so to Kurashiki.

The ricefields were golden, the farmhouses looked prosperous behind high walls, with pine trees curling an arm over the sides. I noticed what seemed to be a characteristic style of building in this region, a decorative treatment of the space under the tile roofs with black bars on the white plaster.

At Kurashiki we made our way through a very old shopping center, where a kind of roof of coarse white muslin covered the narrow street between the shops that jutted out from solid old houses. Every imaginable variety of merchandise seemed to be offered in profusion, including hideous vinyl plastic tablecloths.

Presently we emerged upon a narrow river, to which flights of stone steps descended at intervals. Once, it seemed, Kurashiki was a busy port and these steps were loading places for the boats that came to trade. Along both sides of the river were substantial houses with black tiled roofs and geometrical designs on white walls. The Ohara art museum, which is widely known, seemed out of key with its modified Greek temple architecture; it houses a famous collection of paintings from Rubens to Roualt, but I was not in search of European art today. We crossed a bridge, continued down the street, turned a corner and came to the Mingeikan (Folk Art Museum).

Mr. Tonomura, the curator, met us at the door of the sturdy stone building. Like Mr. Kawai and Mr. Hamada, he wore a hand-blocked homespun kimono and *mompei*. His thin, eager, sensitive face and gentle warm manner reminded me of others I knew who were interested in folk art and I wondered if there was something inherent in this cult that attracted to it only gentle, ardent, imaginative, unworldly but quite determined persons.

Behind the main part of the museum was a stone-paved courtyard and a large rice storehouse, a century and a half old, with enormous roof beams. The collection was an interesting one: hand-blocked, hand-woven cottons used for covering farmhouse bed-quilts, pottery, baskets, ironware, brass-bound chests, all the beautiful anonymous things that common people make for their own use—or once did. Japan seems to be entering upon the cycle that occurred earlier in other countries: the industrial revolution brings in cheap, bright, machine-made wares and the very people whose taste has been so true fasten on them eagerly. Then as the vinyl plastic tablecloths crowd out the hand-blocked cotton ones, intellectuals become aware of the old things and begin to collect them. A movement for their preservation arises, with publications, museums, special stores (Takumi in Tokyo is a treasure-house), and modern craftsmen begin to practice the old arts of the people. The simple objects which the peasants once made for themselves are now priced out of their reach.

This final stage has, happily, not yet been reached in Japan. In country places there can still be found local handicrafts of good design and at low prices; the farmers make their straw raincoats and straw boots on winter evenings; the children have painted wooden pheasants on wheels to play with; people in Shimane Prefecture, and doubtless elsewhere, raise enough cotton in their tiny fields—a cotton field the size of a family vegetable patch is startling to eyes accustomed to the acres of cotton in North Carolina—to make the coverings for their own quilts and cushions, weaving it and dyeing it themselves; and there is a limitless variety of lovely things made by patient, knowing fingers out of bamboo. That appreciation of these things is increasing instead of declining is due in great part to the leadership of the members of the folk-art movement in Japan.

On the way from Okayama to Nagoya we made a detour and went to spend a night on Koya San, the sacred mountain. I had been hearing about Koya San for a long time: the trees, the temples, the chanting of sutras in the dawn, the remoteness from all that was modern, bustling and commercial. Kobo Daishi, who established the great monastery on that mountaintop in 820, was always crossing my path, in books, statues ascribed to him, treasures associated with him in temples that I visited.

He was one of the great saints of Japanese Buddhism, but in

addition to being a saint he was also, to quote Dr. Suzuki, "a profound scholar, an ascetic, an extensive traveler, an artist of the first class, and a most experienced calligrapher." In the first substantial history of Japan that I read—Sir George Sansom's *Japan: A Short Cultural History,* probably the most completely enthralling single volume that I have ever read about any country, with the possible exception of Edith Hamilton's *The Greek Way*—I had long ago learned that Kobo Daishi was according to tradition the inventor of *hiragana,* the fifty-odd symbols representing syllables that form a kind of substitute for a Japanese alphabet and modify the rigors of the Chinese characters.

I had once visited Kobo Daishi's birthplace at Zentsuji Temple in Shikoku, about twenty-five miles from Takamatsu. The temple itself was founded by Kobo Daishi on land that he had inherited from his father, who was a daimyo named Zentsu, and has been rebuilt many times. The oldest part is probably of the seventeenth century. The thing that struck me most keenly about Zentsuji was that though it was a tourist attraction, its Buddhas were not shawled with dust, and its metal lotuses were clean; in fact all its brass and lacquer gleamed, the incense pervading its halls was of good quality, and in general it had the air of a religious shrine actually prayed in and cared for with real reverence, not perfunctorily kept going for revenue. The pool with lotus blossoms was there in Kobo Daishi's day, and the old pine overhanging it is said to be the same one that he climbed upon and from which he saw his face reflected in the water. He painted his own portrait and gave it to his mother before he went to China. The portrait, at any rate, is still there, but it is enshrined in the holy of holies and cannot be seen.

Kobo Daishi went to China at the age of twenty-nine and stayed for three years, traveling and studying under great Buddhist masters, from whom he learned a new and esoteric variety of Buddhism. This he brought back to Japan and established under the name of *Shingon,* or True Word.

From then until his death, he traveled about Japan, spreading his doctrine and searching for a site for the monastery that was his dream. The eighty-eight places where he stayed to rest are all recorded and revered. The place where he would build his monastery, he said, must be remote; it must be on a mountain, but the mountain must have a flat top with plenty of room for expansion; it must have an ample supply of pure water. In the end, it took not one miracle but two to find it: a Buddhist implement which he had thrown into the air in China he found again lodged in a tree on Koya San, to which he was led by two dogs, one black and one white, and a mysterious light.

When he died, in 835, he did not really die but entered into *samadhi;* his uncorrupted body lives on, it is believed, in the sanctuary on Koya San waiting for the coming of Maitreya, the Buddhist Messiah.

In years gone by, pilgrims to Koya San were carried up the mountain in palanquines, or if they really wanted to obtain merit they walked. It is easier now. We took an electric train from Osaka, which began almost at once to climb through steep, heavily wooded mountains, past woodcutting villages where wooden houses crowded along the tracks, and high valleys with terraced ricefields. At Koyashita we left the train and got into a cable car for the last sharp climb to the top of the peak that loomed above us.

The station at the end of the line was still some distance from the temples; we were lucky to get a taxi. My first impression of Koya San was the trees, the massive towering boles of cryptomeria, pine and fir, the spreading branches high overhead. Here and there gleamed the black curves of a temple roof or a pagoda pricked through the clouds that eddied and swirled about us like smoke.

Once there had been more than a thousand temples of Koya San; the number now has dwindled to a little over a hundred, plus a university where Buddhism and especially the doctrines of the

Shingon sect are taught. Until 1872 no women were admitted, but today probably most of the visitors are women and they are even permitted to stay overnight in the temples, since there are no inns on the mountain. Shojiin had been recommended to us.

It was a fascinating experience, not only for the beauty of the mountaintop, the glory of the great trees, the ancient buildings with their treasures, and the kindness of the priests who showed us about, but also the simple, homely fact of spending a night in a temple and being served by young Buddhist monks.

Our rooms were large, looking out on a big garden with an arched stone bridge over a stream, where small twisted pines hung over the water and the leaves of the maples on the little hill were beginning to turn russet. Rain was falling when we arrived, but for a few brief moments, the sun came out and the light diffused through the slanting rain glistened on every leaf.

Soon after our arrival there we were invited to have tea and cakes with the head priest in a small room fragrant with sandalwood incense, looking out on a garden. His father had been head of this same temple and he expected his son to succeed him in turn. The son, now in high school in Kobe, was a gifted storyteller and had had considerable success on the radio. Storytelling is still a recognized art in Japan, practiced in theaters and other places. The priest's son had even been in the movies and was beset with offers, but his father was sure that he would return to Koya San to become a monk just the same. I could not help feeling that there were heartaches ahead for both father and son.

Kongobuji is the main temple on Koya San and the mother temple of the whole sect. Our priest took us there to call on the abbot, a tall man with a long humorous face, a turned-up nose, big mouth and an easy manner without a trace of sanctimoniousness. Slipping the wooden beads of his rosary through his fingers as he talked, he told us of the visit of Arnold Toynbee and his wife a few months earlier and presented me with books about the history and art of the temple.

From Kongobuji, fortified with goloshes, umbrellas and rain-coats, for the rain was pouring down with dour persistence, we embarked for Okunoin, the temple dedicated to Kobo Daishi's grave. Our priest wore a smart white raincoat over his fine black brocade kimono.

We left the taxi at the sacred bridge in front of the temple and went on to the grave, which was a simple, very old thatched-roof building like a miniature temple set among trees beyond the last of the sutra halls, the temples which contain sacred statues, lamps perpetually burning for the dead, and shrines to the deities of Koya San. We stopped a little distance from the grave to burn incense; the priest prayed; the rain glistened on gold lotuses and shone on the wet black trunks of trees. I was aware of standing at the innermost core of this mountain sanctified by centuries of worship; I felt that the priest whose prayers I heard but did not understand considered himself to be in the actual presence of the founder of the monastery, the saint and genius who in that small thatch-roofed building still sat sunk in a meditation that he had begun more than eleven hundred years ago.

From the grave of Kobodaishi to the Ichi-no-bashi, the bridge where the taxi waited to pick us up again, was a stone-paved avenue a mile and a half long through the cemetery where many of Japan's greatest sons are buried. Beneath lofty cryptomeria and pine trees were literally thousands of graves and monuments; here are buried or memorialized Hideyoshi, the great general of the sixteenth century, Basho the poet, part of the ashes of the Forty-Seven Ronin (the rest are in the Sengaku-ji in Tokyo), the Kabuki actor Ichikawa Danjiro, and countless others. I cannot pretend that a walk of a mile and a half through a graveyard in a downpour of rain is an exhilarating experience, but I will say that it is an unforgettable one, and that I truly appreciated the kindness of the head priest of Shojiin, who went with us every step of the way and managed at least to awake in us sympathy for his own reverent enthusiasm.

We asked to be called in the morning in time to hear the monks chanting the sutras, or Buddhist scriptures.

Our attendant monk came before seven, a young man with shaven head, black robes, and a purple brocade stole, who led us along the wooden corridors from one part of the temple to the big prayer hall in another part. It was chilly and dim in the morning mist, lit with candles and heavy with incense. There were three altars in the vast room, one to Amida Buddha, one to Kobo Daishi and one to some other deity. A red baize cloth was spread out on the *tatami*, the thick springy straw matting that covers the floor, for us to sit on, which we did in the Japanese style, going down on our knees and then sitting back on our heels. Usually one has a flat cushion for comfort, but this was a temple and the red baize was austere.

Five monks behind a sort of screen knelt before the altar to Amida Buddha. One voice began the chanting, others joined in, their voices strange and bell-like. The sound swelled, died away, rose again. The tempo quickened. A gong emphasized a climax; cymbals clashed; a tinkly bell like a triangle rang; rhythmic thumps on a hollow wooden object made an undercurrent of emphasis. It was impossible to catch the words they were saying, though I recognized from time to time the prayer-ending *tamae*. At times they were all saying the same thing very fast; at other times each appeared to be reading something quite separate on a venture of his own; yet there was harmony.

Long before the beautiful and mysterious hour was over, I was in agony from my knees, which were not accustomed to the discipline they were getting. I kept wriggling my toes behind me surreptitiously, to keep my feet from going to sleep, and concentrated on sheer endurance.

At length, about eight o'clock, the gong rang for the last time, the final voice died away, and we limped back to our room for breakfast.

It was a brilliant, sunny morning after the rain and the long aisles of the trees were splashed with golden light. There was time before we left to see the museum with its art treasures, and some of the other temples and pagodas. I should have liked to stay longer, not to look at statues and paintings but to walk at will in the forest, looking for the rare ferns and wild flowers that abound there and listening to the birds.

From Nagoya we took the Chuo Line back to Tokyo. It was a second-class train, I was warned, quite a different matter from the Tsubame, but the route lay through the Japan Alps and I was willing to sacrifice comfort to beauty.

We had seats together in a car filled with brides and grooms. October, it seems, is a good month for weddings. I was interested in the pair who sat facing us: the groom very happy and anxious to please, the plump bride with a face like a peach and inscrutable eyes plainly quite dubious about the whole affair.

Though nobody brought us tea or hot towels, there was a boy assigned to the car whose job was to keep the floor swept and the window sills wiped clean. When we lost a little time in one of the steep climbs, a loudspeaker at each succeeding station announced that the train was three minutes late, apologized for the delay and hoped that the time would be made up later. Station officials with white gloved hands came out and walked briskly up and down, appearing very busy and efficient, and what was still more impressive to one accustomed to the indifference and negligence of our passenger trains in the United States, full of respect for their work.

The beauty of the country through which we climbed more than met my hopes (no billboards here): the Japan Alps jagged against the sky, the leaves of the lacquer trees yellow and scarlet on the lower slopes, the waving pampas grass, the Kiso River winding beside us, and toward sunset, miles and miles when we saw a sea of golden ricefields stretching toward mountains indigo in the late light, and Fuji floating above huge and blue in an amber sky.

As we drew near Tokyo I remembered earlier homecomings, when our handsome young chauffeur, Takenaka San, used to meet us on the station platform, all welcoming smiles. I had not seen him during this visit as I had hoped to do. After we had gone home to America he had driven for the Imperial Household for a time, but, his work for me having taken him out of the regular line of progression in the hierarchy, he had no chance of driving for the Crown Prince; and he found it dull to fetch and return a minor official each day. For a time he had driven a truck, but now he was a salesman in a sewing machine company. One of his regular trips had taken him away from Tokyo at the time of my visit.

Shinjuku station, when the train pulled in, was boiling with a noisy, plunging, turbulent crowd of home-goers. Seeing no porters, we lifted our heavy suitcases. Suddenly my bag was taken from my hand—and there was Takenaka San, smiling. At the same moment Sato San, the driver lent to me by the Imperial Household, took care of Tané's burden, and they led us off to the waiting car. Takenaka San, having returned from his trip, had got in touch with Sato San, and there he was. No, he had not married yet, he told me, blushing a little, when I asked him in Japanese. I hoped that the blush indicated at least an interest. Some girl will get a prize.

7

Mrs. Ikeda

PRINCESS ATSUKO, or Yori-
nomiya Sama, as the Japanese call her, who is two years older
than the Crown Prince, was married in the fall of 1952. I had already left Japan, but I heard about it from letters and newspaper
accounts. I saw photographs of her, beautiful in her formal
eleventh-century wedding robes, and trim and smart and pretty
in the wool suits she wore in her new home.

She had married a farmer, the word came, who had a "ranch"
outside of Okayama City, more than four hundred miles from
Tokyo. She was living in a small modern "bungalow" and helping to feed the stock, which the newspapers enumerated: 1,000
chickens, 300 canaries, fifty dogs, ten pairs of pigeons, nine Hol-
stein cows, forty pigs, ten turkeys, and nine goats. She got up at
six-thirty to get her husband's breakfast, she knit sweaters for
him, and she loved the simple life.

Her husband was Takamasa Ikeda, eldest son of the former
Marquis Ikeda, grandson of the daimyo of Okayama. In 1868 his
grandfather had yielded his feudal domains to the Imperial government; in 1947 his father had lost his title through the new
Constitution and most of his property in the capital levy. Takamasa, a Peers' School graduate of the postwar generation, had
youth, energy, determination—and a farm. "I want to be a good
businessman," he was reported as saying.

Princess Atsuko had been Mrs. Ikeda for five years when I met her again at dinner at the Palace, soon after the P.E.N. congress had ended. That there were no children I knew was a sorrow; but that her life was interesting and that she was deeply content was obvious. She had been a dreamy girl, rather silent; now she was alert, aware, animated.

I asked her about the animals on her farm and was startled to have the answer, "Lions—a baby llama."

This was not my idea of either a ranch or a stock-farm. Still under the spell of the newspaper account I said, "Do you feed them?"

She laughed and shook her head. "Come and see."

From Kyoto Tané and I took the train to Okayama, a city with a population of about 200,000 in southern Honshu close to the Inland Sea. When we got out on the station platform, there was Princess Atsuko, who with her lady-in-waiting had come to meet us. She was wearing a cherry-colored woolen suit with a red feather pinned on the lapel. The Community Chest drive had started a day or two earlier and she had taken the chief part in the opening ceremony. Okayama City, I learned, was very proud of its princess and she was much in demand for charitable drives and public functions of all kinds.

They took us to our inn in the car they had brought and saw us safely installed. Then the lady-in-waiting left. She was a married woman with a home and family of her own in Okayama who attended the Princess when she went out alone but did not live in the house with her.

The afternoon was well along but there was still time, the Princess said, to see the Korakuen Garden if we would like to do so. So off we went in her car to the famous gardens which had belonged to the Ikeda family and had been given by them to the city. It was a beautiful park, large and artfully made to look even larger than it was, with winding walks, ponds, bridges, pines and artificial hills. Other people were sauntering along the paths.

Now and then, recognizing Princess Atsuko, one would come and ask permission to take her photograph.

Our inn, the Koraku, was named for the garden. Prince Masahito had stayed there when he came to visit his sister. We had the same pleasant room that he had had and were waited on by the same elderly maid, who had been in the inn for twenty-five years. Princess Atsuko had dinner with us there and told us more about her new life.

Mr. Ikeda was away on a business trip, but he would be home tomorrow. Mr. Ikeda, his wife told us proudly, was very busy. He went all over Japan, selling the animals he raised, buying others for the zoo. A few months after their marriage, he had decided that a city the size of Okayama should have a zoo, and so he had turned part of his farm into a zoological garden.

All eyes and ears, we set out in a taxi the next afternoon for the Ikeda *Bokujo* (farm). Okayama City itself, I thought as we bounced along its straight, sunny, dusty, treeless streets, was like a western boom-town. The old city had been destroyed by bombs; the new one, hastily built, was still raw, full of activity and noise.

By-passing the public entrance we followed a winding lane up a steep hill on the edge of town, hearing bits of music borne to us on the wind from an amplifier. We came out at last on a level space in front of a wall with a big wooden gate, which opened to admit us. Princess Atsuko, with three chihuahuas titupping at her heels, came out to welcome us.

The house, which sat on a ledge on the mountainside, was a low white concrete one with a big enclosed verandah, half of which had been partitioned off to make a room for tropical fish. There were tiers of glass tanks that contained darting forms and green tendrils. A battery of wires and tubes emerged from the tanks and there was a little stove in the room to keep the temperature tropical. These were some of the creatures that Princess Atsuko fed and Mr. Ikeda sold.

She showed us the rest of the house, the living-dining room, the bedrooms, the kitchen where a very young maid was at work. All of the house was furnished in the Western style, except the spare room, which had *tatami* on the floor and blue curtains patterned with the Imperial chrysanthemum in white.

When we returned to the sun porch Mr. Ikeda arrived, having taken a train at four-thirty in the morning in order to get home in time. He was a rather tall, slender young man, with the engaging kind of face that we call "bull doggy," squarish, with a strong chin.

After tea, for which Mrs. Ikeda brought out a big platter of fancy sandwiches which she had made herself, we went out to make a tour of the place. It was humming. The cows had come down from the pasture up the hill and someone was leading them off to milk them. In the big chicken house were the incubators, from which thousands of chicks were sold all over Japan. In another building were the birds, not only canaries of every shade but several varieties of brilliant little tropical birds which, like the fish, were being raised to sell in the United States as well as Japan. The eggs are hatched by plainer birds so that the exotic creatures with the vivid patches of green and scarlet and electric blue could continue to lay, undisturbed by family cares. "The breeders wouldn't take the trouble to do that in the States," I was told.

Farther down the slope of the hill were the cages and pens where the lion, the llamas and their baby, the kangaroos, zebra, blue-bottomed baboons, monkeys, ostriches and the rest attracted admiring attention from the crowd of visitors. A new building, tiled inside with colored ceramic tiles, had a pool for an alligator, a fountain copied from the famous Brussels one, and cool feathery palms where parrots preened and squawked. From a distance we heard the cheerful music of a merry-go-round and over some trees I saw a flying boat swing into view and out again. A cable car carried successive loads of people to the top of the hill, where there was an observatory and a wide view.

As we walked about the Ikedas pointed out to us the things achieved and the things planned, which included a dormitory for the workers, already under construction. People turned now and then to look at Princess Atsuko, but there was no craning of necks, no following crowd. We returned to the modern, well-equipped little house for more talk, and then in the car which Mr. Ikeda drove himself they took us into town to a *sushi* restaurant for dinner.

It was a tiny place and one which I cannot imagine existing anywhere else than Japan. Aside from the uniquely Japanese food that was served, there was about it a knowing simplicity, an exquisite neatness and cleanliness, a flair for the artistic use of local materials, all on a very small scale, that made it distinctive.

We went through a bamboo gateway and a miniature garden, with a rock or two, white pebbles and a bit of green, into a room which held a counter and five or six stools. The counter was made of white cedar wood, spotless, with a narrow copper-lined trough through which water was running. This was to dip our fingers in, and we had small pieces of white cotton torn in squares to dry them on.

Behind the counter a man and a girl in white clothes prepared the *sushi* expertly and swiftly and put them before us. *Sushi* was what we went there for and *sushi* was what we had, every possible kind of it, with dishes of soya sauce and big mugs of hot tea. The gray and green and brown pottery was handmade, crude and rough and lovely.

Sushi—they call it *o sushi*, with the honorific *o* that precedes also the words for tea and sugar—is made of cold rice and vinegar formed into balls and wrapped with bits of fish, either raw or cooked. It takes a knack to get the rice just right, so that it does not fall apart, and to prepare the fish. The man and girl behind the counter worked with flashing hands, making the balls, slicing the fish, putting the combination down on the counter before us, one after another. We took them up in our fingers, dipped them in the soya sauce, ate them, rinsed our fingers in the little trough of running water, took a sip of tea and like a row of hungry fledglings on a branch watched expectantly for the next.

I cannot now remember all the different kinds of fish that came before me in bewildering succession. There was only one that I balked at: prawns sliced down alive and leaping, their tails still twitching on the rice. I was assured that they had a particularly delicate flavor, but I could not eat something that wriggled. All the rest I ate and enjoyed: raw *tai,* or sea bream, raw abalone, something called (I think) *anago,* which was like eel, cooked and tender and delicious, and others that I have forgotten.

We four were the only guests; we chatted with the cooks and with one another. The atmosphere of the place was hospitable, leisurely and quiet. Princess Atsuko, like a good Japanese wife, had little to say in her husband's presence; she looked petite and pretty and radiantly happy. Mr. Ikeda talked about his farm and about agriculture in Japan. He told me that the farmers in Okayama Prefecture were prosperous because they had other work to do besides farming. They could afford scooters and three-wheeled trucks.

I thought of Princess Atsuko as I had known her when she and her sisters were schoolgirls and my pupils. They lived in Kureta-keryo, a good-sized house in the Palace grounds, with a garden of its own enclosed by a high fence, and they went out only in Palace cars and accompanied by Miss Natori, their governess, or one of their ladies-in-waiting. Princess Atsuko was fifteen and Princess Kazuko seventeen when they came to visit me one summer in Karuizawa.

What they wanted above all things was to go for a walk like ordinary people along the streets of the village, to look in the windows of the shops and buy some gifts to take home. We were accompanied by Miss Natori on this daring expedition and followed at a discreet distance by two plain-clothes policemen—or perhaps *plain* is not exactly the word, for they were resplendent in dazzling white linen suits at a time when soap was so scarce that most men were fortunate if their shirts were only faintly yellow.

On Tuesday afternoons in Tokyo when they came to my house for an English lesson and a practice tea party, their long black limousine was parked down the street at the corner, so that they could have the experience of walking up the lane and through the front gate instead of being deposited on the doorstep.

There seemed to be little in Princess Atsuko's upbringing behind the moat to prepare her for the kind of life she was living now, but with what zest and competence she had thrown herself into it! Saying good-by to them on the station platform, where they accompanied us at the end of the day, I thought that this lovable young couple, improbable as it might seem, was in truth very much like scores of ambitious young people in the United States, determined to "get ahead": the husband absorbed in his business, working overtime, the wife helping him where she could, entering into his plans, occasionally going with him on his business trips but more often accepting patiently his absences and the loneliness they entailed. I looked at the young Ikedas, standing there together smiling and waving, and I saw them forging steadily ahead until the little house on the ledge became a big one withdrawn in a garden, and the little car driven by Mr. Ikeda turned into a Mercedes-Benz and a chauffeur. And I could imagine them looking back nostalgically and saying, as so many others have said, "Oh yes, we're very well off now, but the early days of struggle were really the best!"

8

Japanese Inns

THERE are many comfortable and pleasant hotels of the Western style in Japan. In fact, the Imperial Hotel in Tokyo and the Fujiya Hotel in Miyanoshita are on my selected list of hotels which I count the most delightful that I have known for atmosphere, comfort and courtesy, a list that includes the Gritti Palace, Venice, the Halekulani, Honolulu, the Sligachan Hotel, Skye (but that was twenty years ago), and the Highlands Inn, Carmel, California. But it is a pity for people who go to Japan not to stay in some of the enchanting Japanese inns.

I have written elsewhere of the Tawaraya in Kyoto, with the result that people go there and ask to have "my" room, and it remains my home whenever I am in that ancient and fascinating city, but there are other inns in other places which also I love to remember.

All Japanese inns are run according to a certain pattern. You are the guest of the house in a much more personal and less perfunctory way than in Western hostelries. If they know when you are coming, someone will meet you at the station with a car. When you reach the inn and enter through the gateway into a little courtyard with bamboo fence, stepping stones and gravel, green shrubs and a wide open door, you will find an array of maids in bright kimonos waiting to receive you.

You take off your shoes at the door and a boy puts them away in a cupboard. You need not worry about them. Whenever you go out, the news will have preceded you through the house in a flurry of feet on corridors and a rustle of swift-moving kimonos and by the time you get to the door your own shoes will be waiting for you on the front step, ready for you to step into, with a long shoehorn at hand to help.

Stepping out of your shoes on arrival, you step into a pair of scuffs and shuffle down the polished wooden corridor after your hostess or the maid. At a sliding paper door she goes down on her knees, opens it, and invites you in. You leave your scuffs on the threshold and step in your stocking feet on to the *tatami*, the thick, clean, springy matting that covers the floor.

The first room that you enter is a dressing room. Here you find a cupboard that contains your bed-quilts and also shelves and trays for your clothes. On one of the trays will be a freshly laundered cotton kimono, printed in blue and white, for you to wear, and in cold weather a thickly padded kimono also, of some neutral shade. In the room too there will be a little dressing table without legs. Probably of red lacquer, it will have two or three drawers and a tall thin mirror with a silk curtain over it. You sit on the tatami in front of it to look in the glass, and when you are not using the mirror you keep it covered in a seemly way. They will tell you vaguely, if you ask why, that it is to keep the mirror clean, but there are deeper reasons than that.

One of the three sacred treasures of the Imperial regalia is the mirror which was supposed to have been given by Amaterasu-no-Omikami, the Sun Goddess, to her grandson, the first Japanese Emperor. The earliest Japanese, like other primitive peoples, had a feeling of reverence and fear for the mysterious surface that reflected objects and faces. In Shinto shrines throughout Japan today there is a mirror in the main sanctuary. Common as mirrors have become in ordinary life there still clings about them a remnant of the age-old mystery and reverence, and so you have a nice strip of printed silk to hang over your looking-glass.

You do not stay in the dressing room, you go on into the larger room, which is your living room, dining room and bedroom as long as you are here. It will be a lovely room in its proportions and its simplicity. Like all Japanese rooms, it will have a *tokonoma*, or alcove, with a hanging scroll containing a painting suitable to the season, and a flower arrangement below it. In a corner of the room will probably be a low table with writing materials, and in the center a larger table of polished wood or lacquer, about a foot high, where sitting on the floor on a flat, brocade-covered cushion, you will have your meals, spread out your guidebooks and maps and write your post cards and letters. If the weather is cool there will be a brazier beside the table with a few sticks of charcoal glowing on a bed of fine white ash.

The sliding paper doors are probably open on to the *roka*, a narrow balcony with a tiled or wooden floor, where there are a wicker table and two wicker chairs. Scuffs are conveniently placed for your use on the *roka*. Here you sit at the table and look out through glass doors, which slide open in warm weather, onto the garden or the view, whichever it may be. Even in the most crowded cities, there will be something refreshing for you to look at. The tiniest garden is skillfully made, by the use of bamboo, flowering shrubs, ferns, rocks and pebbles, to suggest a cool woodland scene with hidden spaces. Or you may look out at the sea between pine trees or a soaring mountain.

From the *roka* in many inns there is a door to your private lavatory. Your bath you arrange for at a particular time, and you are escorted to it in state, sometimes to a considerable distance.

Reports about communal bathing have frightened many a Western tourist away from Japanese inns, and quite unnecessarily. The saying, "In Western hotels you dine in public and bathe in private; in Japanese inns you dine in private and bathe in public" is only a half truth.

Friends of mine traveling in Hokkaido did, it is true, stay in an old-fashioned inn where the bath was a large one intended for general use. The young wife decided against it but her husband made the plunge. The next day on the street she saw him greet a very pretty young Japanese girl, and asked him, "Where did you meet her?" "In the bathtub last night," he answered airily. Ordinarily, however, by mentioning one's desire, one can have the bath to oneself. Many inns have different-sized baths and sometimes a family will go in together.

Beyond the first sliding door is an ante-room for dressing and undressing, and beyond the second, the bath itself, where you soap and rinse thoroughly first, either in a shower or with basins which you fill at a tap, and then steep up to your neck in a tub of steaming hot water. Sometimes the tub is square, of satin-y wood; sometimes it is a round iron cauldron with a wooden raft on which to sit; sometimes it is beautifully tiled, like a miniature swimming pool.

It is very pleasant to take your bath late in the afternoon, when you are tired and dusty from a day's sightseeing, to put on the kimono provided by the inn, and then, refreshed and relaxed, to sit at the low table in your room and eat the dinner which the kimono'ed maids bring to you.

They kneel to slide open the paper door, move the tray over the threshold, stand to enter the room, kneel again to close the door, pick up the tray and walk across the room to bring you your soup or whatever it is and kneel to place it before you. Up and down, up and down, and each time they kneel there is the swift movement of one hand to smooth the kimono under the knee. No wonder Japanese women are so supple and graceful!

The food that they bring you is delicious and it is pretty to look at as well, with combinations of color, texture and flavor carefully planned, and set forth on exquisite china and lacquer.

There is no need to be afraid of raw fish. It is not a whole fish on a plate just as it comes from the market! It is three or four small, chilled squares of boneless fish with a delicate flavor—sea bream or tuna are the kinds I have most frequently had—with a tangy sauce to dip them in.

Most Westerners know and like *tempura*, the batter-dipped delicacies fried in deep fat which the Portuguese taught the Japanese to cook in the sixteenth century, or *sukiyaki* (pronounced skee-yahki), the meat and vegetables cooked over charcoal at the table, but there are many other dishes that should be discovered and enjoyed. There will be two or three kinds of soup at a meal, for instance, and all good. Sometimes in the clear soup there will be tiny clams in the open shell, a little tricky to disengage with chopsticks, but worth the effort. There is also *chawan-mushi*, which means steamed teacup, and which is an egg-custard made with broth instead of milk and filled with bits of chicken, tiny shrimp, chestnuts or, in season, ginkgo nuts, mushrooms, and the Japanese equivalent of parsley; not all of these things at once, but some little surprises in the smooth, hot custard. In the fall, when the *matsudake*, or pine mushrooms, are ripe, there are dozens of mushroom dishes and sometimes you will get more than one in the same meal. I especially like a kind of broth, which comes in a little gray pottery teapot with its matching cup on its head, but there are many other delicious ways to cook and serve this favorite delicacy.

Spinach usually comes bright green and tender and ice-cold, in little bunches of leaves all the same size, dressed with soya sauce and sesame seed. Three or four edible-pod peas, crisp and young, appear to garnish some other dish; bamboo sprouts and sliced lotus root (like little wheels) in their seasons provide a wonderfully crisp texture and subtle flavor. Tiny flakes of fresh ginger, dipped in some red sauce, appear in unexpected places. With a *tempura* meal, for contrast with the batter and oil, I have had breast of chicken and tart apple grated together.

Rice comes at the end of the meal, followed by green tea. Dessert is not a regular part of Japanese meals but in deference to Western custom fruit is usually provided. The Japanese fruit was a revelation to me. No one had ever told me it was so large and beautiful and full of flavor. One reason for its excellence is that it is not sprayed with chemicals but the farmers and their families patiently make by hand little paper bags to cover each peach or pear or apple or bunch of grapes and protect it from insects. During the years after the war when paper was very scarce, a shipment of Bibles sent by the American Bible Society to convert the rural areas was a great boon to the pear and apple growers of Nagano Prefecture. The thin-paper pages were exactly the right size and weight.

Fruit in Japan is seasonal as it no longer is in the United States, where we can get strawberries from California all year round and apples and oranges and grapefruit have no season at all. You enjoy each fruit in turn for the short period of its ripening and then you do not see it again for a full year. Rosy-cheeked peaches, each one of a size to include a Momotaro (the Peach Boy of a famous Japanese fairy tale) and full of flavor, are followed by pale and juicy pears round as an orange and crisp as cucumbers; figs come in September and then the apples and persimmons of the autumn, and enormous thin-skinned green grapes. There are mandarin oranges for the winter, and for the earliest spring, strawberries grown on stone terraces warmed by the sun and so big that three are a generous serving. *Biwa*, or loquats, a mild, yellow, fleshy fruit, tide one over till the summer oranges, sour and rather like grapefruit, usher the peaches in again.

Feeling replete after dinner and comfortably weary, you go to bed early. The maids pull the "rain doors" out of their cases, heavy wooden doors that make a loud rumbling noise as they roll into place outside the glass doors of the *roka*, and you are shut up for the night. Plenty of air in the daytime is the rule here as in England, but at night the mists and breezes are shut out. It isn't necessary to feel immediately suffocated, for air does drift in through cracks.

The table is removed from the center of the room and the sleeping quilts are brought out of the cupboard. Two thick pads covered with bright brocade go down first, then a cotton sheet. Over them is spread the covering quilt, with a sheet buttoned on to it. If it is cold you have more quilts over you. The pillow is small and hard and stuffed, I think, with bran. A square lamp with a frame made of bamboo or lacquer is set at the head of the beds, one or two or three in a row, however many there are in your party. In hot weather, in places where mosquitoes are bad, a mosquito net like a great cage is hung from hooks in the four corners of the room, and you whisk in quickly in the hope of beating the mosquitoes to it.

The first time you sleep "on *tatami*" you realize that that thick springy matting is harder than you thought and that your own bones are nearer the surface. You may even feel a little bruised when you get up. But the second night is better and by the third you are realizing that not only have you slept well but that you haven't really quite been in Japan until you have lived for at least a few days on *tatami*.

You get up when you wake up. It is still dark in your room, but somehow your maid—and there appears to be one who has nothing else to do but to wait upon you—knows when you begin to stir and she appears at once to open the rain doors and the glass doors and the paper doors, air the room and put away the beds while you are dressing in the outer room. When you are ready for breakfast it appears.

Here is another source of fear and dread to Westerners. They have heard that the Japanese eat bean soup for breakfast and they want none of it. They are not strong enough for bean soup so early in the morning; they want their coffee.

During the years right after the war I used to take a jar of instant coffee with me to the inns, as well as my own bread (to make toast over the charcoal brazier) and tinned butter, but now you can get good coffee in any inn. There is plenty of fruit, the Japanese are now making a variety of excellent breads, and they will cook your eggs in any way you want.

The only time I have ever had a real Japanese breakfast was in the temple on Koya San, and by that time I was thoroughly at home with Japanese food. The breakfast which the young monk brought consisted of rice, hot and filling, bean soup, which is not the thick potage we know but a thin, cloudy, rather acid liquid made of bean paste and boiling water, dried seaweed, pickles, cold broiled mushrooms, and green tea. It was all, actually, very good.

The splendid bath at Shojiin gave us a surprise, though we knew from the tourist bureau that it was a fine new one designed by a specialist in bath architecture.

We were the only guests in the temple that Sunday evening, and so even though there was no lock on the door of the famous bath we felt safe from intrusion. There was the usual ante-room for undressing and then the bath itself, tiled in white and blue, with a beautifully shaped pool big enough for anywhere from ten to twenty bathers. The water was fresh and hot and Tané and I were simmering peacefully when we heard the outer door open and then saw the black bulk of a monk filling the clouded glass panel of the inner door. The door began to slide open.

I freeze into speechlessness in moments of crisis, but Tané was vocal. *"Haite imasu!"* she screeched, which meant, "We're in here!"—just as if, she said afterwards, he didn't know that and wasn't coming in, just for that reason, to perform the services of a bath steward. The panic in her voice stopped him; there was a brief exchange of Japanese courtesies, and after he had retreated we resumed our simmering with reminiscent giggles. How often since then I have regretted a lost opportunity, thinking how use-ful it would be to say casually at dinner parties when the conversation needs revitalizing, "When I was taking my bath in the temple and the monk was scrubbing my back . . ."

Of all the charming Japanese inns I have known besides the Tawaraya, I think of three that stand out in my memory. One is Hassho-kan, a longish taxi-ride out of Nagoya, which is set in a large and beautiful grove of pine trees, and which is famous for its combination of the traditional and the modern. Pictures of its new part, which won an architectural prize in 1951, and of the tiny garden which the bath house overlooks, have appeared in American magazines and books on architecture. Air conditioning is concealed under the *tokonomas*, and the bed-quilts on which you sleep are filled with foam rubber. It is fairly expensive, but not unduly so when you take into consideration the beauty and peace of the setting and the perfection of food and service.

Among the tall trees there is a thatch-roofed farmhouse—like all such farmhouses it is "three hundred years old"—open for guests to see. The Japanese acquaintance who first showed it to me struggled to express in limited English the feelings which the age and quiet of the little building awoke in him. "I like to sit here, in kimono, and write a Japanese poem," he said.

In Matsue on the Japan Sea, where Lafcadio Hearn lived for a number of years, I spent a night at the Minami-kan. From our window we looked out on the Shinji Lagoon to mountains beyond. It was a lovely scene in the late afternoon: the blue lake, an old bridge, a point of land with some small black and white houses, a few fishing boats, and the opalescent lights repeating and reflecting each other through the mist as clouds veiled the sunset and at last rain fell and the little boats went home. I hated to leave in the morning and we had to hurry at the last to catch our train. People of southern Honshu make much of the tea ceremony and have it not only in tea-houses with the leisurely formality I had known elsewhere, but also in ordinary rooms to dignify any occasion. Our hostess at Minami-kan was disconcerted to find us dashing for the train just as she prepared a farewell ceremonial tea for us. Undaunted, she pursued us down the hall and I gulped the thick powdered tea from a bowl held in one hand while I wielded the shoehorn with the other.

The Nabeya in Hitoyoshi, the city of our adventures with the Mikamis, is another inn that I remember fondly. We slept in the Kirinoma, the Misty Room, from where we could see the river rushing below, a long arched bridge, and the low hill called the Sleeping Buddha. There was the fresh green odor of new *tatami* in the room and a classical arrangement of pine branches and daisy chrysanthemums in an old bronze vase in the *tokonoma*. After a hot spring bath that did away completely with the chills and sneezes which had been bothering me all day, I fell deeply asleep to the music of the river chuckling with its stones.

The next day we took a luncheon with us which the inn had prepared. Most hotel box lunches of my experience have been substantial and nourishing but scarcely imaginative. This one was a little work of art. When the lid of the oblong wooden box came off, there was revealed an arrangement of food as pretty as a flower arrangement, and decorated with a bit of palm leaf. There were little white rice balls wrapped in shiny black seaweed, pink shrimps, bits of fish dipped in soya sauce and browned over charcoal, broiled mushrooms, pickles, and chestnuts boiled and sweetened.

It is difficult to confine myself to mentioning only three inns out of the many that I have enjoyed. How can I leave out the Hinako in Beppu or the Koraku in Okayama or the one on Enoshima whose name I have forgotten, where we stopped one afternoon for tea?

We had had a picnic lunch on the beach opposite the island near Kamakura and then had walked across the long bridge and up the steep hill to the shrine. The day was warm and the ham sandwiches had made us thirsty. Coming down the steep stone passageway between an unbroken row of souvenir shops on one

side and inns on the other, I saw through the gateway of one inn
a glimpse of sea and mountains, and I suggested that we go in
and engage a room for a time and have tea—which we did.

An old man in a gardener's blue *happi* coat was sweeping the
ground with a twig broom that came straight out of a fairy tale.

"Honorable Grandfather," said Tané politely in Japanese,
"may we come in and look at the honorable view?"

Honorable Grandfather, to whom American tourists were evidently no novelty, continued his sweeping. "O.K.," he said
wearily without looking up, "W.C."

9

Dedicated Girls

WHILE we were in Kyoto our friend Mr. Kozo Sawada invited us to have dinner with him. It was not the first time. Seven years ago he took us to a fascinating restaurant called Hyotei, three hundred years old and run by the thirteenth generation of the same family. In the early days travelers coming in from Osaka stopped there for a meal and to get new straw sandals before going on into Kyoto. More recently, when the present Empress was a girl, she was brought here by her father, then a general stationed in the old capital.

There was a garden with a pool fed by a stream from Lake Biwa, which rippled and whispered beyond the paper doors of the house. Going in, in the twilight, we could see the carp, but when we left, after a tea ceremony and a long and delicious meal, a maid in kimono, carrying a lighted paper lantern, led us along winding paths through an enchanted darkness.

Tonight, however, when Mr. Sawada came for us, looking very distinguished in kimono and *hakama*, the wide, divided skirt that goes over kimono for formal wear, he said, "I am going to take you to a different place this time. Last time, because of your connection with the Imperial Family, I could not introduce geisha to you, and I think your Japanese education has been incomplete."

Toriimoto is an old restaurant in the Gion section of Kyoto, the "pleasure quarter" of the city, where the geisha live. It perhaps needs to be said again that geisha are not prostitutes, but talented women trained to be entertaining, to dance, sing, play the samisen, talk well on current topics, dress well and look charming. Their services are engaged by the hour, at rather a high price, through a "broker" or agent. When a Japanese man entertains a business associate—or foreign guest—he leaves his wife, *Okusama*, Honorable Within, at home and takes his friends to a restaurant, where he arranges for geisha to come and entertain them. There are various ways of looking at this custom— and I have always seen it chiefly through the eyes of the Japanese wife, who scrimps and saves and works hard, only to see the money for which she has made sacrifices spent lavishly on women whose profession it is to charm. On the other hand, it could also be said that the Japanese wife does not have to add to her other jobs, as the American wife does, the strain of keeping the children stowed away while she gives parties, without adequate help, that will convince her husband's superior and his very critical wife that her husband should have a promotion and a raise.

Toriimoto specialized in *gionryori*, a characteristic kind of cooking which was brought from Nagasaki two centuries ago. Soon after we had sat down on the *tatami* in a room with the sliding doors open on the garden and the mild October evening, in walked an enchanting little creature in a pale blue kimono whose flowered skirts, padded at the hem like wedding robes, trailed on the floor behind her, an embroidered obi that swathed her from breast to hips, and the traditional hair-do with floral ornaments and a silver pin that dangled and glittered. She had a face like a kitten, wide at the eyes and cheekbones, pointed at the chin, with a small, turned-up nose, and a kitten's baby look and playful ways. Her face and neck were painted white, except for a small dark triangle at the nape of her neck, which showed when she bowed low, and her lower lip and just a little of her upper lip were scarlet. Her name was Ko-Fuji, and she had an engaging giggle, like water gurgling over pebbles. A little later a second one appeared, slightly taller, more conventionally pretty, more self-conscious. Both of their obis were tied high in the back with long ends that came almost to the floor and swung gently as they moved. Neither one was a day over fifteen. They were *maiko*, young girls still in training to be geisha.

We sat, Mr. Sawada, Tané and I, facing the garden, each with a lacquered tray in front of us, and the *maiko* knelt before us, pouring sake and orange drink, giggling, talking "Kyoto language," which might be compared to a Virginia or a South Carolina accent, asking questions about the Crown Prince and answering our questions about their own life and training.

They had been through the nine years of compulsory education, but in a school in the Gion district that was almost entirely attended by the children of geisha. After sixth grade, they told us, they never cut their hair, so that the sculptured black rolls and loops on their heads were their own, not wigs, as is frequently the case with the traditional coiffures that appear at New Year's time. They had just passed the *maiko* examination, and now were studying flower arrangement, dancing, singing, and so on. Their nights usually ended about two A.M. and sometimes their assignments included going to modern night clubs with their employers.

Though this was actually my first party with geisha, I had heard much about them from other Westerners, and I waited for the samisen, the "baseball dance," the parlor tricks and finger games that I had been told were a usual feature of geisha parties. Nothing like that came forth however; we ate the succession of interesting dishes in this quiet and pleasant room, with these pretty children prattling and filling our glasses. Mr. Sawada, whose business is silk and the designing of new patterns, and whose avocation is collecting old Chinese art, was a very interesting talker, and we did not need to play pat-in and pat-out.

After dinner he suggested that we go walking with our *maiko* through this old section of Kyoto. We put on our shoes again, and they donned *zori* with very high platforms, and off we went, they leading the way, their long skirts held up skillfully in one hand, their long obis swaying behind them.

Old brown wooden houses with latticed windows lined the narrow streets on both sides and over the doorways hung lighted paper lanterns, some small and red, some larger and yellow. It was like a stage setting in its quiet, ancient atmosphere, with none of the sudden stores, the burst of light and noise, the untidy places to be found in most Japanese city streets.

Once we passed a group of university students who turned in palpable excitement to look at our *maiko* but who made no attempt to follow them or to attract their attention. Once I heard a kind of howl that I took to be the equivalent of a wolf whistle, but it did not come from boys. Six little girls in the blue serge middies and skirts of their school uniforms, followed the *maiko* for a while, squealing and giggling, reaching out from time to time to touch them. The *maiko* walked along without giving a sign that they noticed, and the schoolgirls faded away.

Suddenly the *maiko* turned and went through an inn-like gate, and we followed. We were obviously expected, for the door was open and hostesses were there in the lighted entrance to greet us.

We were led to a handsome room with polished wood and a big table in the center. Beer was brought for Mr. Sawada and orange drink for Tané and me. The hostess, a dignified and attractive middle-aged woman, sat with us.

This house was, I was told, a *machiai*, which is not a restaurant but a place for meeting, and we were to be entertained. An older geisha, confident and voluble, came in, talked for a few minutes, and then went out taking the young girls with her. Doors were slid open, revealing a much larger room. The geisha sat down out of sight with her bass samisen and played and sang.

The *maiko* danced a dance of the seasons—spring, summer, autumn, and winter. Their little, pointed, fluid hands, their feet in white mitten-socks managing not to step on their long skirts, their serious expressions and precise, graceful movements, were all charming, and their extreme youth and doomed innocence gave them, especially the kitten, a certain poetry and poignancy.

The house, known as Mantei, was an old and famous one. Oishi Yoshio, the leader of the well-known Forty-Seven Ronin, had visited it in 1702 or 3. The story of the Forty-Seven Ronin is a favorite one, too well-known to bear repeating in detail. Masefield, in "The Faithful Ones," has made an English version. To the Japanese the masterless samurai who avenged an insult to their lord and then were forced to commit suicide in a body, is a romantic and inspiring tale of courage, loyalty and sacrifice; it is the subject of one of Chikamatsu's most beloved plays, *Chushin Gura*. To the Occupation, however, it was a reprehensible exhibition of revenge and the militaristic spirit, and it was banned from schools and theaters alike. Some of the forty-seven, while they were plotting their revenge, to throw dust in people's eyes and create the impression that they were mere frivolous roisterers instead of serious-minded heroes bent on murder, were unfaithful to their wives and squandered money on geisha. Because of Oishi's patronage of Mantei in this operation, there was a little shrine in his honor, which we were shown.

It was the typical small Buddhist shrine, with a draped curtain, flowers, brass and lacquer shining in the darkness, the smell of incense. At the top was an effigy of Lord Asano, with Oishi beside him, and below were ranged the rest of the ronin, forty-six small, old, beautifully fashioned dolls. It was evident from the reverence with which the shrine was approached that the story has a hold over people still.

When we said good-by to our generous and thoughtful host, thanking him for a charming evening, and returned to our inn, I felt that I had seen Japan's unique institution, the geisha, at its best.

The next day I encountered young girls caught in a very different web.

Tané and I went to the Chuguji temple outside of Nara to see again the Nyorin Kwannon there, which is one of my favorite pieces of sculpture in all the world.

It was a warm sunny October day. We drove through ricefields that seemed to march all the way across the plain to the mountains, where pagodas and temple roofs emerged here and there from the billowing green of the trees. In the paddies, where the ripe rice was heavy-headed, tabs of silver-shiny tin strung on wires waved and winked in the sun to scare away the sparrows. White herons rose out of the shallow river as we passed, and black *tobi*—kites—wheeled in the sky overhead. We drove through Nara, past the shops and the park and the temple of the great Buddha, and on to the Horyuji temple, in whose precincts the little nunnery of Chuguji is situated.

We were met by an elderly nun, black-robed and shaven-headed, who took us directly into the room where the Kwannon is housed. It is a larger than life-size figure, carved of camphor wood, dark with time and polish, the product of an unknown Korean artist of the eighth century. Seated, with one foot on a lotus and the other resting on her thigh, the fingers of one hand touching her cheek, her lovely face serene and meditative, she represents the Bodhisattva of Compassion. I say she, for Kwannon is generally considered a goddess, but actually she is sexless. Curtains are half drawn around her, but we were allowed to go close and look at her from every angle.

In contrast to the Buddhas of the neighboring Horyuji, which wore perennial shawls of dust, the Kwannon, cared for lovingly by women, is immaculate. The other treasures in the small room are also cherished and in good order. There is the embroidery

made by the mother of Prince Shotoku and her ladies, early in
the seventh century, which shows Buddha entering into Para-
dise. There is a small shrine with a statue of Kobo Daishi, the
ninth-century saint and scholar, and a still smaller one of Prince
Shotoku at eighteen.

After looking our fill here, we were led back to a reception
room which was furnished with a rug over the *tatami* floor, a
long refectory table and Western chairs, and here we were served
by a young nun first Western tea and sweet cakes with chestnuts
in them, and then ceremonial green tea.

The tea and cakes reminded me of the first time I came to
Chuguji, in November of 1946. It was cold then and damp, and
the hot teacups were comforting to wrap one's numb fingers
around. There were no cakes, so soon after the war, but thin
slices of dried sweet potato, toasted to a delicate crispness.

We had been waited on by two young nuns, and the abbess
who was a former princess had joined us. She had worn a kimono
of rich purple silk, with a kesa, or stole, of bright brocade, and in
spite of her shaven head, bare and uncovered, without any of the
coifs and wimples so becoming to Christian nuns, she was beautiful and patrician-looking. "She had," I wrote home enthusiastically, "that simple and rather gay goodness that the best nuns
everywhere have."

Now, eleven years later, I asked about the abbess, and was
told she had two nunneries to manage and was that day away at
the other one. The name, however, was different. "It must have
been the one before her that I knew," I suggested, and was told
that the predecessor had been very old and saw no one. Then I
remembered. Several years ago *Time* magazine was full of the
story. My abbess had eloped with a salesman who had come into
the nunnery to take lessons in flower arrangement. We aban-
doned that unfortunate topic and settled on the safer one of the
old nun herself, who had a sweet, worn innocent face with the
merriness of the cloistered.

She had come to Chuguji, she told us, at the age of nine, and she had been here for sixty-five years. There were reasons why it was better for her mother not to have her at home.

Were girls so young, I wanted to know, still given to the nunnery before they were old enough to know what was happening to them?

Oh yes, the two youngest nuns out of the ten there now were eighteen and nineteen. One had been brought to Chuguji by her parents at the age of four, the other at twelve.

What about their education?

They must go to the local school for the compulsory nine years. Before the war, when it was only six grades, it was easier. They are required to shave their heads at the end of the sixth grade—just the time when the *maiko* are required to let their hair grow—and they shrink from appearing among the other children with their bare, knobby little skulls. The school, said the old nun, cheering up, makes a special arrangement whereby they can be released from regular attendance at school and have special classes at the nunnery. The study of the sutras and other religious instruction they get from the priests at the Horyuji.

She asked about entrance into convents in America and I told her what I knew about the novitiate and the taking of final vows.

"That is the better way," she said with a sigh. Then she added, "We have found, though, that only those who have been taken into the nunnery as children make really good nuns. Those who come because they have suffered outside and are seeking peace of mind are not to be depended on."

The nuns may be visited by their families from time to time, and once a year they may go home for a day. The rest of their lives they stay there in that small place, rising at five-thirty for prayers, some in the room with the Kwannon, some in another room, caring for the sacred treasures, studying, taking—and sometimes giving—lessons in tea ceremony and flower arrangement.

The nunnery building was once a palace, brought to the temple grounds and set up there as a fitting abode for the Kwannon. The nuns have always come from aristocratic families, and until the end of the Meiji period the abbess was always a princess of the blood. We were led through the rooms and passages to an inner garden, where there was an old, two-story white-plastered house with a black tile roof, which had been the home of the abbess in the old days. Here the Crown Prince had rested when he came to see Chuguji and they had served him a vegetarian lunch.

In the little enclosed garden, of rocks and pebbles and green shrubs, the old nun posed for a photograph with the two youngest nuns. One of the young girls had a white kimono with a black *hakama*, or divided skirt, over it; the other wore a pink kimono under her *hakama*. No, there was no significance. Pink was easier to keep clean than white. There were no rules about it. They were sweet, fresh-faced, cheerful-looking girls.

They came with us to the entrance to say good-by, and we went out of the shady walled compound into the long road, lined with stalls selling souvenirs to attract the tourists, swarming with uniformed school children on study-trips, open to the glare of the sun and the wind-blown dust that stung our faces.

For a long time I carried with me the memory of the two young nuns and the two little *maiko*, turning it over and over in my mind. Victims, all four of them, of parents' sins or indifference or misfortune or ambition, they had been bound before the possibility of conscious decision to a life apart, a life of rigid discipline and obedience. Yet it was not all dark: beauty was accessible to them all, and peace to some, gaiety and some luxury to others. Among the older women who ruled them, whatever dark impulses and hidden cruelty one might imagine, one saw only an outward protectiveness and even tenderness.

Certainly of the two I should prefer to be a *maiko*.

10

Genji the Shining One

I AM never quite sure whether my favorite novel is Jane Austen's *Emma* or *The Tale of Genji*, by Lady Murasaki Shikibu: it depends upon which I have been reading last. Both belong on any selected list of the great novels of the world.

Genji, which was written early in the eleventh century and which Edmund Gosse says may be considered the oldest novel in the world, was superbly translated into English in the 1920's by Arthur Waley, and has been recently reissued in a paperback edition. So good is the translation that Sir George Sansom suggests that the book is even better in English than in the original —not because of any shortcomings in Murasaki's work but because "modern English is incomparably richer, stronger, more various and supple than Heian Japanese."

The extraordinary thing about *Genji* is its reality and the psychological truth of its characterizations, the humanity of these imaginary people of an age and civilization so far removed from our own, the humor, the freshness, and the enduring interest of the book. Though it is full of detail of the life of the Japanese court in a day of great formality and aesthetic preoccupations, the scenes are never artificial or unconvincing. Alan Priest of the Metropolitan Museum of Art points out that if this were indeed the modern historical novel that it resembles, reviewers would doubtless question the accuracy of the background and conversation—but Murasaki was there.

Prince Genji, the Shining One, was the handsome and brilliant son of the Emperor by a concubine. He had great position and power in the court, though he was not eligible to succeed his father. Irresistible to ladies (all but one, whom he courted unsuccessfully for years) he had a series of love affairs which led him into many scrapes and once to disgrace and temporary exile. The remarkable thing about Genji, however, was not his amorousness but his loyalty. "It was not indeed in his nature ever to forget any one of whom he had once been fond," and he went to the greatest trouble to be kind to the ladies whom he had once loved and to do it in such a way that they should not suspect him of patronage or charity. The unattractive and absurd frump known by the punning nickname of the Lady of the Red Flowers (*hana*, flower, also means nose) with whom he got involved, actually preened herself upon his continued affection. "He meanwhile was thinking what a uniquely depressing and wearisome creature she was and deciding that he really must make up his mind to be a little kinder to her, since it was certain that no one else intended to take the business off his hands."

The real love of his life was Murasaki (from whose name the author of the book herself has come to be known) who when she first appears is an enchanting little girl of ten. The nineteen-year-old Genji, seeing her in a mountain temple, resolves to adopt her, bring her up and ultimately marry her. Not surprisingly he finds it impossible to persuade the nun, her grandmother, whose ward she is, of the sincerity of his purpose "to be a mother to her," but on the death of the nun the child's nurse yields her to Genji. Some of the most delightful pages in the book are concerned with descriptions of this child and her relationship with Genji, their games, the toys he gives her, including "a doll's kitchen, only three feet high but fitted out with all the proper utensils," and the trouble he took to teach her to write, to paint and to play the zithern.

There are few descriptions of children in early English writings, but in this eleventh-century Japanese novel again and again in a few words a child comes to life: a little girl with a cage of singing crickets or a small, important page boy. Genji's supposed son, Kaoru, at the teething stage got hold of a piece of bamboo sprout to chew; when they tried to take it from him, he "took not the slightest notice and with a great clatter crawled away with his prize as fast as his arms and legs could carry him."

Little Murasaki grew up into a young lady of great beauty and charm and Genji duly married her. Though she was the daughter of a prince, her mother had been only a commoner, and so, even after his wife's death, Genji could not make her his *kita no kata*, his official wife. But she was, as long as she lived, the dominant figure in his palace. He loved her more than he himself realized, he became very dependent on her, but he made her unhappy again and again. She understood him, as an adoring woman will sometimes understand a most exasperating man without losing any of her affection for him, and she took him always with tolerance and humor. But when at forty, under pressure from the Emperor, he brought to his palace a thirteen-year-old princess as his *kita no kata*, Murasaki was struck to the heart. Her pride too suffered acutely, when it occurred, separately, to three women friends of hers that it would be kind to call upon her. "They arrived in rapid succession, thus bringing home to her in the most painful fashion that she had become an object of sympathy." When Murasaki died, evidently of tuberculosis, still in her thirties, Genji was genuinely heartbroken, a sorrow from which he never recovered.

Someone, Somerset Maugham, I think, said of Elizabeth Bennet that she is interesting as a woman's idea of a really attractive woman. The same thing could be said of Murasaki. She had beauty, wit and tact. Childless herself, she took great delight in children, and even her chagrin when Genji brought home his new bride did not prevent her from making friends with the immature child who was her rival. "They met very often or when that was impossible, exchanged little notes concerned exclusively with the behavior of Nyosan's dolls and the fortunes or reverses of her other toys." She had great skill with her clothes as well as in writing poetry and her taste in all things was impeccable. "Though generous and long-suffering" she was nobody's dupe: she was "capable of making judgments that were by no means devoid of sharpness." She had infinite variety. Other women, even young girls, were boringly predictable to the experienced Genji, but Murasaki kept always the power of surprising him.

Genji himself, growing older (that they are all old at forty is the chief evidence that this story is really of a long-past era), lost none of his charm. The Emperor who succeeded his father, commenting on Genji, says: "His face when in repose has now a nobility and dignity that in his younger and more irresponsible days were lacking; but I still think that he is never so attractive as when laughing and talking sheer nonsense." He had an engaging capacity for seeing himself objectively, a modern quality quite unimaginable in heroes of contemporary English literature such as, say "Byrhtnoth's Death." Delivering himself one day of an improving lecture to his young bride he "caught in his own voice a familiar intonation. How often, years ago, those responsible for his upbringing had adopted just this tone and how dreary, how contemptible he had thought their self-righteous homilies. 'Boring old man!' That is what she must be thinking."

It is not only the leading characters in the story who live in three dimensions, but there are also brilliant sketches of minor characters: Genji's lifelong friend, To no Chujo, whose standards "where other people's conduct was concerned" were "singularly exacting"; Lady Rokujo, who thought herself free of jealousy, until she realized that in her dreams there was a fury of emotion which her waking mind would not have countenanced; the boisterous, good-natured, unpresentable daughter of To no Chujo; Genji's steady, earnest, uninteresting son Yujiri; and many others.

Some of the details in *Genji* interested me especially because I found the same thing—or their echo—in the life of the court today. The heir to the eleventh-century throne lived in the Eastern Palace and was, like the Crown Prince now, the Eastern Prince. References to the ceremony of the Putting on of the *Hakama* reminded me of a moving picture of the Crown Prince in his first *hakama* that I had seen one evening when I dined at Kaintei with the Imperial Family. A handsome, solemn three-year-old with black hair in what we could call a Dutch cut, Prince Akihito had been photographed in kimono and *hakama* sitting formally on a cushion, walking about and then being taken off in a car to a ceremony which was not shown. For the modern custom of taking the children of the Emperor and Empress away from their parents and bringing them up in houses of their own I found ample precedent in *Genji:* the various crown princes of the story lived apart from their parents, as did Genji's own son. Ten-year-old Murasaki was different. "Had she really been his daughter convention would not have allowed him to go on living with her, but in a case like this he felt that such scruples were not applicable." People in the court were called "dwellers above the clouds." On my return to Japan for the Crown Prince's wedding, a Japanese friend who had studied at Bryn Mawr when I was there sent word to me that she would have liked to see me but that as I was "so much above the clouds these days" she was making no effort to get in touch with me. The musical instruments mentioned in the book are the same ones still used for Gagaku, the music of the court today as then, flute, *wagon, sho, koto,* drum, and the court musicians then as now provided music for festive occasions, such as the gay party which Genji, having had special boats built for his lake, gave for all the court. The young Empress Akikonomu, a former ward of Genji's, though she was actually visiting in his Palace at the time, could not attend the party, "being now," it was explained, "an Empress, an August Being hedged about by sacred statutes and conventions." From behind the curtains she listened to the fun "with irritation." I think of today's Emperor and Empress, prevented by tradition from attending the wedding of their son, watching it by television.

Murasaki Shikibu, the author of this fascinating book, was born in 978, the daughter of a provincial governor. A bright child, she learned Chinese by listening to the lessons given her brother. Still in her teens she married a lieutenant in the Imperial Guards, and after his death she became at the age of twenty-six a lady-in-waiting to the Empress, a serious-minded young woman who had a secret longing to learn Chinese. This unfeminine accomplishment Murasaki taught her in secret.

It is not known exactly when *Genji* was written. Some say it was between her husband's death and her arrival at court. Arthur Waley believes that it was begun in 1001, when she was only twenty-three, continued at court during holidays and spare time, and completed in 1015 or 1020. It was mentioned as a finished novel in a diary of 1022. Traditionally some of it, at any rate, is held to have been written at Ishiyamadera, a Buddhist temple on Lake Biwa.

Ishiyama is mentioned twice in the book, once in a passing reference to the "compassion of the Ishiyama Buddha" and once in connection with one of the important scenes of the story. Genji on his way to a celebration at the Ishiyama Temple, with his out-riders, his train of courtiers and noblemen in gorgeous robes, meets the procession of a provincial governor and his wife and all their chariots returning to the capital. The road is narrow and the governor and his train draw off to one side, the oxen, unyoked, browsing under the fir trees. The governor's young wife, who had been one of Genji's flames, and Genji, behind the curtains of his coach, do not meet, but they are deeply stirred by each other's presence. He sends her a veiled message by her brother, who is a captain in the Imperial Guards, and afterwards they exchange poems. This episode is a popular scene for artists who have illustrated *The Tale of Genji,* and in the Metropolitan Museum collection there is a seventeenth-century screen depicting the road and the trees, the oxen, the coaches, the courtiers on horseback.

The chariots in which the high-ranking people rode were small, two-wheeled covered carts, beautifully decorated, drawn by oxen, and entered by a door in front between the shafts. An exquisite small replica in silver of such an eleventh-century coach was brought to me by the Crown Prince when he visited me in Philadelphia.

With Tané I made a pilgrimage to Ishiyamadera in October. It is about nine miles from Kyoto, at the southern tip of Lake Biwa. We left the car at the gate and walked up the steep, winding path under trees so immense and so thick that very little light came through; one moved in a green gloom. Here and there were buildings, a bell, a storehouse, and flights of stone steps. At the top of the hill we came to the Kondo, the main hall, which dates back to the eighth century. Parts of it were twice rebuilt, once in the thirteenth century and again in the sixteenth, but they tell you that the oldest part is intact and indeed it looks as if it might be.

Remote as the temple seemed, it was crowded with visitors: women with small children by the hand, schoolboys in uniform on an "educational excursion," cheerful and clattering, and a few old men with brown lined faces. Part of it was built out from the steep slope on a foundation of great beams and wooden pillars, and as we stood on that platform we felt that we were actually among the branches of the huge cryptomeria trees that surrounded it. Here the sun came splashing through the dark green foliage onto the purple trunks. There was an atmosphere of great age and of sacredness accumulated through the years, in contrast to the dark and dusty interior where cheap incense rose in clouds and charms for every kind of ill were sold at a counter.

A small contribution admitted us into the oldest part of the temple, where there was a statue of Kwannon, goddess of compassion. It was a copy of the original one, which is contained within a shrine and is so precious that it can be seen only once in thirty years. Then the doors are opened and the Kwannon is revealed, seated on the living rock on which the temple is built.

In cases around the hall were sutras that Lady Murasaki copied in gratitude to the temple, and a colored picture scroll, a seventeenth-century copy of a thirteenth-century one that depicted the building of the temple. It was full of movement and humor, with vivid sketches of the workers, the foremen, the priests, the nobles, as recognizable, in spite of the differences in costume, as their counterparts today. The loafing workmen, the avaricious contractor, the crotchety priest, the pompous benefactor who wants his money's worth in deference: all are there.

We came at length to Lady Murasaki's two rooms, an inner room reached through an outer one. Both were small and bare and dark, like two old wooden boxes. In the inner room a window looks out over Lake Biwa, where it is said she saw the moon reflected in the water and was inspired by its beauty. The trees have grown so high that the view is marred, and the little rooms are empty of everything but age. In contrast, the world which that woman of genius created through the power of her imagination is vibrant yet with life and youth and color.

11

The Koizumis

IN the course of my quiet and —except for one unforeseeable and much-publicized interlude— obscure life, I have been privileged to know three, or possibly four, great men. I do not mean great in the sense of unsung homespun heroes or village Hampdens, but men to whom at least a portion of the world at large would apply the term. One of them was Rufus Jones, the Quaker philosopher and saint; another is Dr. Shinzo Koizumi.

We met for the first time in March, 1948. He had recently become a member of the Crown Prince's council, and he came to my house to talk with me and to find out what kind of American was taking so confident a part in the Crown Prince's education.

As far as sports went, I was an immediate disappointment. Dr. Koizumi himself had been a famous tennis player, as well as one of Japan's leading intellectuals, whereas I was about as unathletic as it is possible for any one later than a Victorian miss to be.

Did I play tennis? he asked.

No. Theoretically I knew how but nobody ever wanted to play with me after the first attempt and I had long ago given it up as a bad job.

Then I played golf, of course?

No.

Did I swim?

You had to be able to swim the length of the pool twice to graduate from Bryn Mawr.

Then what was my sport?

I was a member of the fencing club at college, I said with relief. And so I was, and loved it, but it is not a sport that one gets many opportunities to enjoy in later life, though my fencer's wrist is very useful when it comes to opening screw-top jars that are too tight.

When I mentioned fencing Dr. Koizumi looked amused. I knew why and I laughed. The Occupation had banished fencing from the Japanese schools because it was too militaristic!

The atmosphere seemed easier as we went on to the next question, which was, What did I think there was in the education of the Duke of Windsor that made possible the disaster of his marriage and abdication? I replied that I thought possibly his teachers had not had as good material to work on as Prince Akihito's teachers had.

When Dr. Koizumi left, I was not at all sure that I had passed the examination, but afterwards I heard by the grapevine that it was all right.

Early the following year Dr. Koizumi took charge of the Crown Prince's education. The grand chamberlain, Dr. Hozumi, resigned to become a member of the Supreme Court and was succeeded by the vice-grand chamberlain, Mr. Koichi Nomura, a most lovable man. Dr. Koizumi was asked, he has said, to "help Mr. Nomura," but actually, as everyone knew, it was far more than that; he was asked to be the person really responsible for the Crown Prince, not only for his education but for the direction of his life. It was one of those cases, so frequent in Japan, where one person has the title and someone else has the real authority. I don't know what Japanese word is used to describe his position; in English he has been called the chief councilor to the Crown Prince, the standing councilor, and most frequently of late, the tutor, none of which gives any idea of his real function. From the beginning he has once or twice each week given the Prince an hour's instruction on the duties of a Crown Prince, but as the years have passed he has become much more than a tutor: a wise and devoted—and loved in turn—friend and mentor.

Shinzo Koizumi was born in Tokyo in 1888. His father was one of the first disciples of Yukichi Fukuzawa, that astonishing genius who probably did more than any other one man to bring Japan into the modern world after the two-and-a-half-century seclusion of the Tokugawa regime: he was a member of the 1860 mission, the first one ever to go from Japan to the United States, he established the first bank in Japan, the first newspaper, and, in Keio Gekijo, the first liberal, independent university. When Shinzo was six, his father died and his mother was left with three little girls and one boy to bring up. The boy was educated at Keio School and College, and was then sent abroad to study. He had a year in London, after which he went to Berlin, where he studied sociology and economics. When the outbreak of World War I blew the Japanese students out of Germany, he landed at Cambridge and had another year there. He returned to Japan via the United States, spending nine days in New York and going to the opera every night.

He was professor of economics at Keio until he was elected its president in 1930. In 1936 he attended the Harvard Tercentenary as Keio's representative. During the war, when a rival scholar, Dr. Kinnosuke Otsuka, professor of Economics, was driven from Hitotsubashi University because of his radical views, and forbidden to use the Library, Dr. Koizumi arranged for him to have the freedom of the Keio library. In 1945, the year of the death of his only son, a youth of rare promise, Dr. Koizumi's house was burned and he suffered injuries which hospitalized him for the next two years. Even now he walks with a cane. He had expected to spend the rest of his life studying and writing—he is the author of a number of books on economics—

when Mr. Tajima, newly appointed director of the Imperial Household Agency, or grand steward, came to ask him to take charge of the Crown Prince's education.

He refused, not once but many times. He was drawn to a quiet and leisurely life; he felt the burden of his physical disabilities; he questioned whether any one so identified with anti-Communism as he was should be attached to the Imperial Household. Mr. Tajima, patient and persistent, called on Dr. Koizumi fourteen times before he at last got his consent.

Nothing that happened to the Crown Prince—except his marriage, and Dr. Koizumi helped to make that possible—has had so profound and beneficial an effect upon his development as the association with Dr. Koizumi. The Japanese people too are influenced by him; everything he writes is published and read.

In two or three articles in Japanese publications, Dr. Koizumi has referred to me as his "colleague"; I was not, of course, I was his subordinate, and happy to be so. During the year and a half that remained to me in Japan after he came upon the scene, the whole climate around the Crown Prince changed, and it became possible to bring to him new experiences that would have been unthinkable before.

I soon had a chance to know Mrs. Koizumi and their two attractive and charming daughters, Mrs. Kayo Akiyama and Mrs. Tae Koizumi, whose husband was adopted into the Koizumi family in the Japanese way. When I was young, in a day when marriage and a career were much more mutually exclusive than they are now, I used to look at the married couples of my acquaintance, especially the older ones, with an appraising eye, deciding which were a recommendation to the institution of marriage and which were not. My standards were exigent: a vegetable contentedness was not enough; there must be some fire and beauty in their happiness. Had I known them at that time, the Koizumis would have had a high place on my very selective list.

Mrs. Koizumi has a flower-like personality—a flower with the grace and fragility of a *kikyo*, or bellflower, and the staying powers of an orchid. Gentle and self-effacing, she is mistress of her own house and runs it with notable competence. She is gifted artistically. Her flower arrangements are among the loveliest that I have seen; I remember a very hot evening in August and a bowl with a few small zinnias (that very uncompromising flower) which by the effective use of that essential but subtle element in the Japanese art of flower arrangement, *space*, she had made to look airy and cool. She designs her own kimonos and obis, but more than that, she designed the beautiful room which they had built on to their house.

Wholly Japanese in construction and taste, it is furnished with a rug over the *tatami* and modern chairs and tables of simple lines and beautiful craftsmanship. There is a wide *tokonoma* with a flower arrangement and some lovely ornament—once it was two etched Steuben glass plates on stands—and the sliding paper doors open to include in the room a small garden with evergreens and flowers. The proportions of the room are so true that when you first go into it you think of it as a small and intimate room, but you find that there is just as much space for ten people as there is for three.

The flower-like Mrs. Koizumi has a passion for baseball and *sumo*, that incomprehensible form of wrestling engaged in by mountainous men with long hair done up in topknots—an unexpected and endearing trait which she ascribes to having grown up the only girl in a family of boys.

The Koizumis are among the Japanese friends whom we have rejoiced to see in Philadelphia. When the Crown Prince went to Europe for the Coronation, Prime Minister Yoshida suggested to the Koizumis that they go to Europe too, not to travel in the Prince's suite but to visit the countries he visited at the same time. After some hesitation Dr. Koizumi agreed, "thinking that the Crown Prince's educator should have an up-to-date knowledge of the postwar Europe and America, keeping pace with the pupil prince." When Prince Akihito visited me, they came to Philadelphia, too, staying at the Barclay and joining us in some of our activities.

After the Prince left for New York, where I was to join him the next day, the house was suddenly and startlingly quiet and empty. The Prince and his suite were gone and with them the men from the State Department, the diplomats from the Japanese Embassy, the representatives of the Mayor's office, and all the newspaper, radio and television people; the policemen who had been guarding the house back and front, day and night, departed; the watching crowds of neighbors drifted away; our borrowed butler went back to his own job. Violet and I sank down on the sofa, blissful because everything had gone well and the Prince had been safe and happy, but too tired even to "talk it over." At that moment a taxi drew up in front of the house and the Koizumis got out; they had come to say good-by. They took in the situation at a glance—and we have often laughed about it since, both together and apart.

The following spring Dr. Koizumi came back alone, to receive an Honorary Doctorate of Humane Letters at Columbia's bicentennial celebration. His citation read: "A friend returned; chief administrator of Keio University; later bringing life to another, younger school at Fujihara; a scholar whose faith in mankind and whose ties with kindred colleagues of America survived the cruel flames of war; honored in his homeland for thoughtful and courageous leadership in the advance of his countrymen toward free and enlightened citizenship; trusted adviser today of prince and people alike; a man of peace in whose lofty mind there is an abiding hope for that future when all men will be brothers."

Both in 1957 and 1959 the Koizumis put aside other engagements and devoted themselves to doing beautiful things for me. In both years they took me on a little trip to the Hakone mountains in their car.

There is an old Chinese saying to the effect that it is very difficult to get three things together: good weather, beautiful scenery and a mind at rest. If you add to that congenial companions, you have something really rare and fine. On the first trip we had everything but the weather, on the second, all four. That country through which we traveled is lovely in rain or sunshine, at any time of the year. In April there were the tiny new green leaves on the trees and the cherry blossoms, already past in Tokyo, foaming white and pink on all the mountain sides; in September the *higanbana*, spidery red flowers, bloomed in all the ricefield ditches and along the roadsides. We passed through Odawara and the hot-spring resort of Atami and stopped at Kawana, on a headland where through pine trees we could see the surf creaming over rocks. We climbed up to Jukokku Pass and took a cable car to the top of a mountain, from which we could see not only the "ten counties" of the name but on one side Sagami Bay, with its islands and on the other the silver curve of Suruga Bay. We saw Hakone Lake with scudding sailboats and Fuji floating high and misty blue above it, drove along the old Tokaido Road to the famous Barrier, which appears in Noh and Kabuki plays and in the woodcuts of Hiroshige, and saw the great avenues of cryptomeria trees. We stayed at two of Japan's finest hotels, the Kawana and the Fujiya at Miyanoshita, where the rooms are named for flowers—mine was the Thistle one year and the Pomegranate the other.

The first time we went, Tané made the fourth, and the second time, Taeko Koizumi. There were long leisurely hours for good talk and laughter, and quiet times to rest, and a feast of beauty the whole way.

On the way back from both trips we stopped at Oiso to have lunch with Mr. Yoshida. Mr. Yoshida has often been called the Churchill of Japan, and it is easy to see why. Both men are honest, fearless, strong in purpose and vivid in speech; both have undergone in their political lives violent alternations of ups and downs and have remained throughout calmly and triumphantly themselves. Both are aristocrats and autocrats; both are liberal as only true conservatives (as distinguished from reactionaries) can be; both have a free-swinging humor, and something of the same physique.

Mr. Yoshida invited me for dinner in 1947 just before his government fell, and again in 1949 and 1950 when he was once more prime minister. He is now at eighty retired and living at his villa on the seacoast some forty or fifty miles from Tokyo.

When we stopped there in 1957, secret service men were milling around because Princess Chichibu was coming for lunch too. With Mrs. Matsudaira, her mother, she arrived a little later. Mr. and Mrs. Mitani and Mrs. Yasuda were the other guests. Before Count Makino died, I used to send him English detective novels, which he had told me he enjoyed very much and had missed during the war; when I learned that his son-in-law, Mr. Yoshida, was also a fan, from time to time I supplied him with a "who-done-it" or two. On this occasion I was prepared and I said to him, "I have brought you a murder." He replied promptly, "Mrs. Vining, I will revenge that at once"—and gave me a copy of his memoirs, which had just been published. ("Is it selling well?" someone asked him. "Very well," he replied, "I buy so many copies myself.")

As we sat in the drawing room before lunch, he said suddenly, "Mrs. Vining, I have a complaint to make. In your book you told that I said baseball was a coolies' game. That did me a great deal of harm. My government fell as a result."

I professed suitable sorrow, and Mr. Mitani came to my rescue.

"When did your book come out?" he said to me.

"In 1952."

"And when did your government fall, Mr. Yoshida?"

"In 1954."

"So then," Mr. Mitani closed the trap, "it took two years for even that powerful battering ram to bring your government down?"

Mr. Yoshida's rambling house, which is filled with treasures from many countries, has a lovely view from every room—on the fringe of pines through which the blue waters of the bay can be seen, on the garden, on the waterfall, which does not, however, run constantly but is turned on for occasions—and I noticed that each window has an easy chair so placed that the view can be enjoyed in comfort. He had also, to my delight, five lively little cairn terriers which wore the cocky look of dogs that know they have house and master well under control.

When we left, in 1959, he came out into the sunshine to see us off, and that is the last picture I have of him: a smiling, indomitable figure in black kimono and *hakama* with a little cloth beret on the side of his head.

12

The International Christian University

D<small>R.</small> YUASA brought out two very old ceremonial tea bowls to show us, one from Korea, the other from Kyoto, Raku ware. The Korean one, shallow and open, was for summer use, allowing the tea to cool; the deep, black-glazed cup from Kyoto, which kept the tea hot and gave the drinker something warm to wrap his cold hands around, was for winter use. Both were larger than the ordinary teacup, unadorned but beautiful in shape and subdued color.

We were sitting after lunch in the president's house at the International Christian University, looking out at the view and talking about folk art, of which he is a connoisseur and collector. Beyond a row of blue and white drip-glazed jars originally made to hold bean-curd that stood in front of the big window, the ground fell away sharply in a steep bluff, and down below was the university farm with its model herd of cows that provided delicious milk for the university and the ricefields where experimenting was being done on planting the seed directly in the place where it is to grow, instead of the traditional back-breaking work of sowing it first in a seedbed and then transplanting each separate seedling into ankle-deep mud. If the day had not been enveloped in pale mist, we should have seen Fuji in the sky beyond.

Dr. Yuasa had left Japan at eighteen, he told us, and was abroad studying for a number of years. Returning to teach in the Imperial University of Kyoto, he found himself completely out of touch with Japanese culture. His colleagues at the university were not only scholars in their own field but were connoisseurs of art as well. He had had a feeling of inferiority and had sought some area in which he himself could achieve a degree of mastery. Being in Kyoto, where so much great porcelain had been made, he chose ceramics, but he soon found it too difficult and expensive. Then, somehow or other, his attention was directed to folk art. He took to getting up early in the morning and going to the flea market, where he bought inexpensive articles of native, honest beauty made by the people for their own use. The flea market itself was an eye-opener to him; it introduced him to a kind of life he had never glimpsed before, a life of people so poor that a worn toothbrush, a single *geta*, was something not to throw away but to buy and sell.

One woman wrapped her wares in a *furoshiki* of handmade, hand-blocked cotton which he liked. She refused to part with it, however, for she needed it to carry her things home again. He persuaded her to sell it to him the following week and they settled on a price. The next week when he got there, though it was early, someone was ahead of him. He stood on one side and watched the newcomer offer the woman twice what he had agreed to pay for the *furoshiki*—and saw her refuse because she had already given her word. This woman's honesty typified folk art for him—its integrity, reality, usefulness and beauty. The fact also that it comes from the life and needs of the people and so is much the same in all lands appealed to him. He had found the field in which he could take a knowledgeable interest, and the finding of it had been for him a spiritual experience.

I had first met Dr. Hachiro Yuasa in 1946 on the *Marine Fal-*

son on my way to Japan. He had been in the United States at
the time of Pearl Harbor and had decided not to return on the
exchange ship but to stay on. After the war he returned to his
own country to resume his interrupted presidency of Doshisha
University in Kyoto. When the International Christian University was founded he was called to be its first president.

A Christian, interdenominational graduate school, with non-
Japanese in both faculty and student body, was a dream of
missionaries as long ago as 1900. After the war Japanese and
American Christians, more than ever convinced that a liberal
university of high academic standards, open to qualified students
regardless of race, creed, sex or nationality, was more than ever
necessary to educate leaders in a newly democratic Japan, went
to work to make the dream a reality. The year 1949 is considered the year of the university's founding, because at that
time a board of trustees and council were organized, a constitution adopted, and officers elected. Prince Chichibu was one of the
first honorary councilors, and after his death, Princess Chichibu
is carrying on his interest and support of the university. In New
York a foundation was set up to raise money and support for
the school and fourteen Protestant denominations joined in the
undertaking. In Japan the astonishing sum of 160 million yen
was contributed by people of all walks of life, from the Emperor
down, not more than five per cent of whom were Christians.

In Mitaka, a western suburb of Tokyo about seventeen miles
from the center of the city, 317 acres of land and the few remaining buildings of the Nakajima Aircraft Company, which had
manufactured bombers for the Japanese army, were bought for
the campus of the university. There was one large concrete
building which could be restored and converted into an administration, library and classroom building. A small church was built
immediately, for this was central to the whole enterprise. Faculty housing, a dining hall, a few dormitories followed. In April
1953 the first class of freshmen began work.

It was necessary, because of Japanese law, to start with a four-year undergraduate college before the graduate school could be established. As soon as the first class of the college of liberal arts had received their diplomas, the graduate school of education was started. This will be followed, as soon as it becomes possible, by a graduate school of public administration.

There were 171 students in that first class, a substantial number of whom were girls. They all came from the top five per cent of their high schools, and they all got jobs when they graduated, or were received into other institutions for graduate study—except a few girls who preferred to get married. About ten per cent of them were non-Japanese, from the United States, China, Burma, the Philippines, Germany, Indonesia, Korea. Of the faculty of 178, about fifty are non-Japanese. Instruction is in both Japanese and English, with very intensive language study for freshmen.

One of the American students whom I met there both years was John D. Rockefeller IV, a tall, attractive, able young man with a gentle and eager manner, who has found there his life direction. He came in 1957 intending just to take his junior year at I.C.U. He also worked as an assistant instructor in English. He liked it so well, however, and became so deeply interested in Japanese culture and history, that he decided to stay on, acquire a working knowledge of the Japanese language, and graduate at I.C.U. before returning to Harvard for graduate study in Asian history. He attempted at first to live on the twenty-five dollars a month that suffice the average Japanese student but was later persuaded by concerned elders to be a little less rigorous. He now lives near the campus with two or three Japanese classmates in a small Japanese house presided over by a capable middle-aged Japanese woman who cooks for them and mothers them.

My interest in the I.C.U. was not a casual one, for I am a sponsor of the Women's Planning Committee, which raises money for special projects. I was happy to be able to spend two weeks there in 1957 and a few days in 1959 as the guest of Tané Takahashi.

Tané lived in the Maple Grove House, a small apartment house for unmarried women faculty that I would like to see duplicated at Bryn Mawr. Each apartment has a large living-dining room, a sleeping alcove, a kitchen and bath. Downstairs there is a big, charmingly decorated common room where the inhabitants, half of whom are American, the other half Japanese, have dinner together once a week and entertain as a group. They have, moreover, a kindly and energetic housemother with an assistant, who buy their supplies, stow them away in their refrigerators, clean the apartments and do their laundry. It is almost enough to keep a woman faculty member from marrying! The apartment next to Tané's happened to be vacant at that time, and so I slept there and had happy meals with Tané—whenever I was there, which was not as often as I would have liked, for my engagement calendar was as full as any debutante's.

Tané's library occupies part of the second floor of the main building and the weight of the books threatens to take the floor down to the basement. It had been thrown together during the frenzied years of preparation just in time to meet the minimum requirements for a university charter. When she returned to Japan in 1954 to take command she had to do more than start from scratch: she had to back up and start considerably behind scratch and subject the chaos to some kind of order before she could begin to create. A multilingual library on that scale offers problems peculiarly its own.

When I saw it that September I felt that I would have known it anywhere to be Tané's library: like her apartment it bears the stamp of her personality, serene, ordered, welcoming. Her staff of fourteen, plus many more student assistants, works together harmoniously; the sunny rooms are filled with students concentrating peacefully. It is the first and perhaps still the only university library in Japan to have open stacks, and the students value highly the privilege of going straight to the shelves and browsing for what they need. The trust in them and the degree of maturity expected of them are, Tané believes, part of the process of democratic education.

Her title is still "acting librarian." No university in Japan can bring itself to name a woman, and a young one at that, librarian, not even one that is international and coeducational and Christian. A university librarian in Japan is usually a distinguished figurehead who leaves the real work to someone else. But still, she is the only woman to have a seat on the university Senate, and she herself is entirely content with her title; she feels that it gives her greater freedom than the higher title would, and she values freedom above prestige. Besides running the library, she also teaches a course in library science and is adviser to a number of undergraduates. When I was there she was about to meet with the architects who were planning the much-needed library building, for which ground has as last been broken.

I.C.U. is a delightful place to stay. Besides the Yuasas I was glad to see again Dr. and Mrs. Maurice Troyer and Dr. and Mrs. Glen Bruner and be entertained in their lovely houses on the bluff. Dr. Troyer and Dr. Bruner are vice presidents of the university. There were walks in the woods, through a neglected formal garden that had belonged to the owner of the aircraft company, to the university farm. And always there were the students, alert, purposeful, happy-looking young people who were having the inestimable experience of being part of a great institution in its pioneering days. Though they themselves might be more consciously aware of the lack of a gymnasium, an overcrowded library and insufficient dormitory space, they would in later life, I was sure, look back upon their college days as a time of intellectual excitement and the zestful fellowship that comes with blazing new trails. The cheerful sound of hammering and the rattle of the cement mixer from the new dormitory and the

Student Union building that were under construction were a constant reminder of the steady physical growth of the university.

One morning as Tané and I were having a leisurely breakfast, Miss Taira arrived, the flower arrangement teacher from whom my sister and I had had a lesson each week for nearly two years. Violet, indeed, had become so proficient that she acquired a certificate and a professional name—Kofu, Shining Maple. For the first time I saw Miss Taira in Western dress; otherwise, except for a little added weight she had not changed at all in the seven years: she was tiny, spectacled, shining and indefatigable as ever. She had brought us sweet potatoes, cooked in a special way, fruit and flowers. The flowers she proceeded at once to arrange in two vases, one for each of our rooms. In mine, with swift sure motions, she created an effect of airy beauty with yellow and white chrysanthemums and the red-tipped grass called *ware-mo-ko*. She invited us to a vegetarian lunch at a Zen temple, and then with many bows she departed, to an appointment on the other side of Tokyo—and Tokyo is an enormous city. She gets up at five-thirty every morning, goes to early service at her church, which belongs to one of the small evangelical sects, and from then on till late in the evening she weaves her way back and forth across the city by train, bus and tram.

Seishoji, the temple to which we went a few days later, has a restaurant attached named Daigo, which consists of a series of serene Japanese rooms built around a garden. Five of us, Miss Taira, Miss Hana Natori, formerly the princesses' governess, Mrs. Togasaki, Tané and I sat around a low table which had been made by fitting four little black lacquer temple tables together. Five beautiful maidens in mauve kimonos with sage-green obis, who had been trained in the tea ceremony, waited on us with austere grace, bringing us exotic vegetarian delicacies on hand-made pottery. There were, for instance, bamboo sprouts no more than an inch long, served whole, a ripe fig deep-fried in a batter made of the pounded rice used at the time of the New Year, and the seeds of some tree—I did not catch the name—fried in a batter of powdered green tea.

One evening five of my former students invited me to dinner at the University Club. They had all been classmates of the Crown Prince at the Peers' School and four of them had at different times shared one of his private lessons each week. The fifth I had several times suggested to the Crown Prince but he had always turned him down on the grounds that his English was entirely too good. I made a point each term of selecting one boy whose English was better than the Crown Prince's and one whose English was less good, but Inokuchi San, Prince Akihito maintained, carried excellence too far. They had engaged a private room and ordered a delicious dinner; afterwards we sat around the table talking.

Michio Inokuchi was now a graduate student in nuclear physics at the University of Tokyo; Akira Hashimoto, a reporter working for Kyodo; Tomohiko Sekine, a graduate student in economics at Hitotsubashi University; Masao Oda had just got a job in a bank; and Nobuhide Suda was doing nuclear research for the Mitsubishi Shipbuilding Company. Oda San had recently returned from a year at Stanford University, and Sekine San, though he did not know it then, was to go to McGill two years later. All were attractive and well-set-up young men. All spoke English so well that I forgot it was not their native language and did not bother to speak slowly or to choose my words. We talked about Japan's economic situation, Germany's prosperity, and the race problem in the United States. The Little Rock episode was at its shocking worst at that time, and they pushed me hard about it. I was delighted that they did and considered the discussion at least in part the fruit of my efforts in teaching them; I was glad also to have a chance to disabuse them of the idea that they firmly held that this sort of discrimination and violence was going on in every city in the United States where there were Negroes. We also talked about less controversial things, the P.E.N.

meetings, modern novels, drama, and music. When at last we broke up, Sekine San insisted upon escorting me all the way back to the Maple Grove House. Altogether it was an evening to fill a teacher's heart with happiness and pride.

Mitaka was near enough to both Jiyu Gakuen and Keisen Junior College for me to visit both again. Jiyu Gakuen, or Freedom School, was conceived, established and run by Mrs. Motoko Hani, Japan's first woman journalist who used the profits of her magazine, *Fujin no Tomo*, to finance her remarkable school. The beautiful buildings were designed by a Japanese pupil of Frank Lloyd Wright, the extensive grounds are kept in order by the students, the boys work in the attached farm, the girls prepare the school lunches. In fact, students "do everything," as Miss Hani says, "but pay the teachers' salaries!" One day a week is devoted to music. Every child in the school learns to play an instrument, every child has a turn at conducting an orchestra. All this—and much more—is fitted into a normal academic program.

Since I had left Japan both Mrs. Hani and her quiet, strong husband had died, leaving their daughter Keiko to carry on the school alone. It was a heavy responsibility, but Miss Hani was equal to it. Her somewhat fluttery feminine manner is deceptive: she is steel within. She studied at Cambridge University before the war and has had a year in England and other countries since; she has taught at the school for many years, working closely with her parents, and, since she spoke English and they did not, she has been the one to meet the many foreign educators who have come to the school to see and admire. For some time after her parents' death, she told me, Mr. Amano, former minister of education, called her every evening at seven-thirty to ask how the school was and to help her with any problems, but now he has discontinued that custom, saying that she has everything in hand. And indeed the school is as beautiful, as original and strong as it ever was.

Keisen Junior College is Miss Kawai's dream: a horticultural college for girls. I had seen it in its early struggles with spartan living conditions and meager financial resources; it was a joy to see its prosperity now and the dedicated spirit of its director, Miss Michi Yamaguchi, who has studied at the School of Horticulture for Women at Ambler, Pennsylvania, and its fine, attractive, sturdy students.

On Sunday Tané and I went into Tokyo to attend Friends Meeting. Once again I saw great changes. For more than four years after their meeting house was destroyed Friends had met in the living room of the Friends Center and then in the Friends Girls' School. Now they had once more a real meeting house on the old site. It was not a beautiful building, but it was useful. Christian church architecture in Japan leaves much to be desired. I know of only two churches that are beautiful, the little Catholic church in Karuizawa, and the little Evangelical and Reformed chapel attached to Aisenryo, an orphanage in Saitama; both have made imaginative use of native materials, bamboo, tile and stone. But if the building was commonplace, the quality of the gathered silence and the fellowship of the dear Friends who met there were deep and beautiful.

Later, at the end of my six weeks in Japan, I went back to spend a few days at the Friends Center with Esther Rhoads and to visit again the Friends Girls' School, which has risen like the phoenix from its ashes and which was celebrating its seventieth anniversary in the newest of the buildings which have been achieved since the war through so much vision, devotion, generosity and courageous hard work.

However far afield from I.C.U. I might wander during the daytime of those two weeks in September, I was glad to return at night to the peace of that country campus, where I looked out of my window at pine trees sharp and black in the moonlight or veiled in white mist and where the last thing I heard before I went to sleep was the singing of crickets.

13

Michiko and Moken

THE Inoue family were an important part of my life in Japan. That first rainy evening in 1946 when I stepped out of the car that brought me from Yokohama, three of them were bowing on the doorstep of the house that was to be mine, Mrs. Ryu Inoue, the cook-housekeeper, her nineteen-year-old daughter, Michiko San, the maid, and Yukio San, her son, who had a government job but who lived in the house and ran the furnace.

The mother must have been then in her early sixties, but she looked older, a tiny, gray-haired woman, always in kimono, sweet, motherly and old-fashioned. Deserted by her husband many years before, she had brought up and educated six children by cooking for missionaries. One son had been killed in the war, the other five children were now grown-up, self-supporting, and still unmarried.

The youngest, Michiko, pretty and capable, was a graduate of Keisen, the excellent private school for girls which Miss Michi Kawai had created. She was our very hard-working, indeed, often overworked, little housemaid. She was gay and eager for life; everything she touched she did with a certain flair: her soufflés were wonderfully fluffy and tender and when she made an ordinary pudding, chocolate cornstarch or Spanish cream, it came out delicious and delicate and different. She could make an arrangement of six violets or three cornflowers look poetic instead of insignificant. When she rebelled against her lot—as she occasionally, very understandably, did—there was fire and pathos in her revolt and generosity in her subsequent repentance. It troubled me that she had so much to do and I thought her mother was too strict with her, but there was little I could do to relieve her.

There was an irreducible minimum of entertaining that went with my job. Every Tuesday afternoon either the Crown Prince's younger brother and sister or his two elder sisters came to the house for a lesson, and afterwards we had tea for them and a lady-in-waiting and chamberlain. Every Wednesday afternoon the Crown Prince and two classmates came, with a chamberlain and a doctor in attendance. Michiko not only must help to make the sandwiches and cookies and bring in the tea-tray but, dressed up in the kimono which she never liked to wear, she must open the door, bowing low when the guests arrived, and be at the door again when they left to bow them off. In the waiting room and the kitchen, chauffeur, bodyguard and local police had also to be entertained. There were other regular groups who came to the house and other guests, many of them, but the Imperial visitors, with the weight of security and protocol of which they themselves were unconscious, brought a peculiar and regular strain.

Some of Michiko's work resulted from the delicate health of her family. At first just the original three lived in three rooms at the back of the house. Later Masako, who had a job in a kindergarten, and Aiko, who was a dressmaker, came to join them, when the room in which they had been living was swallowed up in Tokyo's housing shortage. The eldest sister was at that time in a sanitorium with tuberculosis, and the threat of that almost ubiquitous disease hung over all of them. Flu, pleurisy, and other ills swept through the little family from time to time. The work of the household went on, for they were never all sick at once, but the burden lay heaviest on Michiko, who was sometimes nurse as well as cook and waitress.

The work of a Japanese house, even a Western one like ours, with an electric stove and refrigerator, is complicated and endless. There was, for instance, no hot water system. Bringing to the bedrooms little kettles of hot water before breakfast and dinner and building a special fire for the bath was part of the routine. Moreover, every time I went out or came home, it was invariable procedure for all the Inoues in the house at the moment to assemble on the doorstep to bow.

"*Itte mairimasu*," I would say, meaning, "I am going out and will return," which seemed rather obvious.

"*Itte irasshai*," they would chorus. "Honorably depart."

And, later, "*Tadaima*, I am back," I would inform them, and they would reply, "*O kaeri nasai*, honorably return."

If I was in a hurry, as I often was, they would have to come running, leaving the dishes in the cooling dishwater or the broom leaning against the table, in order to get it said before I had entirely disappeared.

I would willingly have relieved them of this ceremony, though I came to enjoy it, and the younger ones would gladly have dropped it, but Mrs. Inoue's standards were high and she held her children to what she knew was right and proper.

For all the work and the concern about health, we were a happy and affectionate household. After my sister came to join me they gave her the especial respect and petting that is the due of the Honorable Elder Sister. From my own country, now, where service has practically vanished, I look back with wonder on the things they did for us, the loving and thoughtful care they took of us. It seemed as if the regular work of the household was to them just a job but the little personal services which they showered on us were their joy.

They were a Christian family, members of Dr. Toyohiko Kagawa's church, and it was because of them that we had morning prayers after breakfast. They would come into the dining room and sit down at the long table. I would read from the Bible in English, Tané or Michiko would read the same thing in Japanese and then we would have a few moments of Quaker silence, after which we would talk about plans for the day. Even the dog joined in. "*Reihai yo!*" Michiko would say to him in the kitchen, "Time for prayers," and he would come trotting into the dining room to sit sedately at the French window looking out into the garden.

They all had good voices and sang well. They belonged to a choral group which went regularly to hospitals on Sunday afternoons and sang hymns for the patients. Yukio was the leader and on Saturdays the group met in the Inoues' sitting room to practice. I loved to hear them, for their voices were clear and true and the familiar hymns sounded somehow exotic with the Japanese words. One of the best parts of my Christmases in Japan was the early morning carol singing of the Inoues and Tané in the garden under my window.

When I left Japan in 1950 I wondered how they would get along. They would be glad, I knew, to have the rest that they needed, but still, they had had a warm place to live at a time when it was desperately difficult to find even a room to rent in Tokyo, and there had been plenty of food. I need not have worried. Michiko, asked what she would like to do next, confessed a secret longing to work in a publishing house, and the *Bungei Shinju*, a popular magazine which had published some of my articles, found a place for her. Masako went back to her kindergarten; Aiko had her dressmaking and the white spitz dog, which was technically mine but which, as he had given his heart entirely to Aiko, I had left with her; Keiko had been discharged from the sanitarium. All they needed was a house, and through the kindness of Dr. Kagawa, that too was found.

During the seven years that followed, we kept in touch with each other through letters and gifts, and even in less tangible ways. I dreamed one night vividly that I saw Michiko walking down the street. She looked sick and troubled, and when I spoke to her she told me that she was "resting." I woke up with this well-known euphemism for tuberculosis ringing in my ears and a conviction that something was wrong. About ten days later I learned that Michiko had to take leave from her job because of a spot on her lung.

One of the happiest things about my return to Tokyo in 1957 was seeing how some of my friends, who had been suffering from ill health, uncomfortable housing, uncongenial work and other difficulties had come through into prosperity and a satisfying life. The Inoues especially seemed to have found a sunny harbor. Michiko, well and blooming, had married a young man on the *Bungei Shunju* and they had a small apartment all to themselves. The rest of the family, who now included Yukio's charming wife and six-month-old baby, lived in the small house on the edge of Tokyo which they were able to rent from Dr. Kagawa. One day in late September I went to have lunch with them.

The car took me to the *machi* of Kamikitazawa, where Michiko and Yukio were waiting for me. Yukio was carrying his daughter, Katsumi, on his arm. A healthy, handsome child with absurd resemblance to some of the baby pictures of the Crown Prince, she was wearing a smart costume of pale blue wool—pants, dress and bonnet—embroidered with cross-stitch in pink, which had been designed and made for her by her Aunt Aiko. Guided by them we crept through crowded streets with open-fronted shops displaying paper lanterns, dangling strings of teakettles, china, toys, books and vegetables, until the road became too narrow for the car; then we got out and walked along a dirt path between high bamboo fences on one side and rice paddies on the other, which stretched away in the sun, pale gold and fragrant with the warm, sweet smell of ripening rice.

The rest of the family were at the gate to meet me: Mrs. Inoue, now positively plump, smiling and a bit tearful, the eldest daugh-

ter, Kiyoko, well and strong, sweet, round-faced Masako, released
from her kindergarten for the day, and Nobuko, Yukio's wife.
The house was a tiny two-storied one, with a small flower and
vegetable garden cared for by Aiko. How six adults and a baby
could live in so small a place and keep it not only exquisitely
clean but uncluttered, is a Japanese secret.

I left my shoes at the door and we sat on the *tatami*, with the
sliding doors open onto the garden and the view of the ricefields
beyond. Shortly after I had presented my gifts and we had exchanged news in Japanese and English, Tané joined us, armed
with a large red celluloid elephant which tinkled music when
you tilted it.

Luncheon, prepared by Nobuko, consisted of *chawan mushi*,
the custard soup of which I am especially fond, *o sushi*, rice balls
wrapped in seaweed and garnished with bits of pickle, fish, ginger, and what have you, tea and big green grapes. It was a broil-
ing hot day and Katsumi-chan (chan is the affectionate diminu-
tive for San) must have been very warm in her wool outfit, but
she bore up with true Japanese fortitude. *"Suteki ne?"* ("You're
very grand, aren't you?") one or another would say to her and
pinch her plump cheeks gently, and she would respond with a
triangular, toothless smile and a bubble. It was plain that she
was the hub of the household.

There was only one cloud over the day's happiness. They told
me sorrowfully that Moken, the dog, was dead. Just three days
after my return he had succumbed to heart worm.

They showed me his grave in one corner of the little garden,
shaded by a broad-leaved evergreen, marked by a white wooden
cross inscribed with his name in Japanese characters and planted
with some white flowers. Every day, Michiko said, people in the
neighborhood came to bow before this grave. He had enjoyed a
measure of fame, both because he was such a handsome creature,
big and white and dignified, with a great white ruff and a tail
coiled over his back like a spring, and also because he had be-

longed to me and I had been the Crown Prince's American tutor. When the Crown Prince had come to my house for lessons, Moken had unquestionably seen him and been patted by him. To know the dog that had known the Crown Prince was a distinction for the whole neighborhood and everyone mourned its loss.

There is something touching about a dog's grave. I thought as I looked at it of the little graveyard on the side of the Castle rock in Edinburgh, where pets of the soldiers stationed there have been buried. The other two dogs that I have loved, Rastus, a cocker spaniel, and Hamish, a West Highland white terrier, died when I lived in an apartment house and have no graves that can be visited. Moken had only tolerated me, regarding me, I always felt, as a dubious foreigner, and so he was not so dear to me as the other two, but he had been the most intelligent of them all and I had looked forward to seeing him again.

It was because of Michiko's encounter with a burglar who broke into our house that I had got Moken in the first place.

One April evening eight years earlier, we were sitting in the living room of my Mejiro home. My sister and Tané were reading and I was preparing my lessons for the next day. Some quiet music was coming from the radio and all was peaceful.

Suddenly we heard from upstairs a shrill scream, followed by running feet. It is strange how long it takes to realize that one has actually heard a cry of distress. My first thought was that Michiko, who went upstairs every evening to turn down the beds, had seen a mouse; my second, that she and Masako were rough-housing. But as the yells increased, drawing nearer down the back stairs, we jumped up and ran out into the hall.

There we found the entire Inoue family and a visitor gathered around Michiko. She was ash-pale and wild-eyed, and she clutched her throat as she poured out her story in a spate of excited Japanese, of which all I could understand was *"dorobo,"* robber, and *"Vining Sensei no heya,"* my room. By bits Tané reported that Michiko had gone upstairs as usual. When she went

into my room, before she could switch on the light a man jumped
out from behind the door and grabbed her by the throat. She
screamed and shook him off; he ran in one direction, she in the
other.

Tané rushed to the telephone to call the police. The Japanese
telephone is the most frustrating instrument in existence. There
was good reason for the admonition posted in the booths in American billets: "Occupation personnel will refrain from pulling the
telephone off the wall." Our telephone elected this moment to go
dead. Furiously grinding the handle on the box and shouting
"*Moshi moshi*" into the mouthpiece, she flew out at intervals to
question Michiko further. Violet and I hovered about trying to
find out more. Meanwhile Masako and the visitor ran to the
police box two corners away and before Tané had given up the
telephone attempt they were back with the policeman.

He was the nice young policeman whom we often saw sitting at
his desk in his tiny office, which I passed every day when I turned
off the main street into the tangle of lanes that led to my house.
The two-room *koban* was also his home, and I used to see his
small daughter playing on the steps in front and his wife, with
the other child on her back, hanging out blue and white diapers
like roller towels on a bamboo pole. Usually, in spite of the domestic air of his surroundings, he was very correct and official in
his blue uniform. Tonight, caught off duty in his shirt sleeves, he
looked tall and slender and boyish—and utterly delighted to have
something so exciting to deal with. Brandishing a revolver, he
went leaping upstairs, followed closely by all the rest of us, who
had become suddenly brave in his presence.

The hall was dark and we turned on lights as we went. We
looked under all the beds and in all the closets, only to find that
the burglar had departed some time earlier via the spare-room
window and the rain pipe. My room was undisturbed, except for
my handbag, which I had left on the top of the chest of drawers.
It was now on the floor, open, and the red wallet containing all

my precious cards, PX, identification, commissary and gasoline, which I had as a special privilege, as well as fifty dollars in Occupation currency, was gone.

From then on till one o'clock that night it was pure Gilbert and Sullivan. Tané had managed to get the local police headquarters on the telephone and five Japanese policemen in uniform appeared, followed by an assortment of shabbily dressed individuals whom we took to be suspects that they had rounded up and brought so that Michiko could identify her assailant. They proved, however, to be plain-clothes men. Several more came from a neighboring ward and the whole crowd, now numbering fifteen, withdrew to the parlor, where they settled down in a circle on the fragile Louis Quinze chairs and sofas upholstered in pale green silk damask, which had been loaned to me from the Akasaka Palace. Michiko had to tell her story again and again, and she and Masako pattered patiently from kitchen to parlor with endless trays of teacups.

Violet, Tané and I sat in the living room and waited. Nothing seemed to be happening, except the serving of tea. At length Tané went to inquire. They were waiting, it appeared, for the arrival of the fingerprinting equipment. At one o'clock we suggested that they call it a day and they departed, but early the next morning they were back again.

Just before I left for school, the chief of police of the district arrived in his best uniform with all his gold braid and buttons, a mild, rather tired-looking middle-aged man, accompanied by a young, round-faced interpreter who knew almost no English. He managed to convey, however, the fact that the chief had come to apologize to me for the burglar's having got into my house. I politely expressed regret for the trouble that the house was causing the police. He promised to watch the house more carefully in the future. I thanked him. We all bowed.

When I returned that afternoon the parlor was again full of smoke and tea-drinking policemen. Michiko was describing my wallet to them and the more talented among them were drawing pictures of it. The next day they came to borrow the new cards which replaced the stolen ones, in order to copy them. The *dorobo,* they told us, had gone from my house to U.S. House 24 next door, but the Colonel and his wife and their Occupation currency were out, and so he had taken only a fur neckpiece. Another day the policemen came again, apparently just to sit on green silk damask and drink tea, my cigarette ration from the PX being now exhausted.

The episode, as far as the police were concerned, ended exactly a week from the day of the robbery, when I received from the police interpreter a gift of a packet of morning-glory seeds and a note which made no reference to the unfortunate affair of the burglar but rejoiced in my good health and ended, "Your affectionately."

That week I went to two Occupation dinner parties and a reception and I found everyone talking burglars. Some Occupation houses had been entered and robbed five and six times. Most of the burglars wanted men's clothing. We went out to dinner one chilly evening and found our host attired in white linen, all that a robber the night before had left of his wardrobe. A well-known general took the precaution of sleeping with a loaded revolver on his bedside table and woke one morning to find that a burglar had made off with all his trousers and his gun too! A force of two hundred detectives was reported to be at work on the burglaries, but while they sometimes recovered the goods they almost never caught the men.

"Japanese burglars are terrified of dogs," Tané told me. "They never enter a house which has a sign *Moken* in front."

Moken, literally fierce dog, corresponds to our Beware of the Dog signs.

"Well, then," I said firmly, "we'll get a dog."

A mental picture of a German shepherd or a large and formidable Japanese *Akita* floated before me, and I began to ask everybody I knew about reliable kennels. We discussed the question one afternoon when the Crown Prince and two of his classmates were at my house for English and tea. Good dogs were rather scarce, it developed, for we were still close to the war, when there was not enough food even for people and nobody could feed a dog.

The Occupation now moved to protect its personnel. A night watchman, a Japanese, was assigned to guard U.S. House number 24 on one side of us and U.S. House number 25 behind us. The watchman, by making a slight detour through our garden instead of going down the alley, included us in his protection, though I had no U.S. number and was, in fact, employed by the Japanese government. Although the watchman frequently woke us up at night by the sound of his heavy footsteps, his whistling, or an occasional shout, we felt very comfortable and safe and grateful, and I forgot about wanting a dog.

One day a neighbor, the mother of one of the boys who shared the Crown Prince's Wednesday lessons, came to inquire whether I really was looking for a dog or whether I was simply making English conversation with the boys. Her dog's puppies, she said, were now six weeks old, and she would be happy and honored if I would accept one of them. I hesitated. A six-week-old spitz puppy was hardly a watchdog, and then there were the Imperial rugs and the green damask chairs to consider. But I looked at the puppy.

It was a round ball of white fuzz, which unrolled into a dainty and perfect miniature of its future adult self: pointed nose with a moist black tip like a blackberry, bright eyes, prick ears, tapering legs, and tail curling over its back to fit into a little depression in its thick white fur.

I accepted the puppy—who could resist him?—and we named him Moken. We all loved him, but he loved Aiko best.

While Moken was still small enough to wear the first little red collar I bought him, the Occupation remembered that my house had no U.S. number on it and decreed that the night watchman must stop making the detour through our garden and go straight down the alley instead.

"It seems odd," I remarked when I heard this piece of news, "that a colonel in the American army and a commander in the navy have to be guarded, but a household of lone women can take care of themselves."

"Perhaps," said Tané with quiet pride, "they know that we are Quaker pacifists and don't depend on outward guards and weapons!"

But Michiko, who had felt the *dorobo's* hands on her throat, took Moken with her on a leash when she went upstairs to turn down the beds.

14

Poetry in Japanese Life

P OETRY in Japan," wrote Lafcadio Hearn, "is universal as the air. It is felt by everybody. It is read by everybody. It is composed by almost everybody—irrespective of class and condition."

This is probably as true today as it was sixty or more years ago when he wrote it, allowing for a slight exaggeration then and now. Poetry societies of all kinds, from the academic to the domestic, continue to flourish. At least a hundred poetry magazines actually keep alive today—and some of them are commercial successes. There are "schools"—the "Yew Tree" school was a famous one some years ago—which, as in flower arrangement or the tea cult, encourage and develop a particular type of performance. Both men and women make a living by teaching other people to write poems. Two of the Japanese writers whom I most enjoyed meeting at the P.E.N. congress were poets themselves and instructors of poetry: Shigeru and Miyoko Goto. Mr. Goto was the teacher of the Crown Prince, and when Michiko Shoda was being prepared for her new role of Crown Princess, Mrs. Goto was the one chosen to teach her the art of writing *waka*. It was interesting to me that though there were less than six months into which to cram the training for which the prospective brides of previous Crown Princes took at least two years, lessons in writing poetry were an essential that could not be omitted. (Other

144

subjects were: court etiquette, English, French, the new Japanese
Constitution, and duties of a Crown Princess.) All these societies,
magazines and teachers keep going because enough people today,
people one knows, read and write poetry.

Japanese poetry is radically different from our own. In the
first place, there is no rhyme. This is because of the nature of the
Japanese language. All words, indeed all syllables, end in a vowel,
or the letter *n*, which is very lightly sounded. Rhyme would be
intolerably monotonous. All the syllables of a Japanese word,
moreover, have approximately the same value; there is no accent.
Therefore there is no metrical system; you cannot scan a line. It
all depends upon the number of syllables in the lines, and upon
certain other devices. Poems are made up of five- or seven-syl-
lable lines arranged according to certain patterns. There are some
long poems, but by far the most used form from the year 400
until today has been the *waka*, or *tanka*, a short poem of thirty-
one syllables, arranged in five lines, 5—7—5—7—7. The first
three lines form one hemistich, the last two another, with a pause
between, as there is a pause between the octet and the sestet of a
Petrarchian sonnet.

The *waka* is delicate, impressionistic, and has inevitably become conventional. It is impossible to create endlessly anew in so
small a scope, with so much inevitable repetition. The first time
you hear "My sleeve is wet" and get the picture of a Japanese
lady weeping and surreptitiously drying her eyes on the long
sleeve of her kimono, you think it exquisite. After reading fifty
more poems with wet sleeves you begin to wish they would use a
handkerchief! One of the best loved of the sleeve poems was
written in the thirteenth century:

> Like a great rock far out at sea,
>   Submerged at even the lowest tide,
> Unseen, unknown of man—my sleeve
>   Is never for a moment dried.*

* Translated by Curtis Hidden Page.

Like all *waka*, this says little directly, much by suggestion. The theme, of course, is probably the same as

> She never told her love, but let concealment,
> Like a worm in the bud, feed on her damask cheek.

Or it might be some other grief. One fills it in oneself.

Onomatopoeia, alliteration, subtle and delicate cadences, have their place in Japanese as in English poetry, but there are two other devices that are much used: pillow words and pivot words. Pillow words modify the words that follow, through an association of sound or meaning. If you speak of using the grass for a pillow, it always means a journey, not simply a sun-bath at home. By the use of one word a whole set of associations is established, a scene laid, thus making it possible to convey a great deal more than thirty-one syllables would otherwise permit. Pivot words are puns, which in Japanese are both respectable and poetic.

Vast numbers of *waka* are written in Japan. The Emperor Meiji, for instance, wrote twenty-seven thousand of them in eight years. As a result there are seldom collections of the work of a single poet. Poems are generally considered the product of a period, and there have been many famous anthologies. The first is still probably the greatest: the *Manyoshu: Collection of a Myriad Leaves*, which was finished in 759, the time of Beowulf, Caedmon, Cynewulf. It contained over four thousand poems, mostly *waka*, in twenty books, by emperors and empresses, courtiers, prime ministers, and also frontier guards and workmen engaged in building a palace. Later anthologies followed. *Hyakunin Isshu*, which means "One Hundred poems by One Hundred Poets," was published in the thirteenth century, and has formed the basis for the New Year's game which is still played by people of all ages. A deck of a hundred cards, each one of which contains the second half of a poem, is spread out on the floor. The leader reads out the first half of a poem and the players scramble to find the card with the remainder of it. The player, or the side, which ends up with possession of the greatest number of cards wins the game. The Crown Prince enjoys it and is very good at it; when his classmates come to his house at New Year's time, they play it together.

Of subjects, nature in all its aspects is by far the most popular, but love and its sorrows, laments and elegies, travel, and the swift passing of life, and occasions of all kinds are also food for poetry.

"The garment is thin," wrote a Lady Otomo in the eighth century,

> "That my loved one wears.
> Oh wind, blow not too hard
> Until he reaches his home."

Yakamochi, who died in 785, a man who held many important government offices and was for one dizzy year commander-in-chief of the army, wrote of the loss of one whom he loved:

> So this was all—
> Though she and I
> Had counted on
> A thousand years.

There is no way of knowing whether or not this was the same lady to whom he wrote:

> By way of pretext
> I said, "I will go
> And look at
> The condition of the bamboo fence."
> But it was really to see you.*

In a selection from the *Manyoshu* containing only a quarter of the total number of poems, I find love poems written by three different ladies to this poet, but it is not disclosed to whom he wrote either of these.

A long "Dialogue on Poverty" was written by a man who had not himself experienced it, having been an ambassador to China, a tutor to the Crown Prince, and Lord of the Province of Chikuzen. Yet his understanding of the plight of the poor peasant

* Translated by Arthur Waley.

comes out in one of the most realistic and grim descriptions of grinding poverty to be found in poetry anywhere:

> On the night when the rain beats,
> Driven by the wind,
> On the night when the snow-flakes mingle
> With the sleety rain,
> I feel so helplessly cold.
> I nibble at a lump of salt,
> Sip the hot, oft-diluted dregs of sake,
> And coughing, snuffling,
> And stroking my scanty beard
> I say in my pride
> There is none worthy, save me.
> But I shiver still with cold.
> I pull up my hempen bedclothes,
> Wear whatever few sleeveless clothes I have.
> But bitter and cold is the night!
>
> As for those poorer than myself
> Their parents must be cold and hungry
> Their wives and children beg and cry.
> Then how do you struggle through life?

A poem on a waterfowl, written by Dogen, a famous and learned Buddhist priest of the thirteenth century, is reminiscent of Bryant's longer poem on the same subject.

> Though going and coming
> Its track does not stay
> The waterfowl never
> Forgets its way.

The Japanese, as always, only suggests what the Western poet states explicitly:

> There is a Power whose care
> Teaches thy way along that pathless coast—
> The desert and illimitable air—
> Long wandering but not lost.

About three hundred years ago another, even shorter, type of poem developed, the seventeen-syllable *haiku*, or *hokku*, which is really the first hemistich of the *waka*, the three lines of five, and seven and five syllables. This expresses the essence of a poetic mood; it is more spontaneous, less conventional; generally it has to do with nature and it must have something in it to indicate the season of the year. The first writer of this poem, Basho, who lived in the seventeenth century, is probably the greatest poet of *haiku;* some would even say he was the greatest poet that Japan has ever produced. Born into a samurai family, he broke away from his background, became a wandering priest and a teacher of poetry; he was mystical, compassionate, a person of almost saintly life, and a lover of nature.

His most famous *haiku* and perhaps the best-known of all *haiku* is, in the translation by R. H. Blyth:

> The old pond—
> A frog jumps in—
> The sound of water.

Simple and even insignificant as it appears at first reading, it has been the subject of legend and discussion and a great deal of learned elucidation. Dr. Daisetz Suzuki wrote of it in his *Zen Buddhism and Its Influence on Japanese Culture,* "This leap is just as weighty a matter as the fall of Adam from Eden, for there is here too a truth revealing the secrets of creation."

Because of its brevity and its dependence on suggestion, *haiku* invites a good deal of explaining and amplifying. I always enjoyed hearing people who really knew their *haiku* arguing about the overtones and undertones of seventeen syllables that seemed on the surface merely factual. During my first years in Japan I used to drive to Koganei for the Crown Prince's private lessons. After the lesson tea was always served me in one of the waiting rooms. The then Grand Chamberlain, Baron Shigeto Hozumi, was usually there, with one or two other chamberlains, and sometimes a visitor. I would have liked to use these times for talk about the Crown Prince himself and his needs, but Baron Hozumi was very skilful in turning the conversation to the drama,

travel, poetry and other cultural, impersonal topics. As he spoke
English well and his mind was a storehouse of interesting knowledge, I enjoyed these sessions in spite of the frustration involved.
One day, I remember, there was a discussion between Dr. Hozumi and a visitor on the meaning of Basho's poem:

> An autumn evening:
> She comes and asks
> Shall I light the lamp?

One of them said that in it the poet perceived as one thing the
inevitability of nature, as shown in the coming on of night and
of winter and perhaps of death, and the warm loving-kindness
of man.

The other saw it quite differently. Two friends, he said, are
talking in the twilight. It is the wife's duty to bring a lamp without being told, but she is sensitive to mood and she understands
that they might prefer the darkness, and so she asks them.

Baron Hozumi was himself an indefatigable writer of poetry,
chiefly *waka*. When he accompanied the Crown Prince on his
first trip to Kyoto, he wrote no less than a hundred and twenty
waka along the way, and read them to the Crown Prince every
night. He presented me with a handwritten copy of his poems
and Tané translated a sampling of them for me. One of them,
which undoubtedly suffered, as poems do, in translation, was:

"When I see our noble Prince visiting the shrine, my heart is
melted with awe."

My first reaction was to question the effect of such an effusion
on a thirteen-year-old boy, but later I decided that a spot of
adulation was perhaps what he needed at the time. Certainly it
did him no harm.

People write poems, as Dr. Hozumi did, to record some experience that has moved them, to express an emotion or an impression. Many are written to order for a particular occasion. At the
time of the Crown Prince's coming of age, for instance, a number

of people were asked to write poems with the title "Chrysanthemum." In my home in Philadelphia I was invited to send one. Many more were written spontaneously, and there was a great exchanging of poems.

Poetry-writing as a form of entertainment has persisted down the centuries. People come together, they choose a subject, write their poems on the spot and then read them. One of the earliest descriptions of such parties is in *The Tale of Genji*.

The Emperor gave the party—in a garden under blossoming cherry trees. (Incidentally, cherry trees and poetry go together to this day. I have seen cherry-viewing parties sitting on a red blanket on the grass under the trees, a picnic spread out before them, and tied to the branches over their heads long strips of paper inscribed with original poems.) The guests in the eleventh-century party were the royal princes, noblemen, and a few professional poets. Each guest went up to the Emperor and received a title from him, chosen at random. Genji's title was "Spring." The professional poets were very nervous; they all wore an expression of deepest gloom. "It was amusing," commented the author, "to see the lively concern with which the Emperor watched their various but always uncouth and erratic methods of approaching the throne." (I used to suspect that their present-day Majesties felt the same lively concern about my own Quaker approaches to the throne.) The poems were written and then read; Genji, the hero, triumphed. Dancing and a banquet followed.

In the court, poems are still written every month or so. I used occasionally to hear the chamberlains groaning over their tasks. Some of them were entirely equal to it and were actually very good poets, but one or two were not gifted that way. Now and then on a special occasion I was asked to join in, and every year I wrote something for the New Year contest.

The Imperial poetry contest is a very old institution, which lapsed for a time and was revived on a bigger scale by the Emperor Meiji. A subject is chosen and announced, usually with a suggestion of newness and freshness in it, such as First Snow, Spring in the Mountains; Dawn. *Waka* are written on a special kind of white paper and sent in. People from all walks of life and all over Japan send in poems, thousands of them. Some come from Japanese living abroad. A few years ago, an American woman in California, Miss Lucille Nixon, who studied with a Japanese teacher of poetry, sent in one that became one of the winners of the contest. A board of judges selects the best fifteen to be read before the Emperor, in a beautiful ceremony which is held in the Imperial Household Building some time in January.

I have been privileged three times to be present at the ceremony. The first time I went, the winning poets were not there. The second time, they were in the next room with a transom open in between, so that they could hear but not see. The third time they were in the adjoining room with the double doors open.

It is a scene of solemnity and formality. The guests arrive first: members of the government, the minister of education, the prime minister. The judges arrive next, then the five men who are to read the poems. They are all descendants of ancient families who have been performing this service for centuries; some of them have come up from Kyoto, the ancient capital, just for the occasion. Members of the court come, Imperial princes and princesses, and at last the Emperor and Empress take their places at tables covered with fabulous brocade in front of gold screens decorated with scenes from *The Tale of Genji*.

The fifteen winning poems are read—or rather, chanted—and then the Imperial poems. The Emperor's, which comes last, is read five times. The poems are returned to their lacquer boxes, the Emperor and Empress withdraw, followed by the guests in the order of their rank.

The ceremony, which has been a cross between a concert and a slow symbolic dance, has taken two hours out of a weekday morning. The poems are all printed on the front pages of the newspapers. What other modern government in the world would take time out of a crowded week for the ritual reading of poetry?

Other formal occasions for poetry-writing include farewells. When I left Japan the two older princesses each composed farewell poems to me, wrote them in their best hands on long narrow pieces of cardboard especially designed for the purpose, and enclosed them in a long lacquer box. The box, which had the faint gold spattering known as *kinmakie,* was long and narrow and slightly curved, like the classic Japanese harp, the *koto*—a subtle reminder of the kinship between poetry and music. The poems themselves were not labored tributes to me; they simply expressed thoughts aroused by my departure. One of them, for instance, referred to a visit which the princesses had made one summer to my cottage in the mountains. We had gone for a walk and it had begun to rain.

"I remember the mountains and the trees, and the rain falling lightly, lightly."

The Crown Prince did not write a poem especially for the occasion, but he had copied out on a gold and white card in his best handwriting one that he had written earlier. The poem itself was in Japanese, but he wrote on another card a translation and explanation of it. It is interesting that while the poem itself was expressed in thirty-one syllables, the English version took two long paragraphs.

It had to do with the return to the Akasaka Palace garden after the war of some beautiful Formosan birds that he had loved when he lived there as a child. He chose this poem to copy partly because his grandmother had given me as a parting gift a painting of the pond in the same garden by the well-known modern painter, Kawai Gyokudo. I have both versions of the Crown Prince's poem mounted on brocade and framed, and of all the gifts he has given me this is the one I cherish most.

Poetry has been the language of love for centuries, not only to celebrate the charms of the beloved, but as a direct means of communication between two people. In the *Manyoshu* there are several dialogues between lovers, and *The Tale of Genji* is full of exchanges of poems to arrange meetings, to refuse to arrange meetings, to reproach and to reject, and to express other relationships as well. When Genji has been exiled, as punishment for an indiscretion, an old friend comes to visit him. In parting, Genji offers the other man a poem:

"O Crane," he begins, the crane being a symbol of good fortune, "who travelest at will even to the very margin of the Land of High, look well upon me, whether in intent I be not cloudless at this new day of spring." By which the crane correctly understands him to mean: You stand well with the Emperor. Put in a good word for me.

When Genji meets in the dark an unknown lady and promptly falling in love with her asks her name, she, quick-witted, puts him off with a poem: "Names are of this world only and you would not care to know mine if you were resolved that our love should last till worlds to come."

There is record of an exchange of poems between Lady Murasaki herself and the prime minister of the time. The chapters of her novel evidently were read to the Empress and court ladies as they were written, and the news of this enthralling story of Prince Genji and his love affairs got about. Accordingly the prime minister, who disliked her, wrote to Lady Murasaki on a piece of paper decorated with plum blossoms, "How comes it that, sour as the plum tree's fruit, you have contrived to blossom forth in tale so amorous?"

To which the lady replied, "Who has told you that the fruit belies the flower? For the fruit you have not tasted and the flower you know but by report." Meaning: You have neither read my book nor won my love.

The gift for quick and witty expression by no means died with the eleventh century, as a recent incident shows. After the war Prince Takamatsu gave up his palace and moved into a small house on the grounds. The mansion and garden were thrown open to be used for meetings, concerts, parties, bazaars, and the like. Miss Michi Kawai went there one day to a bazaar that was being held for the benefit of the Association of University Women, and she met of course many former students and teachers. As she was sitting on a bench talking with old friends, a young woman came up and spoke to her. She replied in the kindly condescending language that a teacher from her pinnacle uses to a former pupil, "Now, let me see, who are you?" The next moment she was overwhelmed to realize that she was speaking to Princess Takamatsu herself, the sister-in-law of the Emperor. A very different type of language was called for in the circumstances! Miss Kawai was numb with confusion, but a little later she got a chance to put it all in a poem. One of the money-makers at such a bazaar is a table where for a fee you write or draw on plain white plates, which are then fired. In a clever and graceful *waka*, no doubt with several puns in it, Miss Kawai expressed her chagrin at not having recognized the Princess in her own garden. A little later the Princess coming along saw the finished plate and in great delight insisted upon having it for her own.

Once when Michiko, our little maid, was in trouble with her mother, I got her for her birthday, and to cheer her up, the gaudiest box of American cosmetics that I could find at the PX. This gift transported her with a delight that prose could not contain. That afternoon a poem came in on the tea-tray, to the effect that she would try to express her undying gratitude in more virtuous living.

Even in recent times poems have been put to more serious uses than to cover social errors or acknowledge benefits. The story of the Emperor's using a poem by his grandfather to express his opposition to the war has been told elsewhere but it bears repeating here. In a meeting in September, 1941, the Japanese Cabinet informed the Emperor of its unanimous decision to go to war with the United States if the negotiations in Washington proved unsuccessful. They were not asking his advice, they were demanding his approval, which was always given to a unanimous decision. Instead, he quoted to them with great feeling a poem by the Emperor Meiji which has long been considered the great expression of the universal human desire for peace:

> Surely in this world men are brothers—all
> One family!
> Why then do winds and waves on all the seas
> Rage stormily?

He repeated it a second time, and left the meeting. The members of the Cabinet went away profoundly shaken, but when they were back again among the leaders of the army and navy who had not been present when the Emperor spoke they were quickly restored to their original determination.

15

Japanese Humor

HAVE the Japanese a sense of humor?" people sometimes say to me in a tone of surprise, and, equally surprised, I remember that once I would have asked the same question myself.

"Japanese history began with the laughter of the gods," says R. H. Blyth in his very interesting book, *Japanese Humor*. He is referring to the well-known myth, in which Amaterasu-no-Omikami, the Sun Goddess, outraged by the misbehavior of her brother, the Storm God, retired into a cave, leaving all the world in darkness. All the other gods had a conference about ways of coaxing her out again. At last one of them danced a comical dance (a strip-tease, according to Mr. Blyth) which set them all to laughing uproariously. It was too much for Amaterasu. Out she came to find out what the joke was.

This most famous of Japanese myths is quoted in many contexts. Basically of course it is an eclipse myth. Most often it is told in connection with the belief that the Emperors of Japan are directly descended from the Sun Goddess. On the other hand, the late Baron Kantaro Suzuki, a former admiral and prime minister toward the end of the war, told me that modern democracy in Japan was actually a return to the profound truth of the old legend, in which a group went into conference to meet a problem and settled it by democratic procedure. Only Mr. Blyth, so far as I know, has emphasized this gale of prehistoric laughter. And yet, how human and how Japanese. It was bound to work.

Mr. Blyth, who considers the Japanese the most humorous as well as the most poetic of all nations, to whom "an unlaughing man" is hardly a human being, explores and describes the manifestations of Japanese humor in literature. Puns, parodies, caricature, satire, funny stories, as well as the gentler humor that arises out of character or situation in poem or story, have abounded throughout Japanese literature, and the fact that humorous poems appear in the *Manyoshu* shows that humor has from earliest times been considered worth preserving.

It was more than once lamented at the P.E.N. meetings that whereas the visual arts have universal and immediate acceptance, literature must always pass through the medium of translation, losing something on the way. This is particularly true of humor.

The humor in Japanese art is immediately perceptible. Japanese caricatures, exaggerated and sometimes even savage, are frequently too cruel to be funny—real humor is not cruel—but there are a number of picture scrolls which, simply by depicting human beings as they are everywhere, fussy, eager, excited, greedy, frightened, pompous, important, have a humor as universal as it is quiet. The humor in these scrolls is not primary, it is incidental; the figures are only part of a larger scene, the burning of a castle, the building of a palace, a street scene in Edo. But there are other scrolls whose whole purpose is humorous. The Choju Eiga (animal scrolls) ascribed to Toba Sōjo, a monk of the late eleventh and early twelfth centuries, are the most famous as well as the best art. Painted in ink on paper, these four scrolls depict scenes in which monkeys, rabbits, foxes, frogs and other animals playing the part of human beings make exquisite fun of human foibles. A monkey offering a persimmon at the altar of a frog Buddha, a fox and a rabbit piously reading the sutra, rabbits swimming and frogs wrestling are all so inimitably themselves and yet so human that one cannot look at it without smiling. That it is also superb art in its swift sure economy of line, in composition and movement, in beauty of detail, makes it timeless. When the Japanese government a few years ago sent an exhibit to be shown in five United States cities of a hundred of its most cherished art treasures, one of the Toba scrolls was among them. Thousands of Americans saw the original, but reproductions of some of the scenes appear in every book on Japanese art, and parts of it have been reproduced in a picture book for American children.

The humor that depends on words, however, loses sadly in translation. Puns are by their nature untranslatable—and usually are not very funny anyhow. Funny stories depend so much on a knowledge of social customs, colloquialisms, folk lore and local history that by the time everything has been explained both teller and listener are tired of it all and the point has been lost in the verbiage.

Drama is easier, because so much is made clear in the acting. Though the classical Noh plays are serious indeed, every program of Noh is interspersed with *kyogen,* brief comic interludes, which are lively farcical dialogues between two robbers, or a daimyo and his servant, two old women, a wife and her henpecked husband and so on. In Kabuki the humor is woven into the plays, and though some of it is incomprehensible to a Westerner, much of it is deliciously funny, even though one has not understood a word of it.

There is a brief scene, for instance, in *Shinju Tenno Amajin,* a play about the common people written by Chikamatsu in 1720, which is as fresh and funny as if it were written yesterday. An apprentice boy brings to Koharu, the heroine, a letter filled with bad news. She opens it and becomes at once absorbed in it. The boy lingers at the gate, unnoticed and disconsolate. At length, squirming a little, he suggests that perhaps she has forgotten something. Hastily coming to, she finds her purse and offers him a coin. All surprise and delicacy, he makes a great show of refusing to accept it, all the while edging forward with outstretched hand. It is simple humor, but universal and good in any period, any country—and acted so as to extract every bit of the juice.

The humor in Japanese books, except with the admitted limitations of translation, is unavailable to me, since I don't read Japanese. What I was very much aware of, however, and what was a constant delight to me, was the laughter in daily life.

The humor of every day is fragile, or not fragile so much as spontaneous. How often one hears someone in paroxysms of mirth gasp out, "It wasn't so much what he said as the *way* he said it!" and then return to helpless, speechless laughter. Solemn talk about it, analyzing it, giving examples, is like putting a wetting-agent on a duck; the poor creature sinks at once. Or what seems funny to one person falls flat with another. The story is told of the late Walter Connolly that in playing the part of the comedy uncle in *The Good Earth,* he told funny stories to Chinese children, who sat at his feet and laughed heartily. One day, when he was eating a sandwich lunch on location a four-year-old child came to him and said, "Are you the funny man?" Connolly replied that he was and made funny faces and gestures to prove it. The child said, "Why don't I laugh?"

At the risk of arousing a similar reaction, I am going to give an example or two of Japanese humor, not in books, but as I met it.

It was not based on overstatement, as in the United States, or on understatement, as in England, but it seemed to me usually a simple acceptance of fact, funny largely because it was true and unexpected.

I remember being at a dinner party one evening and hearing a story told that was immensely funny to everyone there. There was nothing in it that lost momentum in the translation, but there was a kind of monumental detachment in both the story and the laughter that left me feeling as if I had had a blow in the solar plexus.

A distinguished scholar, a friend of all of us, was famous for his way of becoming gay and lighthearted on a minute amount of sake. During the war he was dining one evening with some friends who had a handsome gold screen, on which they were going to have a famous calligrapher write some decorative verses. Our friend, after a small portion of sake, insisted upon writing on the screen himself, which he proceeded to do with vigorous and splashy black letters. The hostess was heartbroken. Her husband comforted her by saying reassuringly, "Never mind, it will be burned up in the next air raid anyhow"—and it was. The whole company laughed in apparent delight. All of those who found this story so funny had themselves been burned out during the war. Furthermore, one of them had told the story to the Emperor and Empress, and Their Majesties, who also had been burned out, were equally amused.

As I listened I tried to imagine a scene at home, with a group of Georgians, in the presence of a Yankee guest, making merry over a similar story involving, say, a brocade sofa destroyed by Sherman's army. Ninety years after the Civil War was over, my imagination faltered.

Our little maid, Michiko, as I have written, occasionally rebelled against her fate. One day, completely fed up, she ran away and took refuge with family friends. The next morning, her elder sister, Masako, was sent by their mother to fetch her back. In the afternoon Moken slipped his leash and disappeared. Masako again sallied forth, combed the neighborhood and recaptured the fugitive. At dinner as Violet, Tané and I were quietly chuckling over Masako's day of rescue work, suddenly we heard shrieks of laughter in the kitchen. Tané, making inquiries afterwards, reported that the same thing had at the same moment struck the Inoues as funny and one and all, including Michiko herself, they had burst out laughing.

The last time the Koizumis and I went to Kabuki together, we had lunch between plays in a private room on the second floor of the theater. Before we had finished our meal, the warning bell rang for the next play, *Kanjincho*, of which we did not want to miss a single word.

"Unfortunately," said Dr. Koizumi, "this is unusually good eel."

One of the first things I noticed about the Crown Prince when he was still a little boy of twelve, was his genuine amusement when he laughed. As time went on I came to know and enjoy his sense of humor. Like all Japanese, he enjoyed puns and in time made them in English. He had also that gift for stating a simple, sometimes unpalatable truth so that it produced laughter. For the following instance, I am indebted to his friend and classmate, Kiyoshi Togasaki.

As captain of his school riding team, he had to make a speech welcoming new members. "At present, we have only one horse for the whole team," he told them, "and no addition can be expected with the increase in membership. If everyone of us rides this one mare, she will be literally worked to death. Therefore, as far as this team is concerned, we welcome those members who will be faithful in the payment of their dues and be good loyal loafers in their practice."

The word humor, according to the Oxford Dictionary, originally meant moisture or juice and only fairly recently, that is to say from the seventeenth century, came to mean that quality of action, speech or writing which excites amusement, or the faculty of perceiving what is ludicrous or amusing. As anyone who has experienced the lubricating effect of even a small joke in a household well knows, humor still has an element of juice. It keeps life from drying up, gives it freshness and flavor.

Some laughter can be cruel. Directed against a person, it hurts and shames. A dog dressed in a plastic raincoat is perfectly happy until someone laughs at him; after that he will never wear it again and he will growl when he meets the one who has mocked. One of childhood's bitterest wounds is the experience of being laughed at by the grown-ups. Adults, schooled in pretense, will join in laughter at their own expense, but often they carry resentments that come out much later in small acts of secret revenge.

Shared laughter, on the other hand, is healing. It dissolves tension and unites hearts. Christopher Fry, the poet and playwright, goes further: "Laughter may only seem to be like an exhalation of air, but out of that air we came; in the beginning we inhaled it; it is a truth, not a fantasy, a truth voluble of good which comedy stoutly maintains."

16

The Search for the Ox

EARLY in my very first year in Japan, I met Dr. Daisetz Suzuki, the great Zen Buddhist scholar. With several others I was invited to visit the temple in Kamakura where he lived and to attend a tea ceremony.

Enkakuji is one of the oldest and loveliest temples in a city famous for beautiful temples. It was founded in 1282, after Kublai Khan's emissaries had been beheaded and his invading army defeated and driven away, like the Spanish Armada, with the help of a providential storm. The Regent, Tokimune, a young man in his twenties and an ardent Zen Buddhist, built the temple called Enkakuji for the consolation of the departed spirits on both sides of the war, both Japanese and Mongolian.

Zen Buddhism, which has recently become so popular in the United States, is not, as many appear to think, the sole form of Japanese Buddhism. It is one of many sects and is neither the oldest nor the largest one, though it might well be said that it is the most vital and influential one in Japan today. It arose in India in the sixth century A.D. and was taken from there to China in the seventh century, where it absorbed many Taoist beliefs and practices. Reaching Kyoto in the early thirteenth century, it was opposed by the aristocratic priests there. In Kamakura, however, it made an immediate appeal to the rising military class. The warriors approved the indifference to death and pain

which it helped to develop; practical, direct, simple men themselves, they liked its simplicity and its intuitive rather than intellectual basis. Its discipline too and the emphasis on asceticism,
self-reliance and single-mindedness were congenial to them.
Archers, fencers and swordmakers found it not only a religion
but an incomparable training for coordination of eye and brain
and hand. To artists and poets Zen was an experience of reality
and a method of getting at the essence of what they wanted to
paint or say which released them from all fumbling or overstatement. They found congenial the fundamental aim of Zen, which,
in Dr. Suzuki's words, "is to throw off all the external parapher-
nalia which the intellect has woven around the soul and to see
directly into the inmost nature of our being."

That December day Dr. Suzuki was waiting at the entrance
to the temple of Enkakuji to welcome us, a small, venerable,
kimono-clad figure against the background of the huge thatch-
roofed gate and the lofty cedars. The first thing one noticed about
him was his extraordinary eyebrows, jutting out over the deep
sockets of his eyes with a vitality of their own, like two small
pony-tails; the second, his unmistakable look of enlightenment,
in the Buddhist sense. One knew at once that he had had the
experience called *satori*, that breaking through the mind barrier
into the wholeness of understanding which is the goal of the Zen
devotee. Light and love seemed to stream from him; his gentleness was clothed in simplicity, his austerity touched with humor.

Before lunch we were taken on a tour of the temple. Walking
up the long flights of shallow stone steps through the cryptomerias and pines, Dr. Suzuki talked of war and peace ("Buddhism never stopped a war," he said ruefully, "—but then it never
started one either"), of Quakerism, of Zen meditation, and of two
well-known Friends, Rufus Jones and Howard Brinton, who had
visited Japan at different times and had meditated with Zen
monks. Hearing about it years earlier in Philadelphia, I had felt
something like awe just to know people who had had such a re-

mote and mysterious experience. Now as we passed the Meditation Hall, where the monks were doing a three-day stretch of *Zazen* (meditation), Dr. Suzuki slid open the door and let me look in.

I saw a rather dim room with a corridor down the center separating two long platforms floored with *tatami*. Sitting on their heels on the *tatami* two rows of young monks faced each other, motionless in meditation. The atmosphere of concentration in that room was as palpable as the old, cold, knife-like chill which struck our faces when the door opened and was shut in again when it closed.

"Here the monks face each other," said Dr. Suzuki as we strolled on again in the December sunshine and pine-fragrant air. "In some temples they face the wall. This way they are not so cut off from one another. It is more like the Quaker meditation, I think."

In fumbling words, answering his questions, I tried to explain the corporate silence of Quaker meeting, which is not meditation but worship. The relationship, I said, was not only vertical, between man and God, but horizontal too, between man and man. The resulting silence was more than the sum of the individual silences. It was like a *hibachi*. If the sticks of charcoal burned alone, they would give little heat; gathered together in the brazier, the glow of each was intensified by the touch with the others. Though he asked questions, he did not need to hear this from me; he knew it already. Out of this conversation, nevertheless, was to come months later one of the most extraordinary experiences of my life.

The tea ceremony was held in a tea-house belonging to Mr. Riisuke Saito, a connoisseur and art dealer who lived close to the Temple. It was not my first tea ceremony. I had already taken part in one in Kyoto, at the headquarters of the Ura Senke School, performed by Mr. Sen himself, the descendant of Sen Rikyu, friend of Hitoyoshi and founder of the tea cult as it is practiced at the present time. I knew that tea itself had been brought to Japan by a Zen monk—the same one, in fact, Eisai, who brought Zen Buddhism to Japan from China—and that the spirit of harmony, reverence, purity and tranquility which the tea ceremony seeks to evoke is also the spirit of Zen. I knew something of its form, by which simplicity and naturalness had been preserved in the amber of a rigid ritual, and I had an inkling of the years of study and practice it takes to enable one to perform precisely and self-forgetfully those unvarying motions with the dipper, the square of folded silk, the bamboo whisk and the cup involved in the preparation, the offering and the accepting of the ceremonial drink. But this was my first tea ceremony in a purely Zen setting, and I found the atmosphere more relaxed and the conversation more interesting. Conventional politeness about the flower arrangement, a single camellia in a celadon vase, or the tea bowl, which looked colorless and rough but was old and Korean and immensely valuable, died away in a room where Dr. Suzuki sat talking about the meaning of *wabi* (translated as tranquility, but much more) and Zen in daily life.

Later Mr. Saito brought out some of his priceless treasures to show us, and Dr. Suzuki explained the meaning of a wonderful old scroll, a Japanese copy of the Ten Oxherding Pictures painted by Kaku-an, a Zen master of the Sung dynasty, to illustrate the stages of Zen discipline. In the first scene, the young man is hunting for the ox, which may be interpreted as the spiritual life, or *satori*. In the second, he finds its footprints: that is, by study and effort he has come to a beginning of understanding. Then he catches a glimpse of it among the trees. "All his senses are in harmonious order." He captures the ox, but controls it with difficulty. In the next stage he has subdued his thoughts to the point where he can lead the ox by a string through its nostrils. In number six he has mounted it and is riding home on its back, playing the flute as he goes. "The struggle is over. He is no more concerned with gain and loss." Then the ox disappears, but this does not disturb him; he sits dreaming. In the eighth both man and ox have vanished. Dualism is gone. And here Dr. Suzuki quotes Meister Eckhart: "He alone hath true spiritual poverty who wills nothing, desires nothing, knows nothing." The ninth picture shows what the youth sees: water, mountains, an old tree trunk and plum blossoms. Abiding in the "serenity of non-assertion," he watches things growing. In the tenth, "carrying a gourd (symbol of emptiness) he goes out into the market; leaning against a staff he comes home. He is found in company with wine-bibbers and butchers. He and they are all converted into Buddhas."

For the further exploration of Zen in more modern terms, Dr. Suzuki gave me a copy of his own altogether fascinating book, *Zen Buddhism and Its Influence in Japanese Culture,* and later, of his *Living by Zen,* in which he wrote: "The great discovery we owe Buddhism and especially Zen is that it has opened for us the way to see into the suchness of things. . . . Zen sees with its satori-eye things as they are in themselves."

Two or three months later he asked me to speak on Quakerism to a group of laymen (including Admiral Kichisaburo Nomura, the ambassador to the United States at the time of Pearl Harbor), who met regularly at Enkakuji to study literature and philosophy, and the following July he asked me to repeat the talk to an assembly of Zen monks.

On a gray, dripping Sunday near the end of the rainy season I went to Sojiji, one of the two largest temples of the Soto sect of Zen. It was a busy temple in Yokohama with a number of buildings with black-tiled roofs like great wings and much coming and going across the courtyards. No meditation was going on that day, for it was nearing the season when the spirits of the dead return to visit the earth, and frequent services were scheduled. In Buddhist temples there is no regular congregational worship as in Christian churches and Jewish synagogues, but at special times or festivals appropriate ceremonies take place.

The little group of us who went down from Tokyo that day attended two such rituals. One was a memorial service for the founder of the sect, the poet-priest Dogen, in which the monks chanted prayers, sometimes kneeling and sometimes marching about in an intricate rhythm, and the abbot in a brilliant brocade robe and a tall hat to match with a long streamer down the back, read from the sutras in the strange, loud "open-throat" voice of all ancient Japanese expression, whether drama, song, storytelling, or prayer.

The second service, called "Feeding the Hungry Ghosts," was a kind of memorial mass for the dead, ordered and paid for by living relatives. Amid more marching and chanting, real food was brought to the altar to be spiritually consumed by the unseen guests. The names of the dead were read out; three monks placed in front of the image of the Buddha three small lacquer tables with a bowl of incense smoldering on each. Three at a time the relatives drew near, knelt before the tables, and put three pinches of incense powder into the bowls. One of them was a frail-looking young woman with a great heavy sleeping child in her arms. She looked tired and sad and underfed, as no doubt she was, for this was 1947 and even the 1,500-calorie ration was often delayed.

After the plentiful vegetable lunch which the abbot served us in one of the many handsome rooms of the temple, we saw the monks eating their dinner in the meditation hall. Each one had his regular place on *tatami*-floored platforms like those I had seen at Enkakuji. From their sleeves they took out lacquer bowls and chopsticks and a wide china spoon and set them out in what was obviously the prescribed way. After more chanting the food came, in huge bowls carried by monks serving as waiters. There was a thin watery gruel of rice and barley, three pieces of yellow pickled radish for each one, and some moist lumpy gray salt, which they dipped out with their china spoons. After two helpings of the gruel, they got hot tea, with which they rinsed their bowls before they drank it. This was all they had, and it was the big meal of the day. They wiped their bowls at the end with squares of cotton cloth, then wrapped them in the same cloth, and returned them to their sleeves.

Though they were referred to in English as monks and though at the temple they lived a monastic life of study, meditation and physical labor for the upkeep of temple and grounds, they were not monks as we understand the word. Some were permanently attached to the temple, some were preparing themselves to be priests, others were priests with temples of their own, often married men, who had returned to the mother temple for what might be called a retreat.

They were very thin, most of them, and a gray pallor lay over their faces. I thought, as I so often did when faced with groups of Japanese, whether children or adults, of the absurdity of the western cliché that all Orientals look alike. These men with their uniform coarse black robes and shaven heads still showed a variety of facial types and bony structure so wide that they might have represented a dozen different racial strains. There was the face with small, wide-set eyes, high cheekbones and long upper lip; the long, classic oval, calm and aristocratic; the square, bumpy face under a bulging forehead; the round merry countenance with plump cheeks and a button nose. Of the familiar Western caricature with the protruding teeth and receding chin I saw not a single example.

Some of the younger ones, I had been told, were returned soldiers who had found no openings in civilian life. Japan was not kind to her veterans. Along with war itself they were discredited and their fellow citizens, struggling with defeat and the occupation, wanted only to forget them. Young men who would under ordinary circumstances have had no interest in the priesthood were drawn to it by economic necessity.

Such were the sixty-odd men who about two o'clock filed into one of the large, handsome, incense-smelling halls of the temple and sat down on the *tatami*, facing a wide *tokonoma*, or alcove, decorated with a forbidding bronze ornament and a large picture-scroll. One of the treasures of the temple, it was a famous painting of an Indian Buddhist sage, whose name I did not get (but it was not Dharma, as I had assumed): a frenetic-looking individual clothed in red, shooting fire out of angry eyes.

With Dr. Suzuki beside me to interpret for me, I stood up in my stocking feet between the red sage and the attentive monks, and spoke on Quaker ideals of worship and service and "Living by virtue of that life and power that takes away the occasion for all wars." In the intervals between paragraphs, while I waited for Dr. Suzuki to turn my simple English into scholarly, philosophical Japanese, I wondered if it all was actually happening.

Nearly two years later I plucked up courage to ask Dr. Suzuki if he could arrange for me to take part in a Zen meditation. In May he obtained the permission of the abbot of Enkakuji for me to join the monks one evening during a special, prolonged period of *Zazen* which they were then undergoing. "May is a good month," he wrote me, with the acceptance of practical fact which is so much a part of Zen, "not cold, not too warm, and mosquitoes won't be bothering us."

The sun was setting as I approached the gate; visitors were coming away and silence was sifting with the shadows through the long arches of the trees. In the garden of Dr. Suzuki's house color still lingered in the peonies and a frog went plop into the pond with the water lilies.

The Meditation Hall that evening was open at both ends to the trees. As *Zazen* was continuous all that week, the monks were in their places, motionless in the pale light. In all probability each of them had been given by the master under whom he was working a question on which to meditate, such as "What is the sound made by the clapping of one hand?" I went, however, as a Friend goes to Meeting, prepared only to be receptive.

At one end a chair had been provided for me. The priest who

was my guide indicated it, I slipped out of my pumps and made my way to it as quietly as I could, and the priest disappeared. A little later, as the evening grew chillier, he came tiptoeing back with a pair of slippers which he thrust under my feet, one more instance of the Japanese kindly thought for the Westerner who tries to conform to Eastern customs.

Although I had come not as a sightseer but with a sincere desire to enter as deeply as an outsider can into an experience of meditation among experts in a particularly intense form of the art, I was aware at first chiefly of the external features of the situation in which I found myself. This I accepted as natural and inevitable and I tried to relax to it, so that the phase might pass as soon as possible. I kept my eyes open, and though I did not turn my head or look about me, I allowed my brain to register what my senses reported to it.

The chair on which I sat was an ordinary straight wooden one without arms, of a good height, neither comfortable nor uncomfortable. I found it quite possible to forget my body altogether, and during the hour and a half that I sat there I did not, so far as I know, move at all.

I saw the trees outside the wide door, tall purplish trunks and dark green foliage bathed in a clear greenish light. I saw the still figures of my fellow meditators. Most were monks or priests in black kimonos, but two or three were students of Zen from outside the temple, who wore ordinary business suits. A young monk with a shaven head and an unlined, untested, expressionless face marched up and down the aisle, his black draperies billowing out behind him, a long rod in his hands. I soon forgot him.

Sounds caught my attention next and I closed my eyes. First there was the wind in the pines, the eternal toss and murmur, soothing and evocative. A few birds twittered and became silent. From another of the temple buildings came the chanting of sutras, with the rhythm which is so unlike Western rhythms and the characteristic strange tones. Yet there was beauty in it, too.

Later I heard the sound of the temple bell, slow, deep, mellow and sweet. "How cool the boom of the great temple bell," runs a *haiku* by Buson, "dying away in the distance." With the tones of the bell came a feeling of peace and of release from the pressure of the strangeness of my surroundings.

My first feeling was one of relief amounting almost to elation. I knew that a space of time lay before me in which there would be no interruption. I should not have to turn my attention to any message, however inspired. I felt as if I were on the brink of some discovery, that if I could still all my thoughts, the ineffable light would show at least a gleam to me. The conviction that I was sharing in an age-old universal search for truth seemed to minimize the differences in belief and method that separated me from my fellow worshipers. A half-remembered phrase from the *Screwtape Letters* came to me: "God, not as I think Thou art but as Thou knowest Thyself to be." Layer after layer of the conscious mind seemed to be folded away as I sank deeper toward the Center.

A sudden sharp crack abrupt as a pistol shot broke the silence. My eyes flew open. A young monk nearly opposite me had bent over so that his forehead almost touched the *tatami* in front of him. The perambulating monk stood before him, his arms upraised, the long narrow flexible rod of bamboo in his hands. The next moment he brought this rod down with all his might on the bent back of the meditating monk. After a third resounding crack, the bent monk straightened up and bowed. The monk with the rod bowed in return and moved on.

I had read once in a book about Zen, and had forgotten it, that when the shoulder muscles of a meditating man become stiff and cramped from long concentration in one position, a sharp blow between the shoulder blades relaxes and eases him. I had also heard that when meditators fall asleep they were waked by a businesslike thwack. For the next few moments I watched to see, if I could, what was the purpose of this castigation.

Soon I saw one of the lay students press his hands together in the prayer position, clearly as a petition. The monk with the staff hastened to him, both men bowed, and the three blows were repeated.

I do not want to emphasize unduly this part of the evening's session. What was the effect sought I could not determine. I have since been told that there is an element in it of punishment for wayward thoughts. For me it dramatized the fact which I already knew theoretically, that each meditator was engaged in an entirely separate search. His unawareness of those around him was so complete that he was troubled neither by the noise of their castigation nor by the fear that his own might disturb them.

The depth of concentration which I had felt earlier in the evening I never quite regained. I sought for a sense of Presence but felt only mystery. It seemed to me that each one there was striving, with an austere perseverance that I could scarcely begin to comprehend, to achieve a new dimension for his spirit. I felt that strong, precise and delicate instruments were being forged there that night, but that the Hand which should use them was absent and indeed was not expected to lay hold of them.

The wind murmured in the trees and shook darkness out of them. The beauty and antiquity of the place swept over me and flooded me with awe. When a short intermission came, in which the monks rested and changed their positions, I rose and slipped away.

It is nine years now since I had that unforgettable experience. The impression which it left has not faded and I am increasingly grateful to those who made it possible, Dr. Suzuki and the abbot and the unprotesting monks. As I look back upon it I think that besides the sheer interest and beauty of it, I gained an understanding, or a beginning of understanding, of the East that I could not otherwise have found. Nature mysticism took on a new meaning for me, and also, in a way that I do not understand, I had a fresh experience of Christianity, a vision of our

Lord moving freely in the sunshine, and a realization of the incarnation as the way in which divinity enters into our daily lives.

I am by no means the only Westerner privileged to meditate with the monks, not even the only woman. Anyone who is seriously interested may be admitted. One of the teachers then at the American School in Tokyo was a regular student of Zen at Kamakura and worked with a master. Once when I returned to Enkakuji, not to meditate but to visit, I saw a number of copper-wire screens neatly stacked in one of the buildings. Those, a priest told me, were screens for the Meditation Hall. They had been donated by Mr. X, who had been greatly troubled by the mosquitoes.

"How American!" I thought when I heard it. But two years ago, when I was again at Enkakuji for a tea ceremony, I asked Abbot Asahina about the screens and he told me that they were in use. After all, I reflected, how Zen.

17

Cormorant Fishing

DURING the spring of 1959, the Crown Prince wrote me, he went to Gifu to see the cormorant fishing for the first time. My mind went back eleven years to the time when, because of the Empress's thought of me, I went to see this curious ancient sport. Because the project was the Empress's, everything conceivable was done so that I might see it under the best possible circumstances.

Tané and I left Tokyo in the morning, on an Occupation train. Travel was still very difficult then, and I was thankful to be able to go on the military train and to take Tané with me. The two men from the Imperial Household, who were to escort us, unfortunately had to go the night before on the regular crowded train.

The ride was the same one that I had taken before, on the main line between Tokyo and Kyoto, one that I never tired of. Most of the snow was gone from Mt. Fuji now; she had only a white cap and some white streaks down her blue sides. Though June had not yet begun, the wheat and barley were being harvested, and here and there in the midst of the gold of the wheatfields were patches of brilliant emerald green, the rice seedlings waiting to be planted as soon as the wheat should be gone.

We reached Gifu, which is a little beyond Nagoya, at five, and were met by the two men from the Department of Ceremonies of the Imperial Household, who had gone down ahead to prepare for us. One was Mr. (formerly Baron) Kikukawa, a very charming young man, alert, gentle, lively. He belongs to a riding family, and his wife and daughter distinguished themselves in some of the horse shows and exhibitions of horsemanship that were held in Tokyo. The other was an able and kindly assistant of his in the Department of Ceremonies.

They had got a car from the Gifu prefectural government, and we had about an hour's drive up the Nagara River through lovely wild country and picture-book villages. The late afternoon lights were beautiful, and the river followed us in and out among the steep wooded sides of the mountains, which rise up out of the valleys without foothills. Once we passed one of the fishing boats going up the river, a small boat with a square sail, an oarsman standing at the stern, and on the little deck a basket in which, Mr. Kikukawa said, were the cormorants. We had left Gifu and the Nagara Hotel behind, and were heading for the upper river, where was the best of the three Imperial preserves.

Cormorant fishing is one of Japan's oldest sports, perhaps one of the oldest sports in the world. It was mentioned in the *Kojiki*, the first history of Japan, written in 712. There are many other references to it in poetry and romance, and the early pictures show the same costumes and equipment as those used now.

As there was no hotel or inn on the upper river, it had been arranged that we were to stay at the house of Mr. Nishibe, a rich sake brewer who had often entertained guests of the Imperial Household.

The weather is very important for cormorant fishing. We had chosen that particular week end, because it was dark of the moon, but the night must be clear as well as dark, and as we wound up the valley we saw thunderheads rolling up, and there was a good deal of talk of the possibility of a storm coming.

When we arrived at the Nishibes' house the whole family, Mr. and Mrs. Nishibe, their son, two small daughters, the son's wife and new baby, and the young wife's mother and sister, were out at the gate to receive us. The house was a very large old one with its front right on the narrow road, and an enormous paved entrance through which the sake wagons could drive into the inner court, rather like an eighteenth-century English inn.

There were two or three broad polished wooden steps leading up from the entrance, where we took off our shoes, right into a *tatami*-floored room where there was a low table, surrounded with cushions, some bookshelves and provisions for business affairs, and high on the wall a "god-shelf," where the family gods were honored.

Tané and I were led to the guest wing, where we had a room and a dressing room to ourselves, opening on a charming little garden with rocks and a stone lantern and delicate plants and ferns in a dozen different shades of green. A passageway led down beside the garden to the bath, which was a new one and all ready for us after our long hot day on the train.

The Japanese bath is an institution, a rite, and an esthetic pleasure. When the Japanese government really woke up to the dangers inherent in the soldiers repatriated from Russia after indoctrination in the camps there who came back bitter against the home people who had accepted the American occupation and filled with distorted information and festering hates, they organized welcoming committees and a program right at the port of entry which should soothe their accumulated anger and fear and hurt and restore their love for the homeland before they went back to their villages. One of the features of this welcome was a Japanese bath, not for the physical comfort of it, which must have been great after the crowded journey home, but the psychological overtones, for all the bath meant to them of home, of peace, of ceremony, of civilization, of Japan.

After we had bathed, dinner was brought to us in our room looking out on the garden. Though there were a number of servants in the house, the pretty young daughter-in-law waited on us, to do special honor to the guests of the Imperial Household. Her kimono was a bright soft coral pink, as befitted so young a woman, with lovely designs of flowers on it. We begged her to eat with us, but she wouldn't, just brought us one delicious dish after another, knelt waiting to serve us more rice out of the big round lacquer box, and talked to us a little. Her baby was two months old, she had gone home to her mother in Tokyo for its birth, as was customary with a first child, and her mother and sister, who was a doctor, had made the trip back with her, to help with the baby. The little boy was wrapped in a scarlet kimono, and the senior Mrs. Nishibe carried him in her arms all the time that we were there. The daughter-in-law, gentle, quiet, self-effacing and graceful, was obviously proving herself in her careful attentiveness to the guests.

During dinner the threatened thunderstorm arrived with fury, the rain beat down in the garden, the thunder growled overhead, and for a time it appeared that we had made our long trip for nothing. But gradually the rain slackened and the thunder died away, and by nine o'clock it was all over.

We got into the car again, and drove still farther up the river to the place where the fishing boats and the men with the birds were waiting for us. The leader of the fishermen explained the process to us before the fishing began.

He wore the costume that appears in the old prints: a sort of black linen turban wound around his head to protect it from sparks from the flares, a black linen blouse and trousers rolled high, and straw sandals. He had twelve cormorants, which he loved, each one separately, and trained and cared for tenderly. About ten years is the ripe age for a bird but they work till they are twenty, and then they are retired and live on the fat of the land until they die. Each one is named, his neck is stretched by massage, and his place in the hierarchy carefully maintained; number one takes pride in his top position. A cormorant is a black bird about two feet high, with a long neck and some white about his big yellow bill, with which he scoops up small fish with great efficiency. If a string is tied about the lower part of his neck, so that he cannot swallow the fish, he will go on catching them until from four to eight fish are lodged in his neck; the fisherman then causes him to yield up his catch and he goes out for more. It takes skill to tie the string just tight enough, so that it will not choke him, or allow any but the smallest fish to go down. If he doesn't get some little ones for himself, the game is not worth playing and he stops cooperating. The string itself is a very special one, the part that goes around the neck is made of hemp, then there is a section of whalebone for stiffening, and the rest is a thin rope made of fibre of the cypress bark, strong, yet soft enough to cut in an emergency.

There are four men in each boat, the master fisherman, who manipulates the cormorants, the steersman, the man who tends the decoy fires, and the oarsman. The boats are rather long and narrow, with a high prow, over which hangs an iron arm which can be moved from one side to another, and from the arm hangs an iron basket in which sticks of pine wood are burned to attract the fish. The fish are *ayu,* a kind of smelt which come up the river in schools during the summer months.

There were five fishing boats there that night, and another boat for us. We climbed in and settled down on cushions on the floor in the center. The decoy fires hanging from the prow of each boat were lit, the boats moved into position, the cormorants were let down into the water, and the fun began. In our boat we circled in and out, now among the birds, now directly under the prow of a boat so that the light from the firebasket shone on our faces.

To encourage the birds the rowers beat on the side of the boats rhythmically with the oars and the masters sing to them, a weird, wild sort of crooning. The black, shining, long-necked birds dash about, across one another's paths, diving from time to time and coming up with the fish wriggling in their bills and shining in the light of the fires. The fish disappears and the bird has another bump in the long line of his neck. Suddenly you see that a bird's throat is all bulged out and the bird himself swims about looking distracted, and then the master pulls on the rope, drags the bird into the boat, and squeezing his neck firmly, makes him disgorge his fish into the basket, and throws him out into the water again. The bird swims around very fast, arching his neck and shaking his head, apparently in self-congratulation, and then suddenly dives again. Meanwhile the master is keeping all twelve ropes separate and unentangled, and pulling in one bird after another. It takes great skill on his part.

All the time the boats were moving slowly down the river, five abreast, and we were sometimes behind them, sometimes weaving in and out among them, sometimes withdrawing a little to get the sweep of the whole thing: the five boats and their flaring fires in a row across the dark river, walled in by the steep black mountains. It was one of the most wildly beautiful sights I have ever seen. Then we drew ahead, and our boatmen put up extra boards on the sides of the boat, and cautioned us to sit in the middle of the boat and sit still. What seemed to be a few drops of rain fell, waves rose high around the boat, and I thought another storm had come up. Then I realized that we were rushing along very fast and that the bottom of the boat was scraping on rocks. We were shooting the rapids.

In a few minutes we were out in smooth water again, and then we beached the boat and climbed up on a big rock to watch the fishing fleet come through the rapids, one after another. First came twelve birds, all gleaming in the light of the fires, rising and falling with the water, then the boat with a dip and a swoop and a rush, the fishermen in their quaint costumes black silhouettes in the darkness. One after another they came, and we clapped and cheered each one as it passed.

When they were all through the rapids and waiting in the dark smooth pool beyond, we got into our boat again and went ahead down the river. At the edge of the Imperial preserve, we found scores of village men and boys with nets, up to their waists in water, waiting to catch the fish that got away from the cormorants. I was told that some of them had been there since early morning in order to get and keep the best places.

In front of the Nishibes' house was a boat landing and shed where the catch was counted and sorted. About half of it was packed up in special hampers with ice to be sent to the Imperial Household in Tokyo. All the Imperial Family and many of their friends had *ayu* that week end that I had seen caught. The rest the fishermen had for themselves to eat or sell—and *ayu* sold for the equivalent of three dollars a pound, being considered a very great delicacy. Each of the cormorants got his reward of fish to swallow.

In the Nishibes' house we all sat around a table and drank tea and talked. The Nishibe ancestors had been the lords of this valley until about 1550, when Nobunaga came in and captured and destroyed their castle, after which the family had taken to sake brewing. They were evidently still the influential people of the neighborhood.

Presently some of the *ayu* that had just been caught and broiled over charcoal were brought in and we ate them. They were delicious—almost as good as the trout I once caught in Yellowstone Lake and fried in butter over a wood fire, the difference being due doubtless to my having been twenty years younger and having caught the trout myself.

We slept well that night, between beautiful silk quilts, with the sound of the river faintly in our ears, and woke to a breakfast of fresh eggs and toast made over the charcoal *hibachi* in our room. After breakfast they showed us where the sake was made, though it was not the season for making it then. In the compound behind the house were great barn-like buildings with huge hand-hewn beams black with age and smoke, and enormous wooden vats looming up in the dim light. Sake-making is regarded as a sacred art, and the presence of a woman, when the making is actually going on, is about as popular as a clergyman on a boat is with sailors.

Before we left, guest-books were brought out for us to sign. I quailed when I saw them, for there had been many distinguished guests in that house, and their handwriting was beautiful. Calligraphy in Japan is an art itself, appreciated with as much knowledge and discrimination as a picture. I was always ashamed of my scrawls, especially when I was confronted with a brush instead of a pen.

We drove back to Nagoya, over glorious country, mountains reflected in flooded fields, thatch-roofed farmhouses, blue iris growing out of roadside ditches, stretches of the Kiso River, which has been called the Rhine of Japan, and has at least one castle riding high on a hill above its blue waters.

Cormorant fishing is open now to tourists all through the summer months. Farther down the river, at Gifu, you can get a boat, or seats in a boat, according to the size of your party, and you can have your dinner on the river, while you are waiting for the dark to come and the flares to be lighted.

18

Kabuki

THE first time I went to Kabuki was in January, 1947, and it must have been one of the first of the Kabuki performances after the war. The Kabukiza (the famous theater especially for this kind of drama) was in ruins, and even the Imperial Theater, where the plays were given, was still suffering from war damage. Shabby, dingy and cold, it must have had big holes in the roof behind the stage, for when the curtain was drawn gales of icy wind swept in. We wore our warmest coats, my Canadian friend, my secretary, Tané, and I, and wrapped ourselves in steamer rugs besides. "Off limits" to Occupation personnel, the theater was crowded with Japanese, who, ill-clad, ill-fed, ill-housed in those difficult days, grasped eagerly at this first appearance of the old joys.

Tané, looking about her, spoke nostalgically of the beauty of the old Kabukiza. It was not only the *hanamichi* that was missing, the long ramp through the audience on which the actors made their most effective entrances and exits, but all the gaiety and elegance of the halls filled with shops and restaurants where people sauntered between plays. She was inclined to be critical of the audience too. They were people with "new yen," she thought, those who were making money in the black market or in the sale of building materials at inflated prices. They were quiet and appreciative, however, and many of them were young people who perhaps, like me, were seeing their first Kabuki.

I, who had known Japan only for three months and only in its poverty, accepted the surroundings without question, intent on what I was going to see. Of Kabuki I knew only that it was the popular form of the classic Japanese drama, livelier than the aristocratic and older Noh. I had a short explanation in English of the four plays that we were to see, but reading it over beforehand I could make but little sense out of it. The actions seemed random and unmotivated, not to say overcomplicated.

There was a sudden clapping of sticks together and the curtain was drawn aside. A small Japanese house was revealed, with all its sliding doors open so that we looked through it to a view of Mt. Fuji painted on the backdrop. In the center of the room sat a warrior in armor, his face apparently larger than any Japanese face I had ever seen and painted white with wide red lines curving down and black eyebrows swooping up, in a way reminiscent of American Indians on the warpath. Later I learned that the markings followed the lines of the facial muscles and that they indicated fierce emotions. But at that time I sat there, quietly astonished, and watched this peculiar apparition sharpen the head of an enormous arrow, at least seven feet long and brilliantly painted.

Meanwhile I became aware that music was being made off to one side, by samisens and drums, and that someone was singing in a strange, harsh, half-strangled voice.

A neighbor entered to bring the arrow-sharpener New Year's greetings and to afford opportunities for some effective poses. Each movement was stylized and dramatic, part of a slow dance. Presently the warrior had a vision, in which his brother appeared to him and, informing him that he was imprisoned by an old enemy of their father's, begged to be rescued. Whereupon the fierce gentleman with much warlike posturing and gesturing prepared to go and fight his enemy. One of these exaggerated poses, which he held for a long moment with grim face and shaking head, was emphasized by the same clapping of sticks together that had opened the play. This holding of the pose, I later learned, was called *mie* and was a distinctive feature of Kabuki; it marked a climax of decision or action.

At that moment a peasant came past the house leading a horse laden with giant white radishes of the same kind that I had often seen piled up outside farmhouses. The horse, of brown cloth with a mild face and human legs, was indescribably funny and at this point I realized that the whole play was a parody and that the Japanese were actually spoofing a warrior. This was contrary to all that I had been told or read about the Japanese, and I was shot through with surprise and delight.

The warrior demanded that the peasant yield up his horse. The peasant quite naturally refused, but inevitably lost the argument —and the horse. The play ended with the warrior mounting the spavined creature and galloping off to rescue his brother, lambasting his steed with a radish. With a great clapping of sticks the curtain was drawn.

The play was *Yanone*, The Arrowhead, one of the eighteen Kabuki plays that have long been considered the best. The part of the warrior had been played by Shoruku, an actor already famous in the 1930's, whom I was to see again and whose acting I always found vivid, strong and finished. I realized, thinking about it in the longish intermission, that this brief piece, which belonged to the type called *Aragoto*—rough stuff—had had, besides the humor which surprised me so much, beauty and style and power; that every effect was intentional, every movement of hand or foot, every shade of brilliant coloring, every rise and fall of samisen or drum or voice, was planned for its part in the whole; that it was in short a sophisticated work of art, of a, to me, new and exciting kind.

The next play *Musume Dojoji*, was based on a Noh play, of the kind known as a "revenge piece." Because of its Noh heritage, the setting was simple, with a pine tree on the backdrop and a great bell hanging on stage left. The full orchestra was drawn up for it, drums beaten with sticks, two kinds of drums tapped by hand, flute and samisens, as well as the singers. The members of the orchestra wore a striking costume of dark gray kimono and divided skirt, covered with a sort of green pinafore, with stiff bretelles over the shoulders, called *kamishimo*, a costume formerly worn by all Japanese and now seen only on the stage.

The legend upon which both Noh and Kabuki plays are based involved a girl who fell in love with a young monk and pursued him into the Dojoji Temple, where he took refuge inside a big bell. Foiled, she turned herself into a snake and twining around the bell, melted it with the heat of her fury, destroying both her lover and herself. After a century or two the temple got a new bell and celebrated it with a great ceremony, at which a dancing girl performed with increasing frenzy. She drew nearer and nearer to the bell; it fell with a great crash, and she was revealed as the revengeful ghost of the girl who had loved the elusive monk.

This is one of the best loved of the Kabuki plays, but even after seeing it three times I cannot appreciate fully its brilliance. It still seems to me rather tiresome. The chief part of it centers in the dancing before the new bell, when the girl makes nine changes of costume on the stage, going to one side and kneeling down with her back to the audience, while a property man all in black and therefore invisible, helps her to remove each top layer and reveal the next one. All the costumes and their accessories are beautiful and elaborate and the changing of them is a tour de force.

What was most interesting to me about that first performance of Dojoji was that the part of the young dancing girl was taken by Japan's best known actor—and indeed one of the greatest of all Kabuki actors down the centuries—the venerable Kikugoro, then well into his sixties.

All of the women's parts in Kabuki are taken by men. This

immediately recalls Shakespearean times, when boys played women's parts—and not very satisfactorily either. We are familiar with Shakespeare's complaint of having "some squeaking Cleopatra *boy* my greatness." Though young boys might look more like lovely young women than middle aged or elderly men, their acting was doubtless no more than mediocre, whereas the acting of the men who take women's parts in Kabuki plays is superb. After you get over the first shock of seeing a young girl with a hard, lined and aging face under the white paint and become accustomed to the falsetto voice, you forget that you are not actually seeing women perform. The movements, the turn of a hand or a head, the way of walking, and the emotions expressed through these movements are convincingly feminine.

The last play that afternoon—and by now it was nearly seven o'clock—consisted almost entirely of dancing. The setting was magically lovely—a village park in the late afternoon, a stone Buddha under trees, and in the background a field with a scarecrow and distant mountains against the sky. Some tiny children in bright kimonos are dancing when Onatsu Kyoran comes in. She has gone mad because she fell in love with a servant, whom her brother would not allow her to marry. The children tease her, one of them, in a big straw hat and striped kimono, pretending to be her lover. A drunk comes in with his sake bottle and dances tipsily—funny and restrained and a little sad—until he too is repulsed. Twilight has been coming on. As the first star appears in the sky, the girl is left standing alone, bemused and tragic, with the maple leaves falling around her.

We went out into the raw winter dusk, and I knew then that I had fallen under the spell of Kabuki. Twelve years later, I still have not seen as much of it as I would like to see, though once, by going to the afternoon show one day and the morning show the next, I had eleven hours of it out of twenty-four!

I saw the great Kikugoro once more before he died. By that time they were using the Tokyo Gekijo, a large modern theater with a wide stage and the *hanamichi* which is so important a part of Kabuki.

The play, realistic and poignant, was one of the kind called *Sewamono*, the life of ordinary people. It was the story of an old master potter, an artist, who was determined to achieve a new color in the glaze, and who sacrificed to his ambition his money, his strength, his daughter's happiness. Again and again he failed. Ruin stared him in the face. He had not enough fuel for the kiln. Then, when the fire could no longer be kept up, the despairing old man opened the kiln, and by that chance combination of time and chemistry the miracle occurred: he found on his plates the new color that he had dreamed of, the bright persimmon hue that we see today in old Imari china.

There was no need to understand a word of Japanese, to feel the impact of this play, so perfectly was it acted by the three stars who took the main parts: Kikugoro as Kakiemon, the potter; Baiko as his daughter Otane, and Ennosuke as the faithful apprentice who loved Otane. The whole thing was different from the stylized, even surrealistic plays that I had seen before. It was human, quiet and subtle. Kikugoro *was* the potter, and when I think of him now I see him always as that patient, indomitable fanatic old man, driven by his vision beyond human strength. Otane was no male actor skillfully impersonating a woman; she was the very epitome of the old maid daughter, resigned yet passionate, devoted and drooping. The clumsy, faithful Ennosuke, running off on the *hanamichi*, all legs and arms, was the eternally lovable and comic apprentice.

Kikugoro was actually the sixth of his name. Kabuki actors form a closed circle of related, descended, and adopted persons. The great families, the Ichikawas, the Nakamuras, the Onoes, the Ichimuras, go on from generation to generation, the little boys being trained from early childhood, appearing on the stage before they are old enough to go to school. If an actor has no son of his own, he adopts a nephew or the child of a friend. When an actor achieves an outstanding success, he takes on the name of a famous predecessor.

I was at one of the performances when the new successor to the name of Koshiro was announced. Between the first and second plays the whole Matsumoto family came out on the stage, dressed in formal costume similar to the *kamishimo* worn by the orchestra. They ranged themselves in a line across the stage, the oldest in the middle, the children at the ends, and bowed their foreheads to the floor. The master of ceremonies, who was the father-in-law of the new Koshiro, announced the new name and one by one the members of the family asked the favor of the audience for him.

Immediately after the ceremony, Koshiro VIII took the part for which he is most famous, that of Benkei in *Kanjincho.*

Kanjincho, another of the famous eighteen, is possibly the best known and best loved of all the Kabuki plays. Dr. Koizumi tells me that he has seen it more than thirty times and knows all the lines by heart.

Benkei was a hero of the early thirteenth century, the very embodiment of resourceful courage, wit, and loyalty. His lord was Yoshitsune, the younger brother of the Shogun Yoritomo. In *Kanjincho,* Yoshitsune is a fugitive, disguised as a strolling monk, accompanied by Benkei and four other retainers. Togashi, the barrier keeper on the highway, has been ordered to capture Yoshitsune and turn him over to his jealous brother for execution.

When the five pretended monks approach the barrier, Togashi recognizes Yoshitsune and stops him. Benkei, as the leader, insists that they are true monks, raising money for Todaiji, the great temple at Nara. When challenged to show his subscription book as proof, he reads a list of names from a blank scroll so convincingly that Togashi lets them pass. Just as they start to go across, however, one of Togashi's attendants points out to his superior the noble bearing of one of the monks and they are all brought back again for further questioning.

In desperation Benkei strikes Yoshitsune with his staff, certain that nobody would ever imagine that any loyal retainer could so mistreat his master, even to save his life. This climactic act is done with the *mie*—the held pose—the clapping of the sticks and shouts from the enthusiasts in the top gallery of "I have waited for this!"

Togashi, certain now that he has Yoshitsune in his hands, is so deeply moved by Benkei's painful position and his devotion that he motions them on. A little later, however, he overtakes them and invites them to have a drink with him. Suspecting a trick, Benkei, tense and wary, drains two enormous bowls of wine with Togashi, becomes—or pretends to become—drunk, and then, realizing that Togashi is after all sympathetic, dances a dance of relief and gratitude.

While he is dancing Yoshitsune and the others slip away unnoticed. Released by Togashi, Benkei at last follows them in a most splendid and dramatic series of leaps and hops on the *hanamichi*, while the audience goes wild.

Benkei's costume is traditional, a small black pill-box of a hat tied under his chin, an enormous wide robe of dark damask with a plaid under-robe, box-like wide stiff white trousers, a monk's *kesa*, or stole, with four white pom-poms on it, and a Buddhist rosary, a staff, and a sword. Because this too was a play originally taken from a Noh play, the setting is simple with the great pine tree at the back of the stage and the full orchestra is employed.

When I returned to Tokyo in 1957, the Kabukiza, which I had last seen as a battered shell, had been restored. It seats 3,000 people and has what is said to be the largest stage in any legitimate theater in the world. Outside, it appears somewhat temple-like, with tiled roofs in curves; inside, there is space and beauty. The decoration, unlike the rococo gilt and glitter of many Western theaters, has a quiet elegance. The wide halls are edged with all kinds of entrancing shops where one can look and buy during the long intermissions, and restaurants where delicious meals are served in a short time.

There are two different programs a day, of four plays each, one beginning at eleven and ending at four-thirty, the other beginning at five and ending at ten-thirty. Every month the programs change. The Kabuki devotee sees them all, though how they manage it I don't know. The best seats are eleven hundred yen, about $3.00. In a country where a promising young bank clerk, graduate of Tokyo University, earns $36 a month, and marries on that, I wonder how Kabuki can be often seen, even from the top gallery. But other people's finances are always a mystery.

Whole families go to Kabuki and women who wear Western clothes most of the time will wear kimono to Kabuki because it feels more appropriate. Children up to eight or nine years old sit quietly in their parents' laps and disturb no one. I have seen two seats occupied by four people, all absorbed and happy for five hours.

During the month of April, 1959, to celebrate the Crown Prince's marriage, the programs, morning and evening, were congratulatory in purpose. There was a historical drama about Prince Shotoku, the enlightened sixth-century prince who brought a new era to Japan; an enchanting and lively dance, *Ninin Sambaso*, in which Ennosuke, now seventy-three and his fifty-year-old son Danshiro, who look very much alike and both no more than forty, took the part of twins; *Dojoji; Kanjincho*, with Koshiro again as Benkei; and a new play written especially for the debut of a new actor who, it is expected, will some day hold one of the great names in Kabuki.

Just after the war, when the new education laws were passed, there was much headshaking and gloomy prophecy about their effect upon the future of Kabuki. No longer could the actors' children go directly into the troupe and find their education there. They must attend the regular schools for the compulsory nine years. It was not only the long school hours that would be subtracted from the hours of training in Kabuki techniques that worried people, but the being away from the backstage atmosphere and being exposed to other standards, other ideas. These dark forebodings seem now, twelve years later, to have been baseless. The little boys in the plays, performing after school hours, are as serious and able as ever. Some of the most promising young men, who have continued beyond high school into Keio University, are able to combine their college work with such parts as that of Yoshitsune's followers in *Kanjincho*, and the smaller parts in other plays. One of them played the part of Dr. Koizumi's father in his student days in a new play about Fukuzawa, the founder of Keio University.

The actor who was making his debut this April, however, was so young that he has no school problems yet and will not have any for some time to come. He is the three-year-old grandson of Kikugoro VI and the son of Kanzaburo Nakamura, one of today's stars.

The play, *Mukashi-Banashi Momotaro*, The Old Tale of the Peach Boy, is based on one of Japan's favorite nursery tales, as familiar to every Japanese child as Cinderella is to Western children.

The curtain was drawn on a thatch-roofed farmhouse and an old man working in front of it. Presently along the *hanamichi* came the Old Woman (Kanzaburo) pulling her wash tub, in which there was an enormous peach, which, she said, she had found floating down the river.

They put the peach on the chopping block, near the back of the stage, and the Old Man whacked it open with his ax. As it fell apart, the child, Kankuro, was lifted onto the chopping block from behind. He struck the *mie* pose, and the audience melted in laughter and tenderness.

He was a square-set little boy, wearing the traditional Momotaro costume with short trunks and a sort of halter top that showed his chubby baby shoulders and arms. With his father

right beside him, in the part of the Old Woman, he delivered a
short speech or two in a high, clear, childish voice of considerable
strength.

The gist of it all was that the old couple, who had long wanted
a child, welcomed him and named him Peach Boy, and that he
immediately declared his intention to go to the Ogres' Island and
defeat the ogres. After this he went off holding his father's hand,
while the dog, the monkey and the pheasant appeared and danced,
announcing that they would accompany Momotaro and help him.
They were three young actors with their faces made up to suggest the three animals and wearing costumes in appropriate colors. The pheasant's green and golden brown were especially effective.

Now the whole action came to a halt while Kankuro was formally presented. Kanzaburo, Koshiro and the others bowed low
and requested the future patronage of the audience for the little
actor, and the baby himself called out shrilly, *"Yoroshiku onegai
shimasu!"* (I ask your kind favor.)

In the next scene the revolving stage swung round to show the
Ogres' Island and Momotaro and his three companions arriving
there, Momotaro in full armor with a small sword and helmet
and glaring red lines painted on his face to denote fierceness. The
ogres, all with long red hair, swarmed out to meet them; Momotaro laid about him with his sword and chased them off-stage.
Returning with the two largest roped to him (one of whom was
his father) he took the *mie* pose, and the audience fairly swooned
with delight.

The play ended when Momotaro, having received the treasures
of the island, made a triumphant exit on the *hanamichi*, stamp,
stamp, stamp, in the most absurd and delicious baby caricature
of Benkei's gigantic hops.

I had been invited to go backstage immediately after this
play to have my picture taken with the new actor, and so I sped
down the stairs and through long passages, past the great revolv-

ing stage, which was being swung around for the next play, to a
little *tatami*-floored room where the child was waiting.

In his armor and wide helmet he was about as broad as he was
high, and he was not quite as high as my waist. When I knelt on
the *tatami* in the Japanese way and he stood beside me, our
heads were nearly on a level. I congratulated him in Japanese
and won a smile that broke up all the fierce red lines on his face
and the painted downward curve of his lips. What he really
wanted to do, however, was to wave that sword again. So he
flourished it bravely and held the *mie*, while I stood beside him
admiringly. When the camera was removed someone must have
given him a signal, for he turned to me and said in his shrill stage
voice, "Thank you—berry much!"

His father, who was hastily dressing for his part in the next
play, came rushing out in a towel to shake hands with me, and
then I met his mother, Kikugoro's daughter. She is a beautiful
young woman, with that special quality which many Japanese
women have, of quiet elegance and hidden strength.

Little Kankuro Nakamura, within a month or two of his fourth
birthday, was a full eighteen months younger than the usual age
for a debut. There was a good deal of discussion and speculation
about him. What would be the effect of this very early exposure
to the heady delights of grease paint and applause? How would
he meet the years when his parts would be small and exacting
and no one would pay any especial attention to him? Had he
really the remarkable talent that he seemed to promise? Would
he in time be good enough to win the title of Kikugoro the
Seventh? For win it he must; it does not descend by heredity
alone.

19

The English Club

THE English club still, after twelve years, met once a month. On this April afternoon in 1959 its members had planned the meeting especially for me.

The house where we gathered was a pleasant one with a large garden in the section of Tokyo called Kyodo, not far from Keisen School. The hostess was the young wife of a popular pediatrician. When I first saw her in my class at the Peeresses' School, she was eighteen, a serious, studious girl with long braids over her shoulders. After graduating from school she had taken a kindergarten course and had with some difficulty persuaded her parents to allow her to have a job in the kindergarten attached to her college. Then she had married—an arranged marriage, of course. Now, hair modishly cut and curled, a long submerged dimple much in evidence, slender, vivacious, gay and tender with her children, she looked radiant.

We sat in the living room, which was furnished in Western style, looking out through the sliding glass doors into the garden, where six scarlet-cheeked little boys and girls were playing hide and seek and now and then coming to peer in at us, as if to make sure that their mothers were still there. Two adorable babies eight or nine months old were passed from lap to lap, as we sat and talked and exchanged news.

Eight of the original fourteen members were there that afternoon, with eight children, distributed through five families. Three were in the United States with their husbands, a doctor, a businessman and a young diplomat. One had just returned from New York with her husband and young baby. Another, the mother of one of the little boys playing in the garden, was just back from Bangkok, where her husband had been attached to the Japanese Embassy. One was secretary to the president of the International Christian University; two were teaching. All were attractive, alert, modern young women, vitally interested in their world.

I had known them all well, and some of them had been very close to me. They had written me letters and essays, had given me copies of their diaries and had once for my birthday made me a scrapbook in which each one had written reminiscences of her childhood and pasted early photographs. Two had studied at Bryn Mawr and one at Swarthmore, and during those years I had seen them often; as they matured and became more proficient in English they talked freely about their changing views and their philosophy of life. Through all these means I got a rare insight into the minds and hearts of young Japanese who had experienced the war as adolescents and had grown into young womanhood during the confusing period of defeat and "democrashi." They are not typical, for they belong to a highly privileged group, but they are representative of a class and of a way of thinking that has its own part to play in the "new Japan."

The club grew out of one of the first classes I taught in the Peeresses' School. It was a small section made up of girls who were especially lively, articulate and friendly and so could more quickly break through the barriers of language and custom that separated us. They, or the leaders among them, thought of many spontaneous, charming things to do for me. I remember sitting between classes in the little waiting room that had been assigned to me, alone in my glory, and hearing muffled giggles in the corridor outside. Then they filed in, the class that I had just finished teaching, and with linked arms they chanted in chorus, "We can hardly wait till next week!"

This was the class, too, that gave the play, *Evangeline*, the first autumn I was there. It was a cold, rainy day, the roof of the makeshift school auditorium leaked, and the surroundings were about as dismal as one could imagine, but the girls put on their play with great verve and resourcefulness and the whole affair was eloquent of youth and courage and vitality. Evangeline, who played her part with dramatic abandon, Gabriel, slender, grave and handsome, and the arrogant English captain, actually a particularly gentle girl, who wore her father's naval uniform, all became later able presidents of the English Club.

Through their English diaries and compositions that winter I got glimpses of the struggle that even privileged people must make to live in ruined Tokyo. Several of them had been burned out during the war; one was grieving for her father, who was on trial as a war criminal; all had to combat cold and shortages.

"The sky is gray," wrote one, "it is going to snow. My little brother cries, 'I am cold, I am cold.'"

Another: "After the graduation I want to work to help my family's economy, because in my family there is no man and my dear mother is old."

And another: "After returning from school I helped Mother with supper. Lately because we have no maids we are busy from morning till night in household duties. Today was a clean-up day. We cleaned the cellar. We collected twigs and branches from the garden for fuel. It is like a dream to remember the easy days when we had five maids and a student servant."

Others were amusingly frank about their efforts at cooking: "While I bake the bread with electric appliances I write the diary with rapt attention, so that the bread gets burned." And: "I cooked the vegetable, but it was a miscarriage."

After their graduation in March they wanted very much to go on with their English, and so I said that I would help them with an English Club, which could meet at my house twice a month, on the second and fourth Saturdays.

At first it was primarily for English practice and sociability. Later they began to think of doing something for others, and after making scrapbooks for children in hospitals they adopted a little orphanage in Saitama called Aisenryo, Fountain of Love, and made games, knitted sweaters and sewed baby clothes for the children there. Once or twice a year we went in a body to visit it. After I left Japan the Club continued to meet once a month.

The Peeresses' School was founded in 1887 on the initiative of the Empress Shoken, and until 1946, when it was united with the Peers' School as an ordinary private school, it was administered by the Imperial Household as a school primarily for Imperial princesses and the daughters of peers. One of the paintings in the Emperor Meiji series is of the Empress Shoken, attended by her ladies-in-waiting, visiting the school. The Empress is dressed in the old Japanese style, with a stiff *hakama* (a divided skirt) of scarlet silk, as wide as a hoop skirt, and a patterned over-robe with long kimono sleeves; her hair falls down her back, tied in three places with narrow ribbons. She is standing on a dais before a table draped with brocade, and the schoolgirls, all in plain kimonos and *hakamas* are drawn up in rows facing her, but at some distance. In the space between stands the principal in a frock coat, reading an address which he holds high in front of his face, perhaps to keep him from looking directly on the Imperial countenance. Except the Empress and the principal, everybody stands with bowed head, as if in prayer.

For many years the young peeresses came to school in rickishas, followed by their maids in other rickishas, who waited for them in waiting rooms. Baroness Ishimoto's autobiography, *Facing Two Ways*, gives a vivid picture of the elegance and formality of the Peeresses' School in those days. By the time my girls got there, however, daughters of government officials and

selected business and professional men were also admitted and
some of them at least rode to school on their bicycles, bowling
along through the outer gardens of the Meiji shrine under the
ginkgo trees toward "the great antique gate of our school and a
front garden where an artificial hill and cherry trees were."

"I feel my childhood is behind the heavy iron door called
'war,'" wrote one of them, and indeed all their memories are
bathed in a tender golden light made unearthly by that massive,
impenetrable door. One child, playing hide and seek in the
grounds of a neighboring temple at sunset, was caught up by the
beauty of it; "a great emotion filled my heart, and I was un-
consciously kneeling." They all had gardens, in which they de-
vised flower games, or played with a gentle dog large enough to
carry a small child on his back, or made "watermelon ghosts" on
summer evenings. The watermelons, which in Japan are no larger
than our honeydews, were hollowed out and faces were cut in
them. "Then we put candles in them, covered them with white
veils and hung them on bushes. When the garden was enveloped
with darkness, children went one by one into the dark bushes
lighted only by candles in the ghosts. In the sky black bodies of
the trees formed giants, and the branches played their big harp.
Then children surrounded these ghosts, sang songs, and told
many stories of ghosts." Grandmothers who told stories and
played the *koto*, visits to the seashore and the mountains, winter
nights when all the family gathered in the living room and the
children did their homework under their father's supervision:
these are their memories. "My mother's white pretty fingers
when she played her violin," wrote one, "my father's happy face
when he played golf, and our old school building, how I remember them!"

To all of them school seems to have been pure joy. They took
pride in the beauty of the Japanese-style building; they loved
their teachers. One of them drew a delightful picture of a young
teacher in purple kimono with dark brown *hakama*, tying up her

long sleeves with a cord when she played games with her pupils.
One particularly gentle-hearted girl, whose father, a well-known admiral was regarded by the Western powers as a ruthless and dangerous enemy, described her home life in these words: "I was a happy child in my sweet home of simplicity in the military spirit, with my pious father of honesty, integrity and benevolence and tender-hearted and meek mother." Every Sunday the father took his four little daughters on some expedition, to climb a mountain and see the autumn leaves, to play on a riverbank, or to visit shrines, "which purified our souls with their clean and noble atmosphere." *Bushido*, the way of the warrior, in its domestic aspects, had an appeal.

Then came the war and everything changed. Though it was "a dark, unpleasant memory," they wrote about it reflectively and with, to me, amazing detachment. There was in what they wrote no bitterness toward the recent enemy, the present occupiers. I saw only that realistic acceptance, of which the Japanese seems to me to be more than ordinarily capable, and a groping for the meaning of it all to them.

The Peeresses' School became a factory. The girls went to school every day as usual, but instead of studying they made vacuum tubes.

"It was very delicate work. We gave up our fervor and all energy for service. . . . It was all absorbing for me that with a pincette I picked up mica plates, positive electrodes, cathodes and heaters and put them together. When we worked we forgot everything, and our record and our union became an encouragement to me."

The air raids brought not only terror but the dislocation of daily living. "I worked in the house after our school had burned and all the maids were no longer working for us and we had such an amount of drudgery to keep a large house which had been taken care of by seven or eight servants. Days and nights we had continuous air-raids; people got thinner and thinner from lack of food and lack of sleep and a constant fear. One district after another the houses were burned down. The water system was destroyed and we had to walk miles to get daily water from someone's well. The gas system was also destroyed; we collected wood and broken boxes to make a fire to cook. Some of the rationed food was almost impossible to eat, but we ate as much as possible, but most of the people got indigestion. We dug holes under the ground to escape during the air-raids and day and night we escaped there with the sound of siren."

The great air raid on May 25, 1945, destroyed the school and the houses of several of the girls as well. For one girl it meant the loss in a single night of all the solid institutions that made up her life: her home, her school, the hospital which her father, who was a doctor, owned and maintained, and the church, where she "was given nice mental foods," played the piano for the Sunday School, and acted in Christmas and Easter plays. "Through a series of experiences in my happy days and hard times," she wrote, "I have come to thoroughly realize how valuable it would be to keep the world in perfect peace."

Another girl described that fateful night: "The last day we put all our instruments in a little house that was separated from the school building. We said good-by to school as usual and went home. That night a siren blew. Immediately we got ready. My father went to Tokyo Metropolitan Office. My brother had gone to the base of Fuji San for field work. So my mother and I were at home. After about one hour and a half the airplanes went away, but the fire spread and at last we left our house.

"Next morning we came back to the debris and went to my uncle's. There I knew that my school building had burnt too. I lost my heart. After three days I tried to dig the debris of my room. Just where my desk had been I found ashes of my notebook. I could read some sentences clearly on the ashes. . . ."

When peace came, it was the peace of defeat, not victory. They thought about it a good deal and tried to understand what it meant for them. Brothers had been killed. A grandmother, a sister or two had died. The whole face of life changed.

"The day of the end of the war came. It was a great shock to me. The next day I bowed at the Imperial Palace. Thus I collected myself a little. . . . I found the delight of peace. I thanked it." And then, looking back on the days when she had worked with fervor on the vacuum tubes, she thought that even in service for war, even in the discomfort and anxiety, it was "a welcome gift" that they could give themselves to some work "with all our heart." She had put her finger on a profound truth: the joy and release to the young idealist of using to the utmost all one has and is for a purpose beyond self. The Communists have learned to use the ardor and generosity of the young in peacetime in a way that we in the democracies have not.

Only one spoke exultantly of the new position of women. "If I think of the condition of our society before the war," she wrote, "I know that there was a long despotism which deceived Japan's people and made many groan. Happily it has been vanished. Since democratization of Japan has been going on, individual liberty has been approved and woman also has been given freedom. Each of us can take her own way according to her judgment, courage and ability. These things are indeed splendid new happiness for us."

To another it was all confusion. "When my brother volunteered to go to the army, I wished I could be a boy so that I too could go to the army like my brother. I highly esteemed the spirit of self-sacrifice; especially when one dies for the nation, I thought it to be extremely beautiful, for there is no worldly reward one can expect if one were giving his life. . . . For women it was considered most virtuous to sacrifice themselves to the family. They were submissive, modest, suppressed all desires of their own and just worked hard for others without a word of complaint or excuse." After the war, however, "the beautiful deed of noble soldiers who died for the nation was no longer praised by anyone; virtuous submissive women who silently worked without a word of complaint were no longer considered virtuous; instead, they were demanding their right and freedom and higher position in society. I realized that the idea of the whole country had completely changed. Freedom which they stressed seemed to me as though it was to be abused by uneducated mass as orderless and arbitrary; equal rights of men and women sounded to me as though women were boosting themselves without true knowledge of self. They praised democracy of Americans, who, until yesterday, were regarded as inhuman who wanted to destroy order and peace of Asia."

Discussion with her classmates led only to argument and disagreement, but when a Japanese teacher told her that "in democracy your sacrifice is not only for your nation but for all mankind," she wrote, "Suddenly something hit me. I found it was very true." (How I wish it were.) She met Americans who were not like her mental picture of "hard-boiled Christian types," she came to this country for four years of strenuous but on the whole happy study, at the end of which she wrote, "I realized that I had changed. I no longer held the former conception of Americans who were materialistic, but instead I found really sympathetic and understanding Americans who were genuinely wishing good-will of all mankind. I found narrowness of nationalism and the cruelty of war which results from misunderstanding between the nations. I was most impressed by the action of people, but not by words, when people showed me by heart their true love of humanity; though it was invisible it had the strongest effect on my mind."

It was another one of these girls, who crossing the United States by herself, paid the highest tribute to our Occupation soldiers in Japan that could well be paid. Her train was late reaching Chicago, and she realized that she would miss the connection which would get her to Philadelphia at the time when her friends would be meeting her. Frightened, bewildered, she looked about for help. Did she go to the Travelers' Aid? She knew nothing of Travelers' Aid. She turned to the kind of person that she had evidently learned to trust in Japan—a young man in the uniform of the U.S. army. I held my breath when she told me this! But he found out when the next train went, which happened to be the one that he was taking, telegraphed her friends, took care of her baggage and saw her on to the train, after which he left her alone until the next morning, when he turned up on the station platform to make sure that she was safely met.

They were keen observers, the three who came to the United States to study, and occasionally they would give us a little glimpse of how we looked to them. Of San Francisco on her first day in the country, one wrote: "We went through the orderly and hilly streets: some people were wearing fur coats, though it was the middle of the summer! In a shopping district, people were walking on as though they were marching: they stopped strictly with the red light, and marched on immediately with the green; it was quite picturesque."

The heavy, plain china in our restaurants, paper cups, teabags, machine-knit sweaters, blue jeans, and the universal wastefulness of a "mechanized civilization" startled another girl. "One of the things I feel rather strongly," she added, "is the separation from nature, the lack of sensitivity to nature. I have felt it particularly with food. In Japan we know the change of seasons by the food available as well as by the flowers and trees around. It is a great joy to see the first fish of the season served. We feel we taste the beauty and the joyousness of early spring together with the feast for our eyes. People prize the freshness of young cucumbers in early summer and the smell of matsudake (a kind of mushroom) which brings us the whole flavor of autumn. While here in America I have found that there is less connection between the food and seasons, for one can get almost any kind of vegetables any time, thanks to deep freezers and hot-houses."

I quite agree with her. In my pre-freezer childhood shad, peas, strawberries and asparagus were brief and keen delights associated with tiny leaves on the trees, handfuls of violets and the warm breeze on one's suddenly freed arms and legs. In Japan every season brings its own fruit and flowers to be savored, though I must say that I in my turn was startled on my last visit to find chrysanthemums appearing in the spring.

But my young friend in her time here felt that she began to understand what democracy really means—"not as a theory but as a part of my living experience."

"My two-year stay in America, away from home, has helped to awake in me a sense of individuality. It has also taught me that the final authority for any decision lies nowhere but within me. It is difficult to know exactly what are the factors that have influenced me. Through talking with people here and seeing what they do, it gradually came to an awareness in me. . . . Even small children here have a sense of independence and parents seem to encourage them to be that way. Some time ago I happened to hear a father telling a little girl who had climbed a ladder half way and could not go on, 'Now, you've got your choice. Do you still want to go up, or do you want to get down?' I thought if this had been in Japan, the father would probably have told her to get down or just taken her down without a word. . . . Underneath this pattern of behavior is the concept of the rights and equality of individuals, freedom of choice, which is really the basis of democracy and which is perhaps closely associated with Christianity."

Another girl, who spent one of her summers in Europe with a Dutch friend, got a perspective on both Japan and the United States, and though her conclusions were in no way comforting to her she faced them with penetration and courage.

"The position of Germany in Europe and the big question it involves have been in my thoughts frequently at many places in Europe. The hatred and suspicion towards Germany are still deep in minds of European people. . . . The Europeans, speaking very broadly, know to their bones the agony of wars. They also know very well the danger of Communism. . . . and yet, no one can say that their fear of Communism is greater than their fear of a revival of Nazi Germany. They know the menace of militaristic Germany 'through our own experiences' and they are skeptical towards those Americans 'who don't know much about real destruction' who come and rearm Germany. . . . The resentment and the doubt still remain in Europeans' mind. I've found them hard to be wiped out even with the attitude of 'don't hate men but war itself' or of love and forgiveness."

A discussion on the subject with her Dutch hosts left her shaken. "To make the discussion short, we had to come down to the very basic point of difference, that of our views on life, and it took a glass of fragrant liqueur and good music to cure ourselves from the 'mutual disillusion.' All during this sad argument I was shivering inside. Isn't it true that the position of Germany corresponded to that of Japan in the Far East? Aren't we still deeply resented but do not feel it because we live on islands? So do we have the right to say 'forgive Germans' to those people in Europe? as if to say it is a matter of course for us to be forgiven and to demand friendship? There should be one stage before that which we must go through—maybe of self-knowledge or penitence? As for us as individuals what would that be?"

During the crowded weeks that I spent in Japan in 1957, another former pupil, Asako Tanaka, and I slipped away from Tokyo one morning to spend a night at her family's *besso*, or cottage, at Hayama.

Hayama is a fishing village and summer resort on Sagami Bay about forty miles from Tokyo. In the center, where the level land widens out, is the Emperor's villa, hidden from sight by a tile-roofed white wall and a forest of pine trees. Behind are the mountains, small, jagged hills with twisted pines hanging off their sides against the sky, narrow valleys with rice paddies and thatched farmhouses, little temples and fields of chrysanthe-

mums grown for the Tokyo market. Girdling the lower slopes is
the road, narrow, dusty, and gravelly, and on the steep declivity
below the road are the fishermen's houses and the summer cot-
tages, fitted close together, pressing against each other and peering over each other's shoulders like the houses in Italian hill
towns. Yet each house has its view, its cherry tree or persimmon
or plum, and its privacy.

From time to time a narrow lane runs from the road between
high board fences down to the beach. At the top of one of these
lanes we left the car, which had its garage in a narrow niche off
the road, and walked down to a door set obliquely in the wall, so
that there was, with the most economical means, an effect of
space and a gesture of formality for the entrance. Shiny broad-
leaved evergreens showed above the top of the fence.

My friends owned three houses on the same lot, two larger
ones in modified Western style, rented to foreigners, and a small
Japanese one on the edge of the bluff. A caretaker lived there and
served the family when any of them came from Tokyo. She was
prepared for us, and the little three-room house was open and
welcoming. Beyond the entrance was a good sized room with the
fresh, green smell of new *tatami*, an arrangement of ginger blossoms and marigolds in the *tokonoma*, sliding doors open on a narrow gallery, and down below, the sea. I saw a beach with wet,
dark gray sand, a stretch of mother-of-pearl water, lit with the
faint gold of a sun behind the clouds and edged with white ruffles
of waves. A rocky promontory with three dramatic pine trees enclosed the cove on one side, the island of Enoshima was hazy in
the distance, and scattered over the bay were small boats, some
with colored sails.

O Suye San, the middle-aged, sweet-faced caretaker, brought
us tea. Asako whispered to me, "She's so good and kind. I have
known her since I was a little girl. I could always talk to her and
tell her things. She is *so* good!"

We walked on the beach in the late afternoon in *geta*, which are very good for walking on beaches. The sharp-edged wood ridges on the bottom bite into the sand, and it doesn't matter if you get them wet.

At sunset the little gray fishing boats came home. We watched the families come out to exclaim over the catch and to help pull them in. The men on the boats hopped out and helped the women to turn the heavy windlass that pulled the boats up on the dry sand beyond the tide line. In one group we saw a girl of fourteen or fifteen with a blue and white towel around her head, patched black trousers and a traditional blue and white tunic; in another a young woman in a dark skirt and blouse, gay and smart, who had possibly just come home from a job in the city. A young boy with a serious, responsible air took entire charge of the unloading of another boat, refilling the gas tank and readying the craft for the night.

The catch, mostly gleaming, coral-colored red snapper, was in big baskets which the "boss" of the settlement came to inspect. We followed one family up the lane to the shop where they took their fish to sell. A little crowd gathered quickly. Much of it would go to Tokyo, the rest was disappearing in newspaper-wrapped bundles into the neighborhood. Asako selected two for our supper and we came away. They knew her; somebody must have brought the fish after us to the cottage, for a little later we had them broiled over charcoal.

O Suye San cooked our supper for us and served it on a low table looking out on the view. We had broiled lobster, raw fish with soya sauce, and the broiled fish; rice, string beans, very crisp, soup, tea, and oranges hollowed out and filled with orange ice, which had come down with us from a smart shop on the Ginza.

As the dark closed in and the wind came up a little, the sound of the water lapping on the shore below grew louder. After a hot bath I lay on my quilts on the *tatami* hearing that cool, rhythmic murmur even when the wooden shutters were closed for the night.

Next morning it was dark until the wooden doors were opened with a roar and a rumble, and the whole shining, fresh, seaweed-fragrant, sun-splashed morning world burst on us all at once. "Oh, Mrs. Vining, *look!*" cried Asako. And there across the pale bay, floating between the blues of water and of sky, was Fuji San, huge, serene, mysterious, capped with snow.

I thought, as we ate our breakfast in the crisp sea air, of the years of Asako's growing. Hers is the classic type of Japanese beauty; long oval face, pale skin, large and eloquent eyes, widely spaced and a little slanted. She had studied the tea ceremony and liked it, had been taught to play the *koto,* she had the grace and reserve and stillness of her class and tradition. But she had also rebelled against arranged marriages, had by hard work and determination won her A.B. in anthropology at Bryn Mawr in spite of the time lost in preparatory school in making vacuum tubes, and she had earned her college spending money by working as a waitress during the summers, an experience about which she was always rather reticent with me, with an indulgent air of knowing things which my sheltered life had kept from me. She has what she learned in her psychology course to call a "persistent personality" and she looks her life in the face steadily and honestly. I thought how very satisfactory it is when one's young pupils grow up and the relationship, changing but not lost, becomes adult friendship.

20

Michiko Sama

Ever since the Crown Prince formally came of age in 1952 and was invested as Heir Apparent, court officials responsible for the matter had been considering the question of his bride. From Dr. Koizumi, who was a member of this group throughout the years of their search, I occasionally heard something about the difficulties involved.

The Crown Prince was quite content with the prospect of an arranged marriage. By far the greater number of marriages in Japan are brought about by a "go-between." Moreover, the Prince was well aware that royal marriages all over the world are usually affairs of state. He and Dr. Koizumi read together and discussed Harold Nicolson's life of George V and noted that King George and Queen Mary, though their marriage was an arranged one, had been a devoted couple and had had a warm and close family life.

It was early decided that the choice of the Crown Prince's bride would not be limited to Imperial relatives or daughters of the five powerful branches of the Fujiwara family, as had been the invariable case in recorded and legendary history, all 2,600 years of it, but it was expected that she would come of a noble family and would have been educated at the Peeresses' School.

For several years they scrutinized the records of Peeresses' School graduates and undergraduates without coming to any conclusion. All the while the newspapers speculated busily, even going so far as to follow possible "candidates" to school or elsewhere. The publicity and the comments—was one disqualified because she was too tall, another because she was nearly the same age as the Crown Prince?—must have been very trying to the victims. Some of them went ahead and married other men. Even so late as July 14, 1958, *Time* magazine published the photographs of three girls who, it said, were the three remaining names on the committee's list "after several hundred had been eliminated." Of this article Dr. Koizumi wrote me cautiously, "I am not sure whether any of the three 'candidates' given there is near the mark or not (Confidential!)."

About this time the Japanese newspapers entered into a "gentlemen's agreement" not to mention any names or make any reports until an engagement was announced by the Imperial Household Agency. This was the result of much diplomatic and persuasive effort on the part of Dr. Koizumi, who felt that it was essential to protect any young girls who might be considered eligible from the embarrassment of false reports. He managed to convince the newsmen that the freedom of the press was not involved but that individual human rights were. "The word *candidate* is used in referring to prospective brides for the Crown Prince," he said. "However, it is not a public office that one can run for." The agreement was signed and it was honorably kept, in spite of the intensely competitive nature of the newspaper enterprise and the world-wide interest in the subject.

Three months before the name of Michiko Shoda was known to anybody but the Sacred Heart University and her own circle of friends, the Japanese reporters were certain that she was the one and they followed her every movement—and not only hers but those of her parents, Dr. Koizumi, officials of the court and the Crown Prince's chamberlains.

The rumor reached me in October through some of the young people whom I knew, but I did not believe it. I had heard rumors earlier that came to nothing. On November 9 the first photograph of Miss Shoda, a blurred, distorted one, appeared in American newspapers. *True Story*, a small Japanese weekly magazine in need of a circulation boost, had broken over and named her as the bride-to-be. The edition was quickly exhausted and those who saw it in Japan must have doubted its accuracy when the newspapers still held the line and printed nothing.

At a party in Philadelphia a friend asked me if the Crown Prince would be allowed to marry a commoner, the daughter of a businessman. I answered that I thought it would depend upon the girl herself, her own character and personality, that I thought the Japanese had a very strong sense of worth and that if she were really fine they would accept her even if she were not of the old nobility. So many extraordinary changes had taken place since the war: this would be but one more.

And yet I had a lurking fear that the tragedy of the Duke of Windsor, which had been much in the minds of the people around the Crown Prince when I was in Japan, might be repeated; that the Crown Prince, kept waiting while the officials deliberated, might have fallen in love with someone who was not suitable. But then I reassured myself with the thought that Prince Akihito was a good judge of character and that he would be discriminating in his choice. When I was his tutor, we used to select every term two of his classmates to share one of his private lessons each week. I say *we* for though officially I made the choice I always consulted him. One reason was that I thought his life provided him too few opportunities to make decisions of his own; the other, that I found that his judgment on the other boys, whom he of course knew much better than I did, was sound, and he often gave me sidelights on them that were helpful to me.

After the ninth of November my telephone began to ring—and it rang without stopping almost until Christmas. I think every newspaper in Japan has a representative in New York or Washington and they all know my telephone number, though it is unlisted. They told me the Crown Prince was to marry Michiko Shoda and that the announcement would be made "soon." They were, they said, preparing special editions to be published on the day of the announcement and they wanted interviews, congratulatory messages, articles—all different—and recordings to be used on radio and television.

One reporter, whose English, if limited, was vivid, told me the story of the romance: "I have heard secretly from Tokyo. Crown Prince said, 'I will have this girl [he pointed dramatically] and no other. Miss Shoda was very hesitate to accept this proposal. She afraid Imperial Household and she lose her freedom. But finally she say, 'O.K.' "

The November 17 issue of *Newsweek* came out, about the thirteenth, with a photograph of Michiko Shoda and the Crown Prince taken at the tennis club in Karuizawa, and I fell on it eagerly, not to read the "story" so much as to study the young faces, as if I could draw the truth out of that crowded, slightly blurred, black and white and gray rectangle by the very intensity of my regard.

It had been casually snapped at a tennis tournament. The Crown Prince and Miss Shoda were in a group watching a match; they were not side by side: an unidentified boy sat between them. They were not looking at each other; the Crown Prince had turned completely away, his attention caught by something over his right shoulder. It was not a good picture of him, but he looked unmistakably happy. The girl who sat with her hands loosely clasped on her knees, wearing a white tennis dress and a navy sweater, was smiling, absorbed in the play. It was not, I was to learn later, a flattering photograph of her, but I found in it all that I needed to know. It was an open face with, as has been well said, a madonna-like beauty, and there was in it so much courage, sweetness, intelligence and humor that my heart sang. I knew it was going to be all right.

A week later I heard from Dr. Koizumi. He had written on the morning of the fourteenth: "I hasten to write this letter to fulfill the promise I made years ago that the name of the Crown Prince's bride shall not be made known to the newspaper people before to you. Her name is Michiko Shoda (24) the eldest daughter of Mr. Hidesaburo Shoda, an industrialist very well known in the business world. Last night I went to see the Shodas at their home, less than ten minutes' drive from here, and had their final 'yes.' . . . The engagement will probably be announced toward the end of this month. . . . Miss Shoda enjoys the highest reputation among those who know her for her good looks, fine character and her intelligence. Her non-aristocratic birth (although of an old family of good name) has of course made us hesitate, but after every possible consideration we have decided. It is not only His Highness's but our choice too. (We rather chose first.)"

On November twenty-seventh the announcement was made, and I had a cable from the Crown Prince's chamberlain, Mr. Kuroki. A few days later a big package of newspapers and "graphics" arrived by airmail from *Togushoku*, the Office of the Eastern Prince, filled with photographs of both young people at all stages of their lives, the detailed account of the course of the romance and every conceivable item of interest about Michiko Shoda. Enthusiastic letters from Japanese friends began to pour in.

Becoming at once Michiko Sama to millions of Japanese who had never heard of her before—Sama is more polite and deferential than San—she burst upon the scene like a new comet blazing in the sky. People read about her for the first time in the morning newspapers; two or three hours later they saw her on television.

After her fifteen-minute audience with the Emperor and Empress—and this was the first time the Crown Prince's parents were allowed to meet their prospective daughter-in-law—she had her first press conference, which was televised. Lovely and exquisitely fresh and young in an ivory brocade dress with a mink stole and little white hat, she faced a battery of lights, cameras, microphones and reporters and answered with composure and more than a little skill the assorted questions fired at her. "She spoke very clearly," Tané wrote me, "but in a charmingly modest tone. She did not show any nervousness or embarrassment."

"What attracted you most in the Crown Prince?"

"I was attracted most by his integrity and sincerity. From my heart I can trust and respect him."

"What country impressed you most during your trip abroad?"

"It is very difficult to answer because my trip was too brief," was the diplomatic reply.

"Who is the better tennis player, the Crown Prince or yourself?"

The answer came promptly, "The Crown Prince is."

"Is it true that the Crown Prince told you before you left to be sure to visit Scotland?"

"No, he did not say *be sure.*"

"What is your plan during the engagement?"

"I should like to consult the Crown Prince in everything about our future. I should also like to do my best to improve myself, with the advice and help of other people."

Her parents sat one on either side of her but the Crown Prince could not be there to give her his support. He was at home watching her on television. Later he called her on the telephone to congratulate her and to thank her for what he knew must have been a trying day. He dined with Dr. Koizumi and his chamberlains and doctors that night and she with her family. She had not even yet been alone with the Crown Prince.

It had been an ordeal for her but she had passed her first great test gloriously. "That press interview," Mr. Yamanashi wrote to me, "surrounded by the group of the most wary, scrutinizing reporters dispersed all anxieties completely. Her dignity, frankness, wisdom and above all that gentle, easy grace, not a bit swayed nor tottered in that delicate occasion, charmed all observers. I am therefore quite sure she will be equal to any demands made on her in future. Certainly she will bring perfect peace and happiness to the Crown Prince and honor to the court and the Japanese people."

There could be no possible doubt about the happiness which the news brought to the country at large. "We have not experienced such joy as this as a nation for a long time," wrote Tané, and Dr. Koizumi: "The people's enthusiasm for Miss Shoda was stormy—or, better, explosive." Though the Crown Prince's life history, his character, his achievements were lovingly described once more, the spotlight was directed chiefly upon Michiko Sama. It was her day.

The Cinderella story is always appealing, but this Cinderella, who differed from the original in being born with a silver spoon in her mouth and in being surrounded by a united and loving family, had two peculiarly Japanese obstacles to overcome: the feeling, which she herself shared, of the impassable gulf between the Imperial Family and the ordinary people, and the long-established custom of arranged marriages for everybody, on the grounds that an orderly decision based on background, common interests and family considerations is more civilized than one swayed by passion. Both of these attitudes, it is true, have changed radically since the war. The Emperor in his Rescript of January 1, 1946, renounced all claims (not that he himself ever made any) to divinity, and the new Constitution of 1947 declared him not the source of all power but the symbol of a sovereignty residing in the people. The new position which the constitution also gave to women has resulted in more women in business and the professions, more co-ed students in men's universities, and more love-marriages in consequence. But however enthusiastically the liberal young may embrace new ideas and new ways and whatever a constitution may decree, in the minds of the mass of the people old customs, old paths of thought have a stubborn way of lingering on. The old ice-barriers stay frozen until some unusually sunny warmth comes to melt them. Only a girl of Michiko Shoda's caliber, who could capture the imagination and win the immediate respect and affection of the Japanese people as she did, could have swept away the entrenched attitudes of the centuries. For it *was* a love match. Though the officials approved her from the first, the final word did not lie with them. All the officials' support would have availed nothing if the Crown Prince had not been able to convince Michiko Shoda that he loved her and that she loved him.

She was born on October 20, 1934, when the Crown Prince was within three days of being ten months old. Her father, a graduate of Hitotsubashi University, in Tokyo, was the president of a flour-milling company which he had inherited from his father. He was one of ten children, most of whom found intellectual careers for themselves. One is a well-known mathematician and the president of Osaka University; another teaches mineralogy at the University of Tokyo. I was told that Mr. Shoda himself had wanted to be a professor of economics but had given up that ambition when it became evident that he was the one to take up the burden of the family business. His father, Michiko Sama's grandfather, had himself sacrificed a desire to go into foreign service on the altar of the family business, which was at that time a soya-brewing company in Tatebayashi in Gumma Prefecture.

Her mother, from whom Michiko Sama inherits her beauty—though her father is a very distinguished-looking man—was also the daughter of a businessman. She was educated at Futaba Girls' High School, a Christian school of high standing in Tokyo. Though Mrs. Shoda was educated at a Christian school neither she nor her husband are Christians. Many Buddhists send their children to Christian schools for the sake of the character training that they receive there.

Mr. and Mrs. Shoda, soon after their marriage in 1929, spent some time in both Europe and the United States on business. Their house in Tokyo is built in the Western style—a high-gabled, half-timbered, comfortable-looking house with a deep garden—and their four children, of whom Michiko Sama is the second, grew up sleeping in beds instead of on *tatami*.

A curly-haired, pretty, active, lovable child, Michiko went to Futaba Primary School, was evacuated to Tatebayashi during the war, returned in 1947 to continue her education in Seishin High School and University. Seishin is run by nuns of the order of the Sacred Heart, a teaching order which has its mother-house in Brussels. Mother Janet Stuart, a Scottish girl brought up in the Presbyterian Church, who became a nun, a great teacher and a mystic and whose *Life and Letters* is one of the most interesting books on the spiritual life, belonged to this order. She was for many years head of the well-known School of the Sacred Heart at Roehampton in England. Mother Elizabeth Britt, now the head of Seishin, was on the same ship with me when I went to Japan in 1946, and I formed a lasting admiration and affection for her then.

On both of my return visits to Japan I have gone to see her and she has made time for me in her overwhelmingly busy days. When we met and talked a few days before the wedding of her pupil and mine, it was with an astonished feeling of "What hath the Lord wrought!" My memories of the *Marine Falcon* and that cold, rough, uncomfortable voyage were still fresh. Mother Britt, who was then returning to a convent and school almost totally demolished to start from scratch and rebuild it greater and stronger than before, sat every day in a corner of the bleak lounge on C Deck, tapping away at her typewriter on reports, lists, letters—the administrator's never-relinquished burden. I, sailing toward a totally unknown world and unimagined task, lay in my cocoon of army blankets in a deck chair in the salt spray and wondered. For a few minutes before or after meals I would drop down beside Mother Britt for a refreshing chat. Her face within its fluted white cap and black draperies was serene, keen, kind—and beautiful. She had the complicated mixture of worldly wisdom, tolerance and innocence that deeply religious people sometimes, most engagingly, have, and she had the gaiety of all the best nuns. "The good are always the merry, Save by an evil chance." Saint Teresa could never have said of her as she did of some, "Give me no sour saints." She shared with me her knowledge of Japan and the Japanese, and we laughed together about the peculiarities of life aboard that ex-troopship, the *Marine Falcon.* I remember her saying one day with a twinkle, "Do you know what they called this ship in Australia? The Hell-Ship!" Looking back on those days I said to Mother Britt, "How utterly astounded we would have been then if we could have looked forward twelve and a half years!"

Michiko Sama was happy at Seishin. It has become one of Tokyo's most fashionable schools, and it has a strong international atmosphere, attracting as it does girls from the diplomatic families of many countries, who are posted to Japan. She got a sound intellectual grounding, beautiful manners and almost flawless English. She took the English literature course, wrote a graduating thesis entitled, "A Conflict and its Reconciliation Treated in Galsworthy's *Forsyte Saga,*" maintained an average grade of over 90, was president of Student Government and valedictorian of her class. Though she was devoted to Mother Britt, whose "child" she called herself, she was not converted to the Roman Catholic faith. "It seems she is too reasonable to become a Christian," one of her friends wrote me. With all her splendid qualities, which might seem in the aggregate formidable, she had an endearing sense of fun: *chamé* is the Japanese word.

She had many suitors. In Japan they do not call up and ask for a date: they—or their parents or a friend of their parents— make inquiries of the girl's parents or a friend of the girl's parents. It is known which girls are in demand. Miss Shoda said she thought that all this marrying young was silly and she was in no hurry. She had her tennis—she had won a regional junior championship—her music, her art-appreciation group and plenty of other interests.

On August 19, 1957, a now-famous tennis match took place. The tournament which is the climax of the summer season at Karuizawa was in progress. The Crown Prince and a Waseda University graduate were paired against Michiko Shoda and a twelve-year-old American boy, one Bobby Doyle, who was in Karuizawa on vacation. The score is variously given in different accounts, but the usual one is 7—5, 6—3. The exact score doesn't matter; the Crown Prince and his partner were beaten.

Dr. Koizumi told his pupil without mincing matters that he played deplorably that day. Mother Britt said to hers, "Michiko, what were you doing, to beat the Crown Prince?" To which she replied, "I didn't want to, Mother, but I couldn't help it."

Mother Britt need not have been troubled. The Crown Prince ever since I have known him has had his share both of winning and of losing in contests with his friends and, being a thoroughly good sport, he takes either one in his stride.

The Crown Prince that day was struck both by Michiko Shoda's beauty and by the spirited way she played tennis.

Somebody—possibly it was Michiko Sama's brother—took a snapshot of the game, thinking that she would like a record of what would probably be a unique event in her life. Nobody else appeared to take any notice of it.

They met twice more that fall, both times at tennis matches. One was a private tournament at the Tobitakyu courts outside of Tokyo, to which the Crown Prince invited a group of about twenty tennis friends. Miss Shoda won the tournament and a small silver cup. The Crown Prince took her photograph and sent it to her later. It was this photograph and another one taken by a professional photographer that he sent me for Christmas in 1958. Both were lovely, but the one he took was better: there was a glow in the girl's face which the professional man failed to evoke.

In March, 1958, other schools than the Peeresses' sent in recommended names and Michiko Shoda's headed the Seishin list. The Crown Prince expressed the wish that she be given serious consideration. Besides the Crown Prince's own feelings and Michiko Shoda's ideal combination of personal qualities there were other elements in the officials' decision to put their weight behind this choice: the advisability of adding new blood to a family in which there had been many intermarriages in the past, Miss Shoda's robust health and the fact that her family was a prolific one, and the Crown Prince's conviction, often previously expressed, that marriage to a commoner would bring the throne closer to the people.

In April Michiko Sama happened to join the Tokyo Lawn Tennis Club, of which the Crown Prince was already a member, and throughout the spring they played together there once a week or oftener. On one occasion they played a match with the brother of the Shah of Iran, then visiting Japan, and the wife of the Iranian ambassador. The Crown Prince was now sure of his own heart.

Summer found them both in Karuizawa, playing tennis and seeing each other informally but never alone. A loyal little band of four—three of the Crown Prince's classmates and the younger brother of another—acted as errand boys to arrange chance meetings with Miss Shoda at the behest of the Crown Prince. Another classmate told me that before leaving Japan to go abroad to study he went to Karuizawa to say good-by to the Crown Prince, and was invited to a little dance which the Prince was having at his house that evening. He went, danced with Michiko Sama and other girls, and left without suspecting what was in the air. The zealous newspaper men, however, were quite aware that a romance was in flower, and Michiko Shoda was finding herself an object of an uncomfortable amount of interest.

The first approach to Mr. and Mrs. Shoda by Dr. Koizumi on behalf of the committee brought an immediate respectful but firm refusal—which might have seemed to be Japanese etiquette but which had enough panic in it to be convincing. In a later con-

versation with them, Dr. Koizumi made a moving plea: "Here
is a young man," he said, "of good looks and fine character who
has no secrets. All his life is spread out for the world to see. His
only defect is that he is the Crown Prince." But they did not
yield and Dr. Koizumi reported to the Prince that there were
"difficulties." He did not specify what they were.

The Shodas now took refuge in that ancient resort of distressed
parents: they sent their daughter to Europe. The International
Alumnae Association of Sacred Heart schools was having a
meeting in Brussels on September sixth and seventh. Mother
Britt arranged for Michiko Shoda to attend as the representative
of Seishin. On September third she flew from Haneda Airport.

While she was abroad she visited London, Amsterdam, Zurich,
Rome and Paris as well as Brussels. In most places, she told me,
it was arranged for her to stay with private families instead of
in hotels, which gave her a glimpse of the lives of people which
was unusual for such a short trip and which she greatly appreciated. It was a broadening and stimulating experience for her,
but she carried always in her mind and heart the question that
destiny was hammering in her ears.

At home Dr. Koizumi on the one hand and Mother Britt on the
other were talking with her father and mother. An article in the
Sunday Mainichi, translated for me by Tané's sister Yuki, said
in part, "He did not press Mr. Shoda with the Prince's desire but
one by one he stripped off the layers of fear from Father Shoda's
mind. Always he met with people not as an official but as a private teacher and friend of the Prince. Just as the Crown Prince's
faithfulness in love won Michiko San, Dr. Koizumi's sincerity
overcame Father Shoda's hesitation. Mr. Shoda said, 'I trust
Koizumi San's character and have been helped by his sweetness
to come to the decision.' "

The chasm between the Imperial Family and a commoner, the
prospect of losing their beloved daughter altogether in the rigid-
ities of court life, the opposition she might meet from the old

nobility, the uncertainties of the future in an Asian country so near to Communist China and Soviet Russia: these were the specters that haunted this modest, devoted couple who had brought their children up in a solid, unpretentious, quietly elegant home without the most remote idea that the phoenix would suddenly swoop down from above the clouds and carry one of them off.

At some point, however, "the ice began to melt," and the Shodas wrote to their daughter abroad that the Imperial Household had made a formal proposal on behalf of the Crown Prince. She wrote back this letter quoted in many newspapers:

"I believe the Imperial Household after all is no place for a person of our status to enter. Judging from the royal families of Europe I do not believe it would be to the good of the Imperial Family. I am afraid the Crown Prince would be the one to suffer most."

On October twenty-sixth she returned to Japan, after a brief stay in New York and Washington, where the ambassador was her father's second cousin.

Now the Crown Prince took things into his own hands. He telephoned daily—and sometimes several times a day. She wanted desperately to see him alone just once before she made her final decision but there was no possible way to meet in secrecy. The newspapers were in full cry, keeping a twenty-four-hour "bride watch" on the house, in order to take a snapshot if she so much as stepped out into the garden. They must both have felt, like Genji, that "it was a great inconvenience to belong to that exalted state which arouses intense interest on the part of persons of lesser grade."

In the end, she gave him her answer over the telephone, and a few days later her father sent a formal letter of acceptance to the director of the Imperial Household Agency.

When the announcement was made, a Japanese friend wrote to me: "We rejoice to know that our Prince is a man of determination and also that he is able to discern true values."

21

Are You Going to the Wedding?

ON February 11, 1959, it was announced that the Crown Prince of Japan and Miss Michiko Shoda would be married on April 10. The wedding ceremony would be performed in the Kashikodokoro, the Imperial shrine in the heart of the Palace grounds in Tokyo, and there would be three days of receptions afterwards.

My telephone began to ring again. This time it was mostly American reporters on the other end of the line. "Are you going to the wedding?" they wanted to know.

I could not tell them, for I did not know myself.

For more than two months nearly everybody I knew had been asking the same question, not once but every time they saw me. If I had not known on Monday, surely I would have heard something by Thursday. Now strangers joined in. If I went into a shop to make a simple purchase the woman behind the counter would say archly, "Are you going to that wedding in Tokyo?" Once as I came away from the post office a woman whom I was not aware of ever having seen before called across the street to me, "Are you going to the wedding?"

I found it oddly difficult to explain Japan and the ways of the court to people who thought in terms of a big church wedding or even of a royal wedding in Westminster Abbey. It had been difficult enough earlier to explain why the Crown Prince did not live with his family, why his parents could not see him whenever they wanted to, and why he could not possibly have dates with girls, but this seemed even more incomprehensible to the average American. As he—but more often she—saw it, an old teacher takes up little room in a church pew; nobody has to pay much attention to her, but it is appropriate that she should be there, grateful and beaming, to see this climax in her former pupil's life, and she needs to know that she is going early enough to get a new dress for the occasion.

I knew the Japanese scene. There is no Westminster Abbey in Japan. The Kashikodokoro is small. I had never been inside it, of course, but I had walked around the walls that enclosed the outer compound and I had looked through the gate. I knew that there was not the slightest chance of my being invited to the cere-mony. In Shinto weddings the ceremony itself is performed in the presence of only the immediate families, and the friends and relatives are invited to the reception afterwards. Because I was a foreigner I had been invited once to the wedding ceremony of a former pupil, and I knew how small the shrine was, how intimate the group. While I felt confident that I might be asked to one of the receptions afterwards, I knew of a further complication about getting out the invitations. The date of the wedding had been announced in the newspapers, but the ceremony of officially in-forming the Shodas of the wedding date would not take place until March 16. Naturally no invitations could go out until the bride's family knew when the wedding was to be!

By the first of March, however, I had heard from Tokyo.

Robert Kiyoshi Togasaki, known to all his American friends as Bob, was a classmate and close friend of the Crown Prince's. He was one of the first two boys whom I selected to share the Prince's private lessons. His father, a nisei who had returned to

Japan in the 1930's, was president of the *Nippon Times* (now *Japan Times*) when I first went to Japan; he and Mrs. Togasaki were kind friends to me throughout my stay there. Gordon, the elder son, went to Swarthmore College, where he met Tamiyo Suematsu, one of my English Club girls, and they were married at Plymouth Meeting, near Philadelphia, in 1956. Bob had come to the United States to study at Phillips Exeter, had got his A.B. from Haverford College, had had a year of graduate work at Cornell, and was now back in Japan, where he had become engaged to a delightful girl and was preparing to be married soon after the Crown Prince. Bob, like Gordon and Tamiyo and Asako Tanaka, was one of those whom I called my "children"—Japanese students in Philadelphia colleges who were especially close to me and who came to my house at Christmas and other times. Bob as a thirteen-year-old had been a round-faced youngster with a puckish expression, helpful and eager and sweet-natured. Puck had disappeared as he grew older and struggled with his double heritage—for he was an American citizen—but his other qualities had only grown deeper and stronger.

It was Bob who now wrote to me. He and two classmates had been at the Crown Prince's house for dinner one evening and they had all talked about my coming to the wedding. Hiroshi Kusakari, the Peers' School baseball team's famous pitcher, now working for a brewing company and starring on the company team, and Masao Oda, who had spent a postgraduate year at Stanford University and visited me on a trip east, had both at different times shared the Crown Prince's lessons and had been part of the little group that was in Karuizawa when the Prince visited me there in 1949 and had joined in all the games and picnics.

No invitations to the wedding, Bob wrote, were to be sent out of Japan. Only people actually there in April would be invited. He was "unofficially" assured that if I were there, I would receive an invitation. The three classmates had then gone energetically to work to find a way to offer me an airplane ticket as well as the promise of an invitation. They drew in another classmate, Tomohiko Senge, who was secretary to Mr. Shigeo Mizuno, the president of the Sankei enterprises, which included the hall where the P.E.N. had had its meetings, a symphony orchestra, a newspaper, and the Fuji Television Company. The "Fuji Telebi," Bob told me triumphantly, would pay my airplane fare from Philadelphia, if I would appear on a television program in an interview with the four boys.

This letter and the loyal affection which it revealed touched me deeply. I wrote back thanking the boys and promising to be in Tokyo in April. I was grateful, too, to the Fuji Television Company and would be glad to appear on their program, I said, but my Scotch and Quaker blood had a craving for independence and so I would take care of the expenses of transportation myself. At the risk of getting ahead of my story, I may as well say here that the Fuji Television Company heaped many kindnesses upon me in Japan, putting a car and chauffeur at my disposal the entire time, providing a splendid new television set for my room and many other generous attentions.

Though I had no expectation of going to the wedding ceremony, I thought that perhaps some provision might be made for me similar to what was done when Princess Kazuko was married in the spring of 1950. Then too I had been invited to the reception but not to the ceremony; I had, however, been permitted to see her in her wedding robes.

I hoped that I might be granted some such glimpse of the Crown Prince and his bride; but what I wanted most of all was to see him and talk with him before his wedding, to meet Miss Shoda, and to be in Japan at a time of such significance and such wide rejoicing.

I began hastily to make my preparations for the trip: passport and reservations, clothes, a wedding present.

"What are you going to wear?"

What indeed? I had no idea what functions I would attend or

at what hour of the day or night they would be held. I packed three dresses, suitable for formal wear in morning, afternoon, and evening. By a curious coincidence all three were made of Japanese materials which members of the Imperial Family had given me in 1957.

One was a silk brocade, a gray-blue background with a darker blue pattern of lotus roots and leaves, made simply with a bolero jacket. One evening I had been invited to dinner by Prince and Princess Takamatsu in the charming small house which they have built on the grounds of their former place. Princess Takamatsu is the honorary chairman of the Silk Road Society, and she takes an active interest in the movement to make the traditional Japanese silks practical for modern Western use. A famous French designer was brought to Japan to adapt the old kimono designs and the mills were retooled to weave forty-inch silks instead of the fourteen-inch width used for kimonos. The Silk Road Society headquarters in the Korinkaku Mansion, where every stage of the process of silk-making can be seen, from the cocoon through spinning, designing, weaving and dyeing, is now one of the favorite tourist sights of Tokyo. At the end of a delightful evening, Princess Takamatsu gave me this blue brocade, which I had had made up nearly a year earlier and had worn fairly often.

The afternoon dress was made of printed chiffon which the Empress had given me, a filmy pattern of bellflowers and their leaves in shades of gray and gold, and the black lace for the evening dress had been the Crown Prince's gift.

The wedding present was a much more serious problem. What can one give to a young pair who will be receiving thousands of presents, some of them priceless treasures from heads of state all over the world? I wanted to give something that, however modest, was intrinsically good of its kind, something beautiful, something characteristically American, something that had some significance for the Crown Prince.

After a good deal of thought I went to look at Steuben glass.

As soon as I walked into the shop I saw it: on a shelf by itself against a royal purple velvet background was a glass ornament perhaps eighteen inches high, in the shape of a stylized, slightly modernistic rooster. The Crown Prince was born in "the Year of the Cock."

The twelve signs of the zodiac in Japan are all animals: the rat, the bull, the tiger, hare, dragon, and so on in order to the cock, the dog, and the boar. Everyone knows and sets considerable store by the sign under which he was born. The Empress, for instance, born in the Year of the Hare, has a cabinet full of miniature rabbits of every variety, china, crystal, ivory, wood. One of her gifts to me was an enchanting pair of ivory rabbits rowing a boat made of a slender ivory leaf; and when I went to Japan in 1957 I took her a Royal Copenhagen bunny with a lettuce leaf in his mouth. The Crown Prince gave me in 1950 an ornament consisting of a silver rooster perched on a lacquer drum, with a silver hen and chick on the lacquer stand below the drum. There is in the Seattle Art Museum an early *otsu-e* (wood-block print) of that same group. The story that goes with it is a relative of the Italian legend retold by Longfellow in the "Bell of Atri": an Emperor, wishing to see justice prevail in the land, had a great drum set up in the capital, on which any subject who felt that he had been unjustly treated could thump out his dissatisfaction and obtain justice. So fair and equitable was that Emperor's reign that the drum was never used and even the animals had no fear of loud noises from it; the cock climbed on it to crow and the hen and chickens scratched contentedly beneath it. In the room where the Crown Prince had his first private lessons with me, there had hung a painting of a rooster. I never think of that room without seeing in my mind the painting on the wall, the square table and blackboard under it, and the twelve-year-old Prince's chubby, serious, sometimes bored face as he wrestled with the English language.

All these thoughts in my mind, I bought the glass cock and had it carefully wrapped. When it was ready it was too big to go into any suitcase, too delicate to trust to the baggage compartment of the plane. I should have to carry it in my hand.

On the morning of the sixteenth of March, the Emperor's grand chamberlain, Mr. Mitani, called upon the Shodas and said, "I inform you of the Imperial message that the wedding ceremony of the Crown Prince will be performed on April tenth." Michiko Shoda bowed and replied, "I respectfully acknowledge the message."

Four days later the Imperial Household Agency announced that about a thousand people would be invited to attend the wedding ceremony, or as much of it as could be seen from the inner courtyard of the shrine. All the guests would be Japanese—members of the court, of the government, of the Japan Academy of Arts and Sciences, and so on—with one exception, the Crown Prince's former American tutor, Mrs. Vining.

I already had this thrilling information: Dr. Koizumi had written me that I would be invited to the Kashikodokoro, and the Crown Prince had sent me a heart-warming note which I have put away among my treasures. But it was manna to the press. As far as news about the engaged pair was concerned, there was a lull. Here was a tidbit to fill the vacuum.

Mayor Richardson Dilworth of Philadelphia designated me "Honorary Ambassador of Good Will" from Philadelphia to Japan, invested me with a handsome scroll in a ceremony at the City Hall, and entrusted me with a very nice letter to the Crown Prince.

On the morning of April first I boarded a TWA airliner at Philadelphia International Airport. The pretty stewardess helpfully offered to take my big package from me, and I—afraid someone might drop it or set it down heavily and jar the glass ornament inside—clung to it. The photograph of our brief contest preceded me to Japan. "What was in the box?" became al-

most as well-worn a question as "What are you going to wear?"
and "Are you going to the wedding?"

At San Francisco I changed to a Pan American plane. Gordon
Togasaki, after Swarthmore and the Harvard Business School,
got a job with Pan American, and thanks to his efforts and my
temporary publicity value, I received the treatment usually ac-
corded to leading figures in the UN, multi-millionaires and movie
stars—and I must say it is pleasant. All the minor rubs and discomforts of traveling are made smooth.

After a stopover in Honolulu of thirty-six heavenly hours, I
started on the last lap of my eight-thousand mile trip, peering out
from a flowery necklace of twelve beautiful, fragrant leis.

My arrival in Tokyo had its funny side.

Sunrise on the morning of April fifth was one of the most
beautiful I have ever seen. Below us was a floor of billowing
white clouds, rearing up here and there into fantastic towers and
peaks. The sun came up and flooded it all with gold and orange
light and purple shadows. Away on the horizon there appeared
to be a crimson lake with dark hills on the farther shore.

Near Tokyo the rain began. Yokohama and the checkerboard
countryside around it looked drab as we circled above it. When
the plane's wheels touched the ground and there was a great
stirring in the aisles of people with coats and flight bags, I sat
still, hoping that the others would get off first and I could follow
quietly. But they were all held back and I was summoned.

There to my surprise and joy were Tané and Dr. Koizumi coming up the steps in the rain, followed by Esther Rhoads. Down
below on the shiny wet asphalt masses of newsmen with cameras
came running. The steps were large ones with a landing halfway
up and here we four were halted for the first pictures. A Pan
American official, shorter than I was, gallantly trying to hold an
umbrella over me, hooked my veil with one of the spokes and
hoisted my hat into the air. The rain poured down, the wind

lashed it against us, my hat, disentangled and descending, landed sidewise on my disheveled head.

Somehow or other, still resisting all kindly attempts to wrest my precious package from me, I got to the room in the airport building that had been prepared. My bag, passport, all the formalities of entering the country were taken care of without my lifting a finger. Esther Rhoads competently tidied me up and put my hat straight.

A little more composed, I faced my welcome. Mr. Mizuno was there with a huge armful of yellow roses for me. The four boys who had done so much to bring this event about were on hand, as well as others from their class; Mrs. Koizumi, some of the Inoues, Asako Tanaka, and other friends whom I rejoiced to see.

I had no time to talk with them. The press was waiting. Dr. Koizumi told me afterwards that he counted more than a hundred reporters and photographers in that room. A number of them I already knew and felt that they were friends. One was Akira Hashimoto, one of my own students, now a member of Kyodo, the Associated Press of Japan. The feeling in that crowded room was a wonderful thing to experience: the joyous excitement and cordiality that seemed to be lifting the whole country at this time of their Crown Prince's marriage. Cecil Brown of NBC acted as chairman. I had heard his broadcasts from Singapore in 1941 and read his book, and I was much interested to meet him, but this was no time for social chat. As another press conference was scheduled for the next morning, with many questions and answers, all I had to do now was to read the statement I had brought with me and distribute copies of it, of which fortunately I had had about fifty made.

At last we were in the Koizumis' car, headed for Tokyo and the International House, where I was to stay until the seventeenth when I went to the International Christian University to be with Tané. The International House of Japan is "a center of cultural exchange," a sort of club—but much more than a club—with a

variety of programs aimed at promoting international understanding and intellectual cooperation. With the aid of a grant
from the Rockefeller Foundation, the House, with bedrooms for
fifty or sixty guests, dining rooms, lecture hall, conference rooms,
library and so on, was built on the site of one of the famous man-
sions which was destroyed during the war. It is a beautifully designed modern building, and in its setting of the restored garden,
with its warm, friendly and stimulating atmosphere, it is an
ideal place to stay.

Such a center for international friendship had been the twenty-
year dream of Count Aisuke Kabayama, who died in 1953, when
it was under way but before it could be realized. I had had the
privilege of knowing Count Kabayama in Gotemba in 1948 and
1950, where I heard him say those characteristic words that I
have so often quoted since then: "You know, the *tastiest* thing
in the world is one human being."

I found my room full of flowers to welcome me. I was especially pleased by flowers from the two prospective brides: a
basket of deep purple pansies, with a cordial note, from Miss
Shoda, and an arrangement of lilies and cherry blossoms from
Fumiko Tomoyama, who was to marry Bob Togasaki. There
were also tulips and lilies of the valley from Mrs. Takaki, who
came that afternoon to welcome me on behalf of the Empress.

In the evening Tané went with me to dine with the Koizumis.
There were no other guests, just Dr. and Mrs. Koizumi and their
charming daughter Taeko, Tané and I. It was unspeakably peaceful to be there again in that lovely room, to shed all the excite-
ments and fatigues of the long journey, to talk happily and without reserve among trusted friends.

Dr. Koizumi had my invitations waiting for me: one to the
wedding ceremony at the Kashikodokoro, one to the reception on
the sixteenth. Both were written in Japanese on heavy, cream-
colored cards embossed with the sixteen-petal chrysanthemum.
Each envelope contained also a sticker for the car, a little list of

instructions (private cars will enter through the Inui Mon, men will wear morning coats, women the equivalent) and a card to check and return, indicating whether one accepted or declined.

I accepted.

22

The Days Beforehand

AT the entrance to the Crown Prince's house, Tokiwamatsu, the familiar guards in dark blue uniforms and white gloves saluted as the car swept through the gate and deposited me at the open front door, where the friendly menservants, Suzuki San and Oshitani San stood waiting on the front steps. In the hall inside Mr. Toda welcomed me.

There was something new, I saw at once. In front of the big square gold screen that veiled the hall when the door was open, stood a beautiful and dramatic ornament; from a base, heavy and intricately carved and lacquered in black, projected two great curving horns of polished ivory—whole elephant tusks. It was the wedding gift from Viet Nam.

The Crown Prince received me in his sitting room upstairs and I had twenty minutes alone with him. I felt at once a change in him, of which I became more certain as I talked longer with him later in the week. He was happy, but more than that he had a deep inner confidence, which came no doubt from having wanted something very much, put forth all his efforts to achieve it and having in the end won gloriously. He seemed also to be in a way released, so that he could say more easily than ever before what was in his heart. This was, I found later, not my impression alone but that of the friends who were close to him. He had also, since I last saw him, grown to manhood: there was the initiative, the

236

authority, the sense of direction of one who has taken his life into his own hands and is prepared to be responsible for others.

I presented the mayor's letter to him, he read it carefully and asked me to convey his thanks and appreciation to Mr. Dilworth. Then I delivered at last the wedding present which I had guarded so long. He would have politely opened it at once, but I knew that within the white and silver paper and the white box there was much tissue paper wadding which would take time to undo, and so I suggested that he have one of the chamberlains open it for him later. I told him what it was and asked him if he remembered the picture that had hung over us during the first lessons and he said at once, "Yes. It was painted by Kawai Gyokudo and it was burned when my house was burned." (The simple wooden house in which he had lived for more than two years on the school grounds at Koganei had caught fire one night and burned to the ground, fortunately during the winter vacation when the Crown Prince himself was at Hayama.)

That evening when I saw him again he told me that he liked my gift and later I was made happy by seeing it in the place of honor in his sitting room.

The twenty minutes passed swiftly. Among other things, I asked him about the word *kensho* which I had heard people use in speaking of the Imperial shrine: was it one part of the Kashikodokoro? He told me that both words had the same meaning and signified the whole enclosure as well as the shrine itself. Kensho was the Chinese reading of the characters, Kashikodokoro the Japanese.

This is why it is so difficult to learn to read Japanese. When the early Japanese, who had no written language, took over the Chinese script in the fifth century, they dealt with the characters in two ways: they used them either to record a meaning or as a phonetic sound, with the result that a single character may be read in several different ways. The symbol for mountain, for instance, 山 may be read *yama*, which is Japanese, or *san*,

which is Chinese. Though the character is the same, the Japanese
in speaking of the two mountains, Fuji and Asama, invariably
say Fuji *San* and Asama *Yama*. Only foreigners say Fujiyama.
But how is a foreigner to know which is right? Or take the character for *small*, 小 : it may be read *chisai*, or *ko* or *o*. Just to
complicate matters a little further, the character for large, 大 ,
is also read *o*, as well as *dai* and several other things. Usually in a
polysyllabic word, all the syllables are pronounced in either the
Japanese or the Chinese way, but in names they are sometimes
mixed. Mr. Tajima's first name is Michiji. The *Michi* is Japanese,
the *ji* Chinese. Even the Japanese get confused in transliterating
cases like this; the *Japan Times* always writes his name as *Michi-
haru*, the *haru* being the equivalent of *ji*.

In the Kashikodokoro, or Kensho, the Prince told me, the central shrine is a copy of the great shrine at Ise, and there is inside
it a copy of the sacred mirror, one of the three sacred treasures
of the Imperial regalia. The other two treasures are the sword,
which is at a shrine near Nagoya and the jewels, which are
"somewhere" in the Imperial Palace. There is a set of replicas of
the three treasures, and before the war it was kept always beside
the Emperor and taken with him when he traveled. Since the war
it has been considered too cumbersome and has been left behind.

The costume which Prince Akihito would wear at his wedding,
he said, was the same as that he wore at his Coming of Age ceremony, after he changed from the boy's robe to the adult's. He has
worn it often since then at the regular Palace ceremonies, at the
New Year and other times. At Thanksgiving? I asked. No, not at
Thanksgiving, he replied; he appeared then in the white robes of
a priest. He does not officiate then, nor does his father; they and
various officials merely "attend." I was interested to know of the
difference made between the Thanksgiving ceremony and the
other ceremonies, as if to mark a greater seriousness. It is a court
ceremony in November held in the Imperial shrine when the gods
are thanked for the harvest and the other benefits of the year: a

universal impulse of the human heart, whatever the religion, the race or the period. I knew that the Emperor himself took it more seriously than the other ceremonies, for I remembered one occasion before the Crown Prince was old enough to be present at it, when His Majesty directed the chamberlains to cancel some engagement made for the Crown Prince on the evening before the Thanksgiving ceremony; it was a time, he said, to spend quietly and thoughtfully.

Miss Shoda would wear the wedding costume which Princess Shigeko wore when she was married in the early 1940's. The following morning, Tuesday, they were both to put on their costumes so that the wedding photographs could be taken.

Before I left the Prince showed me the study that had been prepared for the Crown Princess. It was the corner room on the front of the house that Prince Masahito had had when he used to spend two or three nights a week here with his brother, but it had been entirely redecorated and refurnished. Bookshelves and a desk had been designed by Mr. Taniguchi, the architect of the new house now being built; they were made of kiri wood, which is light and dark in streaks. A table in the center of the room, a sofa upholstered in pale green brocade, brocade curtains at the windows, and a brilliant amaryllis on a stand in the corner, completed the pleasant feminine retreat.

Downstairs I met the three ladies-in-waiting who are to attend the new Princess: Mrs. Makino, who is sixty but looks much younger, the daughter-in-law of Count Makino and sister-in-law of Mr. Yoshida, and two younger ladies.

From Tokiwamatsu I went to the Koizumis' house, where I was to meet Michiko Shoda at noon. When the car turned into the narrow lane with high walls on either side, I saw that people had already gathered to see Miss Shoda arrive: mothers and grandmothers and small children, a great many photographers. Inside the house Chise Matsumoto, Dr. Koizumi's great-niece and a classmate of Michiko Shoda's, was already there. I had met Miss Matsumoto two years earlier, when she was not long back from a year of study at the Sacred Heart School at Manhattanville, New York. She is a delightful girl, full of fun, herself happily engaged to be married.

The stir of voices and people moving about outside suddenly increased to something like an uproar, and we all went out on the doorstep to welcome Miss Shoda.

She was wearing a white kimono with a gold thread through it and a rosy obi, and with her dark hair and softly glowing eyes, the play of her expression, she was prettier than even the best of her photographs. To Dr. Koizumi's surprise she and I began to talk before we were introduced, and we continued while the cameras whirred and clicked, the flash bulbs exploded, and the photographers shouted to us to "shake hands once more!"

I felt at once beneath her warmth, her humor, her charm, a deeper level of real strength and steadfastness.

She looked fresh and rested in spite of the grind that she had been enduring throughout the past four months: "lessons" in Imperial protocol, *waka*-writing, calligraphy, French, English, Imperial functions and ceremonies, the duties of a Crown Princess, and the new Constitution of Japan, and the long hours of trying on clothes, so long and exacting that once she fainted. Once a week only she saw the Crown Prince alone, but there was now a direct wire between Tokiwamatsu and the Shoda house, so that they could talk freely over the telephone.

We had a delicious lunch of *o sushi*, sandwiches and dainty small things, sitting in the living room with the sliding doors open on the little garden, where the sun shone on a bush of red camellias in full bloom. Miss Shoda ate very sparingly, and they teased her gently: the Crown Prince likes slender women. "My husband was like that too," I told her, and she answered with mock ruefulness, "Oh, then you know my burden!"

She had brought two photographs of herself for me, and I had brought her a great spray of orchids like butterflies, which a generous friend had given me in Honolulu, and a silver lapel pin handmade in North Carolina.

I mention this very slight offering only because of its sequel. After Miss Shoda went home that day she changed into a suit, fastened the silver pin on the lapel, and had her picture taken in the garden holding the spray of orchids. This photograph she gave me, with an exquisite white orchid, the day I left Japan, when I went to say good-by to her and the Prince. I cannot think of many young brides who would take time and thought before their weddings for such a graceful gesture of appreciation.

The talk at lunch ranged over a variety of topics—English poetry, travel, the Crown Prince, the wedding, children's books, Karuizawa. A good deal of concern was expressed about her mother's health; Mrs. Shoda was in bed with a high temperature, but the doctor thought it was due to nervous exhaustion and that she would be rested in time to go to the wedding.

I heard now the full story of an episode of which I had had only bits before. Before the engagement was announced, the "bride watch" on her house had been so zealously kept that she had ventured to leave the house only twice in more than three weeks. The second time she slipped out with her mother to do some necessary errand. Their car was followed by the newsmen, forced off the street and surrounded by eager reporters who opened the door and demanded an interview.

Somehow the chauffeur managed to get the car started again and with the journalists in hot pursuit they fled to Seishin, which was nearer than their own home. Michiko Sama tumbled out at the main front door of the college and sprinted down the corridor with thirty or forty men pelting after her. Bumping into one of them she accidentally knocked his camera out of his hands and damaged it. "It was dreadful," she told me, "I had to apologize him later." (The omission of that preposition was the only slip in English that I heard her make.)

While the newsmen barged into classrooms and out again, she

found sanctuary in the convent. Dr. Koizumi, learning what was going on, came and pled with the newspapermen, patiently, humorously, sympathetically, promising them opportunities to take photographs later. After several hours of prowling hopefully about and keeping a watch on doors and windows, they yielded and went away.

Today was the day, I learned, when her *o nimotsu*, the chests and boxes containing that part of her trousseau which had not been delivered directly from the shops to Tokiwamatsu, were to be transferred from her old home to her new one. Three new trucks would take the trunks and dressing tables and men in a special uniform of light trousers and dark jackets would unload them and carry them in.

"Are the men from the court or are they your men?" Dr. Koizumi asked.

With only a second's hesitation she answered, "I think we may call them our men."

She has skill, already shown in her first press conference, in gracefully handling questions. Several people told me that when asked which she liked better, bread or rice (a very controversial question in Japan today), she answered, "I am loyal to my father's business."

The Empress, Mrs. Hoshina, her chief lady-in-waiting, and Mrs. Takaki, who besides being interpreter, is mistress of the robes, were there when the *o nimotsu* arrived, to "inspect" them and direct the putting away of them. The Empress does not often have an opportunity to visit the Crown Prince's house; he was on hand to see her, and no doubt it was a great satisfaction to her to have those three hours there with her son before his marriage.

At two Miss Shoda left, to go home and stand at her window, reviewing a "balloon parade" which her neighbors in the Gotanda district were putting on in honor of her marriage. When she said good-by to me, she asked me if I knew the meaning of the word *yoroshiku.* I did, very well, for it is a word one uses frequently. The Japanese seem to have but one word for the message for which we have many: greetings, regards, best wishes, love. "Then," she said, "when you see His Highness this evening, please give him my best *yoroshiku.*"

I delivered the message about five hours later.

The Prince's Peers' School class was having a reunion in his honor at the Akasaka Prince Hotel and I, as one of their teachers, was invited to attend it.

The "Prince" in the name of the hotel refers not to Prince Akihito but to the Korean Prince Lee, whose palace it formerly was. I had gone there in the fall of 1946 to have tea with Prince and Princess Lee and their son, who was two or three years older than the Crown Prince. Prince Lee, heir to the Korean throne, had been brought to Japan as a child when Japan annexed Korea; he grew up in the court and married one of the Japanese nobility. At the end of the war he was in a peculiarly difficult position, for there was no place for him either in Korea or Japan. His estates were lost to him in the capital levy and he was unfitted to support himself in the business world. That October afternoon, when the Lees were still living in their palace, I saw glimpses of what their life had been in the past, the years of golf and tennis, of mountain climbing in Switzerland, the expensive hobbies: we saw his orchid house, which had the perfect warm moist temperature for growing orchids and which had evidently come through the war warm when everybody else, including the Imperial Family, was cold. The son, Prince Rikyu, was a handsome lad with a pale oval face and slanting eyes, a smile at once gracious, humorous and wistful. After his parents lost their palace he was sent to the United States to study; he did well and is now, I am glad to hear, prospering in New York, where his parents have joined him.

As a hotel, the Lee palace has undergone changes; some rooms are divided, other large rooms have been built on at the back

into the garden. I had expected, as one does at functions attended
by royalty, to get there before the Crown Prince did, but he sent
me word that he would be there first and that I was not to come
until six-thirty.

The entrance was swarming with cameramen when I stepped
out of the car. Hiroshi Kusakari and Bob Togasaki were at the
door to escort me into the room where the Prince was waiting.
After posing together for photographs, we turned to go to the
banquet room where the meeting was to be held. I stepped aside
to let the Prince precede me, but he waved me on ahead.

About a hundred Peers' School graduates and their teachers
were already gathered in the big room, where the tables were
laden with a buffet supper of great variety. It was not the first
time I had been the only woman at a big Peers' School affair,
and as I was seeing many old friends—and racking my brains for
half-forgotten or entirely forgotten names—I thought little of it
until the story was published in somewhat surprising form the
next day. Mr. Yamanashi was there, as former president of the
Peers' School, and many of the teachers whom I had known,
with some of whom I had worked closely. The boys whom I had
taught were all grown up. Some of them were unrecognizable.
Some of them had had no occasion to use their English and they
had forgotten it. They gave me deprecating smiles—or looked
the other way—and stayed well out of reach. Others had learned
so much more than I had taught them that I was fairly envious.
They were in all kinds of occupations, banking, television, radio,
business, graduate study, law. One young man was a salesman
in a department store.

One of the young bankers was Hisanaga Shimazu, a primary
school classmate of the Crown Prince's, who had been in my
English class for six months, after which he had been taken out
because of illness. He told me that I had given him the name
"Bobby," during those early dates when I had given all the boys,

including Prince Akihito, English names for class use. His engagement to Princess Takako had been recently announced.

The Crown Prince moved about among his friends, always with a crowd around him, laughing and talking. Trays of beer and orange pop were passed and, when the supper tables had been pretty well ravaged, champagne with which to drink the Crown Prince's health.

It was time for the speeches. Hiroshi Kusakari was master of ceremonies and a very charming and able one. The Prince's health was drunk enthusiastically and he was banzai'ed. Two oak saplings for the garden of his new house were presented by his classmates. Mr. Yamanashi, old and frail now, made a very touching talk, looking back over the years to the first one, when he had come to Gakushuin as president and the Crown Prince as a first-grader. I knew just how the little Prince had looked at that time, for among the photographs recently republished, was one of him at six, striding manfully to school, with a black leather book-bag strapped on his back and sturdy high black shoes with a little tab at the back. Various teachers were called on to speak, and then the Crown Prince.

He spoke without notes, easily, warmly, with touches of humor and an undercurrent of seriousness. He thanked his classmates for their friendship and asked them for their continuing help. After he had finished, he was recalled to tell about his Child Welfare Fund. He and Miss Shoda, concerned about the large sums which various groups were raising for wedding presents, asked that some of the money be given instead to a fund for underprivileged children. It would be turned over to the Ministry of Health and Welfare to be administered but they hoped that it might be used to establish a hospital for crippled children, or a similar purpose. They had decided to give it to children, he said, because children will grow, and are hopeful, they represent the future of Japan.

I thought as I listened what an extraordinary thing—what a

wonderful thing for Japan—it was that the Crown Prince, shortly before his wedding, could have such an evening with his friends, that he had had an education that made it possible. He had experienced with them the difficulties and dangers and discomforts of war and the postwar period, had worked with them, played with them, quarreled and made up, and argued with them about the ideas and questions that are part of growing up. Now that they were all out of school and scattered, he still saw many of them at intervals, and those included not only the future bankers and intellectuals but the one who sold neckties, the one who took care of the properties and ran errands in a television studio, and all the others in jobs that might or might not lead to something in the future. He must have got from them an understanding of the life and thinking of his own generation in Japan that will be of great value to him.

Early the next morning I turned on my transistor radio to get the Far East Network news which came every hour on the hour in English from one of the U.S. bases in Japan. The class reunion got full coverage and a headline summing-up at the end of the five minutes: "American Schoolteacher Queen for a Night at the Crown Prince's Pre-Wedding Stag Party."

I saw him twice that day, which was Tuesday, three days before his wedding. In the afternoon I was invited by Their Majesties to tea at Kaintei, the pavilion where I have enjoyed so many happy occasions. The Crown Prince was there too, and his elder sisters, Mrs. Higashikuni and Mrs. Takatsukasa. Prince Masahito and Princess Takako were both away on trips and would not be back until just before the wedding.

In the evening a little after six I went to Tokiwamatsu to have dinner alone with the Crown Prince. If I were to select out of all those amazing sixteen days in Japan in April, the most deeply satisfying time of all, it would be those three undisturbed hours that evening.

We had an excellent dinner in the small dining room, where I had had dinner alone with him once before, in 1950, as I was leaving Japan. Two dogs, Anastasia, a German shepherd, and Eddie, a Scotch collie, wandered in and out at will. The Crown Prince described the differences in their characters to me: Anastasia deep in her feelings and interesting in her expression of them, Eddie superficial. At Hayama Eddie makes a great fuss barking at crabs, but Anastasia digs them up and kills them. Besides his dogs, he takes a great interest in his tropical fish— rather pallid-looking creatures I thought they were, not bright-colored and exotic as one might expect—which he had in tanks both in the dining room and in his sitting room upstairs. In the garden he has nesting boxes for starlings set up in a row, like an apartment house, and he has experimented with different colors. When the boxes were all the same color, the natural wood, the birds often got confused and attempted to go into the wrong houses, but when the boxes were painted different colors they made no more mistakes. They showed a definite preference for the red box and paid least attention to the green one.

Upstairs in the sitting room after dinner, we talked of Miss Shoda, of their marriage, and of the new house which is being built on the site of the Omiya Palace. The garden is the part of it that interests Prince Akihito most. It is to be a wild garden, he said, rather than a formal one, and he will continue his experiments with birds and with trees and shrubs from other parts of Japan.

The house itself, which is designed by Professor Yoshiro Taniguchi, will be Japanese outside and Western inside. It is going forward rather slowly, he said with a smile, because they had had so many new ideas and made so many changes in the plans.

He told me about the emblem which was chosen for his bride. Each member of the Imperial Family has a special emblem which is used to mark his or her possessions. The Emperor's is a young bamboo, the Empress's a peach, the Crown Prince's the character for prosperity. When Miss Shoda came to choose hers she selected modestly the wild chrysanthemum, but the Crown Prince demurred. He wanted her to have the white birch, which grows so beautifully in Karuizawa. She protested that the flower of the birch is not attractive, but the Prince, persisting, had an artist design a little medallion with birch leaves and catkins which delighted everybody.

The wedding ceremony following the old court tradition would be different from the usual Shinto ceremony, even though the court custom has itself been modified in the last century. Up until about 1850 it consisted of a formal dinner served in a ceremonial hall in the Kyoto Palace, after which the bridal couple went to another room where a number of rice cakes, equaling, he said, the combined ages of the bride and groom, were placed in special containers. Here there was a ceremony of drinking wine. This custom was changed by the Emperors Komu and Meiji, who began the practice of drinking the wine inside the Imperial shrine. At court weddings the bride and groom each sip their wine separately, instead of exchanging cups as is usually done in Shinto rites. The formal dinner of tradition has now become a symbolic meal with Their Majesties after the ceremony, and the rice cakes, in four silver dishes, would be placed in their bedroom for three days—"but not to eat." The custom of the rice cakes came down, he said, from the dawn of history, "when the man went to the woman's house and her mother prepared food."

Wednesday and Thursday he was to spend seeing ambassadors and receiving the gifts they brought from their governments. A tight schedule had been worked out: fifteen minutes were allowed for each country, and of that ten were used for having the gifts unwrapped and set up on a stand, five for the exchange of congratulations and thanks. I heard later what some of the presents were: 270 pieces of Venetian glass from Murano, in a complete service for thirty-six; a collar of Burmese rubies for the bride; a stole of Canadian mink; an enameled coffee set and a flagon of perfume from Soviet Russia; a Steuben glass bowl engraved with roses from President Eisenhower.

I remembered reading of the evening after the Prince's Coming of Age ceremony and how the people in the neighborhood of Tokiwamatsu, carrying lighted paper lanterns, had come walking down all the dark winding lanes into the courtyard of the Prince's house, where they called for him, and how he had appeared on the balcony with a lantern in his hand and acknowledged their greetings. I asked if there would be anything like that on the evening after the wedding.

"I hope not," he said. "Miss Shoda will be tired after a long day beginning at six in the morning."

He was beginning already, I thought, to be a good husband.

All day Thursday the rain poured down and the wind blew it in gusts into every crack and crevice. Neither umbrellas nor raincoats were much protection.

I went in the afternoon to see Princess Takako, who had got back from Shikoku the day before. After both her elder sisters were married she had moved from Kuretakeryo, which now seemed big and empty, into a smaller house in the Palace grounds.

Even after all these years I am still amazed by the number and variety of buildings and activities within the 247 acres of land enclosed by moats and walls that make up the Imperial Palace. Entering by the Sakashita Mon, one sees first the big white Western-style Imperial Household Building, where there are not only audience chambers, halls, drawing rooms, dining rooms, waiting rooms, private apartments for the Emperor and Empress, a concert hall, but offices for the director of the Imperial Household Agency, the grand chamberlain, and all the department heads, and for the host of clerks and secretaries who keep accounts and answer telephones and pound typewriters. At some distance—twenty minutes if you walk by wooded paths—is O Bunko, the converted library where Their Majesties have lived since the Palace itself was burned during the war. Then there are the little hospital which was made over into a house for Prince Masahito, the Emperor's Laboratory, the Empresses's silkworm buildings, the Kashikodokoro, the houses of ladies-in-waiting, the Music Hall, which contains the red lacquer stage for Gagaku, the great drums and the other instruments, the priceless ancient costumes, concert and practice rooms; the greenhouses, the garages for the fleet of cars, the carriage house with rows of state coaches; stables for the horses, storehouses, workshops, meadows and pastures, and, tucked away on winding lanes, in gardens behind fences, such buildings as Kuretakeryo and Princess Takako's new small house.

It was a Japanese house with *tatami* on the floor, but in the little drawing room, at any rate, Oriental rugs over the *tatami*, and chairs and tables.

Princess Takako is now twenty, tall and slender, spirited and lovely. She knows and likes clothes, she dresses beautifully and wears her clothes well. She has had two years at Gakushuin College, which is coeducational, and she spends her summers in Karuizawa, playing tennis in the tournaments and joining in other activities with Prince Akihito, whose favorite sister she is. Michiko Shoda was a tennis friend of hers, and Princess Takako wrote me after the engagement was announced, "She will be my wonderful elder sister!"

She is the darling of the women's magazines and the weeklies, which write about her frequently and sometimes attempt to picture her as a Japanese madcap version of Princess Margaret of England. But she is not anybody's copy, she is very much herself; if she is high-spirited she is also demure; she is warm-hearted and capable, and she is preparing herself to be the wife of the young bank clerk, a second or third cousin, who has been chosen for her. It will be an arranged marriage, but she has had opportunities to know Mr. Shimazu and she is obviously happy.

She herself made the dainty, open-faced sandwiches that we had for tea. To my delight Princess Atsuko was there too, having come from Okayama for the wedding, and Miss Natori came in. Miss Hana Natori, who retired as the princesses' governess several years ago and was succeeded by Miss Takeda, was always with the princesses when I was in Japan before, and I had been very fond of her. We were all very merry, talking of old times and of the wedding next day. Especially of the weather.

It was still raining when I went to bed that night. I turned on the radio and got the weather report for the last time: it was just the same. "Cloudy with showers, clearing in the late afternoon."

The late afternoon would be too late. The wedding was to take place at 10 A.M.

23

At the Kashikodokoro

AT five o'clock on the morning of April tenth it was still raining, but at six the sun was out and everything sparkled. I turned on the television set in my room at quarter past six to watch Michiko Shoda leave her home to go to Kuretakeryo, where she would be dressed for the wedding.

In the street outside the Shoda home in Gotanda people were gathering. A carful of ladies-in-waiting rolled up to the gate and they went inside; the car moved off and was followed by a long, square, high-topped limousine, with the Imperial chrysanthemum on the door, which came to a stop down the street and waited. The neighbors waved their paper flags, and a girl reporter with a pony tail and a microphone went about speaking to the bystanders at random and asking for their "impressions."

Presently the Shoda family appeared and stood in a row beside the gate, Mrs. Shoda slim in a formal dark kimono, with her head bowed. The entrance was one of those often seen in Tokyo with a sharp turn just inside the gate, so that the front door of the house was hidden behind the trees that showed over the top of the wall, but through the new small green leaves a stir could be seen, a flicker of white. Michiko Sama came into view, wearing a light dress with a full skirt, her mink stole, and a small light hat. She bowed to her younger sister and her brothers and then very low to her mother and father. The restraint of those low bows was poignant. The deep emotion held in leash, the sense of finality, the realization of destiny hovering over the scene, made a tension that reached even to a twenty-one-inch screen in a bedroom several miles away.

She turned away, facing the cameras while the car was being brought up. Behind her I saw her mother quietly brush away a tear at the corner of her eye with the tip of her finger—that classic gesture of the Japanese woman. The cameramen kept Michiko Sama standing there for several minutes to photograph over and over again the brave, rather watery smile that she summoned for them, and I wanted to plead, "Let her go! Oh, let her go!" At last she was allowed to climb into the back seat, Mrs. Makino took the jump seat facing her, and the car moved slowly away down the narrow street between the high gray walls.

The Crown Prince, I heard later, at his own house was also watching this scene on television.

At eight o'clock Dr. Koizumi came for me and we drove across Tokyo to call for Mrs. Matsudaira. The city was in gala attire, stands festooned with paper cherry blossoms, blown-up copies of photographs of the bride and groom in shop windows, flags everywhere. The weather, we exulted, was perfect: sunny and mild with a light breeze.

Mrs. Matsudaira, wearing a pale gray kimono with a quiet, small-figured obi, was bowed off at the door of her house by two or three maids. Her hair was gray now and she complained of a stiffness in her knees, but she was the same indomitable, wise, infinitely seasoned *grande dame* whom I had known and admired from my earliest days in Japan. The widow of Mr. Tsuneo Matsudaira, ambassador to the United States and to England, President of the House of Councilors, she was in demand for many public affairs, from the Peeresses' School Alumnae Association to the Foreign Office, which arranged for her to give lessons in Western etiquette to the wives of young diplomats. She had been chosen to teach Miss Shoda court procedure and she told me that the previous evening Michiko Sama had called her up with a bad case of jitters: she was nervous about today, afraid that she would make some mistake. "I told her, never mind. You will be just right. There is nothing to worry about."

It had been reported in the United States that Mrs. Matsudaira, who is Princess Chichibu's mother, was strongly opposed to the choice of a commoner for the Crown Prince's bride. If this was at any time true, it was no longer so: Michiko Shoda had won Mrs. Matsudaira as she had others by the quiet power of her personality. All the time that I was in Japan and in all the letters that I received, I never heard a breath of dissatisfaction from conservatives about the Crown Prince's bride, either of herself or her status. What criticism I did hear came entirely from the opposite direction, from young people who did not "believe in the Emperor system" and who objected to "spending so much money on a royal wedding."

We entered the Palace through Inui Mon, one of the main gates but on the side away from the center of downtown Tokyo. From the gate runs a long straight driveway between two rows of pines, maples and cherry trees, which provide beauty at any season of the year. The cherry blossoms were just over, but the tiny rosy buds of the maples were like flowers. On one side of the drive was an inner moat, on the other a green bank sloping up to a stone wall. Along the bank bushes of mountain kerria were fountains of golden bloom.

At the front entrance to the Imperial Household Building we were each given a slip of paper with a number and the Japanese character, *i*. Those who were designated *i*, I learned, were on the court side, those who were *ra* were of the government.

Every detail had been planned with the utmost care and things moved along without the slightest hitch. When later in the day I saw Mr. Minoru Kuroda of the Ceremonies Department and congratulated him, he was positively jubilant about the weather. They had spent all the day before, he told me, making an entirely new set of plans that could be substituted if the rain had continued.

We were escorted to a large waiting room where chairs clustering about round tables made several circles for friends to congregate. After a short time we were ushered outside to waiting buses, where we took seats bearing the numbers we held. The buses were new and shining and decorated with paper flowers, and each one had a bright little girl in a new uniform to help the guests on and off.

As each bus filled up it went off along the familiar road past the wall of the Fukiage garden and the entrance to Kaintei and O Bunko, past the greenhouses and the famous collection of dwarf trees, one of which is a thousand years old, past the Emperor's laboratory and the ricefield, to the entrance to the outer compound of the Kashikodokoro. Here we got out and walked across the grass under huge pine trees to big black and white marquees, the *i* group to the one on the left, the *ra* group to that on the right. Here again we waited pleasantly, drinking green tea in little blue and white china cups and talking to our friends.

There were few women: more on the *ra* side, where there were a number of women Diet members, than on the *i* side. In Japan wives are not invited to a function like this as a matter of course, as they are in Western countries. The women who were there, were there in their own right. Included with those who had some connection with the court were members of the Japan Academy of Arts and Sciences. I saw former chamberlains whom I had known in the past, Dr. Abe, president of Gakushuin, Mr. Tajima, the former grand steward, Mr. Tamon Maeda, a member of the Tokyo Friends Meeting, a former minister of education and now chairman of The Japanese National Commission of UNESCO, Dr. Chuji Tsuboi, the distinguished geophysicist who used to be the youngest member on the Crown Prince's Advisory Council and who now, somewhat to my surprise, was ten years older and heavier, and many others.

Between the two marquees under the trees was a permanent wooden building with a tiled roof and sliding glass doors, containing the waiting rooms for the Imperial Family. When the chief guests emerged from here, preceded by a *Go-Sendo*, or Honorable Leader of the Way, we all stood up to see them pass.

First came Prince Masahito, in morning coat and striped trousers, high silk hat and white gloves in his hand. He looks older than the Crown Prince now, for he wears spectacles and is a little heavier. It was hard for me to realize that this sober dignified gentleman had ever been the smiling child whom I had taught. When he and Princess Takako, aged eleven and nine, used to come to my house for a lesson and a tea party, it always amused me to watch their covert sparring for the preferred seat on the sofa and the complacent triumph of the winner. After him came the grown-up Princess Takako in a full-skirted white brocade dress and white hat, Princess Chichibu, Prince and Princess Takamatsu, Prince and Princess Mikasa. All of the Imperial princesses were in white gowns, some with a pale blue or a pale green cast. Court regulations of the Meiji Era stipulated that the ladies of the court should wear Western dress at court functions, and a much older law required the princesses to wear white when they approached the shrine. The other ladies who followed, the Crown Prince's elder sisters, now technically commoners, the ex-royal aunts and cousins, and members of the Shoda family all wore formal Japanese kimonos, dark, crested, and most beautifully patterned on the skirt.

After they had passed, the rest of us followed, two lines streaming from right and left, going under the tile-roofed gateway and separating just beyond it to go to the right and left in the inner courtyard.

The courtyard was rectangular. Opposite the gate was the main shrine, flanked by two smaller ones. The sides consisted of buildings that I can only describe as loggia: they had roofs and back walls but were open in front. Here several long rows of folding canvas stools had been set up.

The Imperial Family, the ex-princes and princesses and the Shodas (father and mother and eldest son and many relatives) sat in the section on the left nearest to the shrine, the rest of the *i* group followed. I was fortunate to have a place in the third row from the front, quite close to the shrine. The center of the court-yard, which was floored with fine white pebbles, was shaded by a roof supported on wooden pillars; beyond it the loggia on the opposite side was occupied first by a section of court musicians in white, then by the heads of government, Prime Minister Kishi, Foreign Minister Fujiyama, and the rest of the Cabinet, the Supreme Court, and then the Diet members. To the right of the gate as I looked toward it, were the television cameras and a few selected newspaper correspondents. Three Westerners had been included to represent the three wire services, AP, UPI and Reuters; they and I were the only non-Japanese present.

The parents of the bridegroom were not there. It was an old tradition that the Emperor and Empress should not be present at the wedding of their son, and there was a practical reason for not changing it. "The shrine is too small," the Crown Prince told me. I suppose it was unthinkable that they should sit among the congregation, even in the center, even in bigger and better chairs. Once again, as I had seen it happen so many times, these two loving and sensitive human beings were victims of their own majesty, compelled to smother their natural wishes and submit to a meaningless convention—or even, sometimes, the convenience of others. They were watching it all, I was told, on television.

For many minutes there was utter stillness in the Kashikodokoro.

The shrine, made of golden, unpainted wood, had a wide flight of steps up to the front door and was encircled by a high gallery. In one corner of the gallery knelt a priest in white, wearing a black lacquered silk headdress with a long stiff arching streamer which rose and fell gently in the breeze.

All those thousand people sat there in silence, the musicians with their instruments motionless in their hands. All one could hear was the twittering of sparrows in the trees, occasionally the hum of an airplane or the popping of a firecracker somewhere in distant Tokyo.

The silent attention suddenly quickened. A second priest with black headgear and the white, enormously wide stiffened trousers of the old picture scrolls, came around the far corner of the gallery, walking very slowly. This was Mr. Osanaga Kanroji, the chief ritualist of the shrine. Behind him—I caught my breath—was the Crown Prince.

He wore a similar black headdress and over his wide white trousers was a robe with flowing sleeves, made of silk brocade of a brilliant, soft, glowing shade of orange. He carried in his hand the piece of polished wood called a *shaku*, an emblem of authority somewhat like a scepter. From his waist in the back stretched a long white train. This was carried by his chamberlain, Mr. Toda, who wore purple trousers and a robe of intense, gleaming black. The contrast of the black with Prince Akihito's orange and the vermilion worn by Mr. Hamao, the chamberlain who followed bearing the Crown Prince's sword, was dramatic. The black and the vermilion represented different ranks, I learned later. The sword was of the Heian period and was 900 or 1,000 years old; it has been given to each Crown Prince in turn upon his investiture as Heir Apparent. It was sharp, Prince Akihito told me when I asked him, but not two-edged, as later swords were.

The Crown Prince, preceded by the priest, bowed low at the door of the shrine and went inside. The two chamberlains knelt on the gallery outside, Mr. Hamao still holding the sword on a level with his forehead, to signify respect.

Meanwhile another white-garbed priest had appeared, and following him came the bride.

Her black hair was stiffened with camellia oil to form two wings which framed her face; it was her own hair, not a wig, but a switch was attached behind to make the necessary long tresses, tied in three places, hanging nearly to the ground. On her forehead was a three-pronged gold ornament, the ancient equivalent of a tiara. Her robes, called the *juni hitoe*, meaning the twelve-layered garment, though actually not a dozen separate garments, were still numerous enough and heavy enough to weigh forty pounds.

The top one was a deep violet, decorated with medallions of several colors. Under it showed the edges of scarlet and green layers. Under them was the garment called the *nagabakama*, the long divided skirt. There is no equivalent for this in any other part of the world; it is unique. It is a pair of trousers, very wide and very long, so long that when the wearer stands inside them, her feet come to where the knees would be if a giant wore them. When she walks she shuffles along inside them at imminent risk of tripping and falling. To move forward smoothly in this rig without stumbling and still keep the rest of the trouser-legs trailing evenly behind, is extremely difficult. Kabuki actors can do it to perfection, but they have years of drilling and practice. Michiko Sama had two ladies-in-waiting in crimson robes, crouched at either side of her, hopping along bent almost double, moving the *nagabakama* forward and straightening it out behind.

In her turn, the bride bowed low at the entrance to the shrine and vanished inside. I could see the white robes of a priest but no more.

The priest on the gallery gave a sign and everybody stood up. I knew what was happening within the sanctuary, if I could not see. The priest gave to each of them a spray of the broad-leaved evergreen called the *sakaki*, the sacred tree, and having received it they bowed and gave it back. The Crown Prince then took a scroll from his belt, unrolled it and read the vows for both of them.

The breeze stirred the trees beyond the courtyard wall. There was no other sound. I could hear the Crown Prince's voice, clear and strong and earnest, from within. The words he read were in ancient Japanese. Translated, they were something like this: "On this auspicious day we shall respectfully conduct the ceremony of matrimony before the Kashikodokoro. We promise to live faithfully in conjugal harmony all our lives. For this we ask divine assistance." When his voice stopped, I chanced to look up at the sky. There in the deep blue overhead wheeled a flight of wild ducks.

Inside the shrine they sipped their sake, and at the first sip Michiko Shoda became Princess Michiko.

They came out as they had gone in, the Crown Prince first, Princess Michiko following, and they vanished around the corner of the shrine.

Prince Masahito walked out to the center of the courtyard and bowed toward the shrine. He went up three steps to the first landing and bowed again. As he bowed we all bowed with him. He was representing all of us; otherwise every one of the thousand guests would have had to go and bow their respectful thanks individually.

We went back through the towering gateway and walked across the grass under the trees to the waiting buses.

At the Imperial Household Building Dr. Koizumi and I were whisked away immediately to a room where thirty or forty reporters waited to get our "impressions."

"Mrs. Vining, will you compare it to a Western wedding, please?"

Without premeditation I heard myself saying, "Actually, it was more like a Quaker wedding than anything else." The absurdity of that struck me at once: a Quaker wedding with orange, scarlet and violet robes, white-clad priests, a sword-bearer and a shrine? Then I thought of the deep silence, that earnest young voice reading the vows without a priest's administering them, the simple words of the promises, and I knew that what I had said was true.

The cars and buses were streaming away from the Palace, but

we stayed on, for we were to watch the departure of the procession later and it seemed best not to attempt to struggle through the traffic jams and back again. As we sat in the waiting room eating our sandwiches and talking, I mentally followed the course of the newly married couple. First they went to the two subsidiary shrines to report their marriage and for this rite, I understood, there was ancient music. After that the Princess was taken back to Kuretakeryo where she would have the oil washed out of her hair with benzine, and have it reset and arranged in the pretty way she wore it daily; she would change the *juni hitoe* for a modern evening dress. She and the Prince would have a sandwich lunch, and then go up to one of the drawing rooms in the Imperial Household Building for their first audience as man and wife with the Emperor and Empress and the ritual drinking of sake. At two they would leave the Palace in the open state coach and drive in procession over a five-mile route to Tokiwamatsu.

Towards two o'clock the waiting room filled up again. Mr. Takatsukasa, Princess Kazuko's husband, came in with a friend, and then a group of the Shoda family, including the younger brother and sister who had not been eligible to be invited to the wedding ceremony. I was introduced to the parents. Mrs. Shoda looked beautiful and fragile and pale, as if she still had not quite recovered from her recent illness.

From the windows in the hall we saw the carriages getting ready in the driveway below: the beautifully lacquered and decorated one for the Prince and Princess, the plainer ones for the chamberlains and ladies-in-waiting. The horses for the police escort were coming up.

A great many people had been invited to see the procession start, enough to line both sides of the broad avenue that leads from the Imperial Household Building to the Double Bridge, the Palace gate which is used when the Emperor and Empress go in or out and on other special occasions. The avenue passes between the outer wall on one hand and on the other the great open space which is the site of the palace that was burned. Even in 1950 it had still shown the scars of rubble and broken foundations; now all that had been cleared away and there was a wide green lawn with a fountain in the center. The volunteer workers had done it all, Dr. Koizumi told me.

It had been Mrs. Motoko Hani's idea, very soon after the war, that volunteers from villages all over Japan might come and give two or three days' labor to tending the grounds of the Imperial Palace, now that armies of gardeners were no longer employed and there were arrears of wartime damage and neglect to be caught up. For the past thirteen years they had been coming faithfully, fifty or more at a time, the women with enveloping white aprons over their kimonos and *mompeis,* to work at weeding, raking, sweeping, digging, seeding, carting away; their reward the experience of being inside the Palace walls, of rendering loyal service, and of being thanked by Their Majesties in person.

An ample place near the upper one of the two bridges had been assigned to the volunteer workers to stand and watch the procession. Classmates of the Empress's, friends and relatives of the Shodas', former employees of the Imperial Household Agency, diplomats and their wives, and members and relatives of the Imperial Family stood three or four deep along the drive. The sun shone down or was briefly hidden by moving clouds and the breeze stirred the trees.

The first outriders appeared on prancing horses, then the Imperial carriage. The Crown Prince in formal evening clothes, and the Crown Princess in a white brocade gown and a stole to match, a diamond tiara on her dark hair, smiled happily and waved. In a moment they were gone and I was gazing at the backs of the two bodyguards, dressed in kneebreeches, ruffles and cocked hats, standing on the footmen's perch behind the carriage. The two other carriages followed swiftly and more men on beautiful horses. It seemed a very short procession, but in the plaza outside a number of bands, including the United States Marine band from Hawaii, were waiting to follow them.

The guests along the driveway now broke ranks and went streaming across the grass towards their cars, mingling and talking in the spring sunshine like wedding guests all over the world.

Late that afternoon Tané and Asako Tanaka came for me and we went to Hibiya Hall, where the Sankei Orchestra gave a concert to celebrate the wedding, and the Gakushuin Choir sang a song especially composed for the Crown Prince.

Tané and Asako had been watching television all day and were full of it. They told me about the parts that they had seen and I had not. When the Crown Prince and Princess Michiko first appeared in their modern evening clothes on their way to the carriage, he naturally preceded her—but he kept looking back over his shoulder to make sure that she was coming. When they got into the carriage, her bouffant skirts billowed up around her and he helped her to tuck them in. These two small, significant incidents I heard about many times during the next two or three days. People were delighted. Wasn't it natural, wasn't it charming of him, wasn't it *real*! This could not possibly have happened *before*.

There was one untoward incident in the day. Very little was said about it in Japan, but the Western newspapers played it up. As the procession was making its way through the crowded streets, a nineteen-year-old youth broke through the police lines, hurled two stones, one of which sailed close over Princess Michiko's head and the other made a dent in the side of the carriage, and tried to climb into the carriage. It was over almost before anyone realized what was happening. Princess Michiko flung herself across the Crown Prince's knees, the bodyguards pushed the youth away from the carriage, five policemen were on him at once and he was led off. The Crown Prince and Princess went on waving and smiling as if nothing had happened.

The boy, who was mentally unbalanced, had come to Tokyo

from his home in Nagano Prefecture. According to one story he had failed his entrance examinations to two universities and was embittered. Another story was that his school had burned down and the rebuilding had been delayed; that he wanted to pull the Crown Prince down to the ground and tell him that it was wrong to spend so much money on a wedding when some Japanese young people had no school. There was some speculation about what would be done to him. Before the war there were laws about lèse majesté with savage penalties, but nothing like that in the new Constitution. In the end he was given psychiatric treatment and sent home; because he was a minor his name was not released in Japan.

That evening the wedding photographs taken on Tuesday morning appeared everywhere. The Crown Prince in his robes with his *shaku* in his hand and the new Princess in hers, with her fan, stood side by side in front of a gold screen. Both were young, beautiful and dignified. I studied the picture of the Crown Prince with deep satisfaction. The costume, the pose, the raised *shaku*, were exactly the same as in the photograph taken for his Coming of Age ceremony six and a half years before: the face was different. In the earlier photograph he might have worn a mask, serious, poised, remote; in this one, there was a light in his face.

24

Festivities—and the Second
Wedding

THE day after the wedding
was, fortunately, the anniversary of the death of the Empress
Shoken, the wife of the Crown Prince's great-grandfather, and
so the bride and groom had one day in which to rest and be alone
together before the post-wedding formalities began: the receptions, a civic mass meeting, and the trip to Ise, which was a
ritual duty and could hardly be called a honeymoon.

The first reception on Monday, the thirteenth, with Their
Majesties as hosts and the Prime Minister present, was the most
important. Two hundred of the outstanding social, political and
diplomatic figures in the country were invited to a formal luncheon. There were speeches and toasts. The next day the members
of the Diet were invited. Because of the larger number, they
were served luncheon in three rooms and Their Majesties and
the Crown Prince and Princess went to each room in turn and
bowed.

On Thursday, the sixteenth, came the party referred to as "the
intimate one"; at this the Crown Prince and Princess were themselves the hosts, and Their Majesties did not appear. This was
the one to which I was invited. The guests were friends of the

Crown Prince's and of the Shodas': former teachers, chamberlains, relatives, family friends and business associates.

Once more we gathered in a big reception room to wait and waiting met our friends. Esther Rhoads, R. H. Blyth and I were the three Westerners, all former tutors of the Crown Prince. Esther Rhoads, Principal of the Friends Girls' School and American Friends Service Committee representative in Tokyo, also goes to the Palace once a week for Her Majesty's English lesson. Mr. Blyth teaches at the University of Tokyo and other schools and writes scholarly books on Zen Buddhism and Japanese culture. Mr. and Mrs. Goto, whom I had met at the P.E.N. Congress, I was glad to see again. Mrs. Goto had been teaching *waka*-writing to Princess Michiko and reported that she was extremely gifted in that as in so many other things. Mr. Sumikura, Mr. Sakaki, and Mr. Shimizu, all of whom had been the Crown Prince's chamberlains when I first went to Japan were now, respectively, in business, in the law, and in education, Mr. Shimizu having succeeded Miss Kawai as Principal of Keisen School. Mrs. Takaki, the Empress's English interpreter and mistress of the robes, and Mrs. Kawai, Her Majesty's French interpreter, joined Esther Rhoads and me.

When the Crown Prince and Princess came in at the farther of the two doors, we all stood up and formed a great semicircle around the long room. The Crown Prince, in morning clothes, and the Princess, in kimono, then went around the circle, bowing to each separate person in turn. Some of the guests gave their names, others the Crown Prince recognized at once and presented to his wife, otherwise nothing was said until they reached the three Westerners, with whom they shook hands and said a personal word or two. When they had bowed low a hundred times, they went out through the second door and on to another drawing room, where a hundred friends of the Shodas waited to bow and be bowed to. Two hundred low bows in succession, I reflected, is strenuous physical exercise—and the Crown Prince and Princess

Michiko had already been that morning to a big civic rally at the new Metropolitan Gymnasium, where they had had to stand in a drizzle of rain to receive the congratulations of the governor of Tokyo, listen to speeches, and respond to the banzais of several thousand people.

While the second group was being greeted we moved on into the banquet room and found the places assigned to us. The main table stretched across one end of the room and from it at right angles like the prongs of a fork were four tables holding fifty people each.

My place was next to the main table with Esther Rhoads beside me and Mrs. Takaki opposite. It is always a joy to be with Mrs. Takaki. I had met her the day I had my first audience with the Emperor and Empress and the Crown Prince nearly thirteen years ago, and had seen her regularly twice a week or oftener during my four years in Japan. Whenever I saw Her Majesty, Mrs. Takaki was there, and I saw her many other times besides. I ate my first sukiyaki at her hospitable house and went to many another delightful party there. A widow, she had lived in the United States during her married life, and two at least of her daughters had been born there. She had hosts of American friends, both in the United States and among the Occupation in Tokyo, and she has made an incalculable contribution to international understanding and friendship. Woman of the world and of the court though she is, she has a most endearing simplicity, spontaneity and warmth, as well as impregnable calm and poise. Her face is of that type, in any country, that I think of as the pansy face, wide and lovely with a serenity touched with merriment. She too was one of those who gave lessons in court ways to Michiko Shoda during the months of preparation.

After the Shodas and their friends, among whom I saw the Yoshitaka Mikimotos, with whom I had had many happy meetings, had come in and taken their places, the two eldest children of Prince and Princess Mikasa, a girl of thirteen and a boy of eleven, were led in and seated at the head table, opposite to where the Crown Prince and Princess Michiko would sit.

I had met them in 1957 when I had had dinner at the Mikasas' house. Prince Mikasa is the Emperor's youngest brother, and the most original and precedent-breaking of all the Empress Dowager's sons. He and his wife live in a simple, comfortable house, and they have kept their five children with them. Prince Mikasa drives his own car, a small Japanese model. He is an enthusiastic folk-dancer and a leading spirit in a society that promotes folk-dancing in Japan. During the war he was an officer in the Japanese army; after the war he studied Biblical history and Hebrew literature at the University of Tokyo and now teaches at Tokyo Christian College for Women. He is the author of at least one book and a number of magazine articles, in which he expresses his ideas freely. He has been quoted as writing, "There can be no war for righteousness now or in the future. . . . I say this as a confession of a soldier who once went to war believing it was a war for righteousness."

That rainy evening in September at the Mikasas' house we sat in the living room before dinner talking, when there was a peremptory rattle at the doorknob and in marched a very small boy, perhaps a little over two. A woman's voice murmured, before the door was shut behind the child, that he wanted to see the company. He climbed confidently onto his father's knee and offered us some affable remarks in baby talk. A little later the four older children came in sedately in the order of their ages, Yoshiko, eleven, first, followed by three others, two years apart in age; they all shook hands politely and said "How do you do?" After dinner Princess Mikasa showed us the color movies that she had taken when she and her husband had visited Ceylon a few months earlier. Evidently even the wedding reception of their Imperial cousin had not kept the Mikasa children from school that morning, for they came in wearing their dark blue serge uniforms and heavy black school shoes.

After they were seated, other, older, Imperial cousins who were to sit at the head table came in, and finally the Crown Prince and Princess. Everybody rose and the Crown Prince read a short speech of welcome—while the footmen all stood along the walls with reverently bowed heads. A toast was proposed and drunk and three banzais were decorously shouted.

We sat down and began to eat.

The food served at all of the receptions was exactly the same, and I had heard something about the preparation of it. Akiyama San, the Emperor's chef and the head of the Cooking Department in the Imperial Household, had had eighty cooks working under him in big tents set up in the Palace grounds. The procuring of a thousand *tai* (sea bream) all exactly the same size had been a problem. Then the preparing of some of the dainties with extra salt and others with extra sugar, so that they would keep until the guests, even those who lived far from Tokyo, got them home to share with their families, also required care and thought. Mrs. Takaki had seen Akiyama San after the first of the luncheons, and he was rejoicing that everything had gone off so well.

At each place there was a beautifully arranged wooden box, fastened with red and white silk cords and tassels, containing a full meal: a broiled *tai*, decorated with a gold quill; several slices of pink and white *kamoboko* (a smooth fish sausage which looks like the Necco wafers of my childhood but is rubbery in substance); slices of wild duck ground and pressed (this was sweet); salmon galantine (salty); sweet chestnuts, and bean paste. This box was to take home. What we ate there was on the tray in front of us; raw fish, red rice (congratulatory), soup, green tea and sake. Beside each place was a beautiful little round silver box decorated with phoenixes and the Imperial chrysanthemum, a box of cigarettes, a box of pink and white court cakes (pretty to look at but dry as dust) and a white *furoshiki*, in which to tie it all up and take it home.

Where I sat I was directly opposite Mrs. Shoda, two tables dis-

tant. Like Mrs. Takaki and others, the parent Shodas had been
invited to all the receptions. I could not help seeing and being
touched by Mrs. Shoda's expression as she sat eating little or
nothing and watching her daughter: there was in her face a look
of such tenderness and wonder.

After the party was over Dr. Koizumi came for me to take me
to call on the Prince and Princess. They had already got back
when we reached Tokiwamatsu and were expecting us in the upstairs sitting room. The conversation, after my congratulations
and thanks for the party, rambled easily and came to the subject
of kimonos, and obis, how tight they are and how uncomfortable.
Princess Michiko confessed that she had seldom worn kimono
before her engagement but had worn it a great deal since, because the Japanese people liked it and it photographed well.

"Why don't you go and change?" suggested her thoughtful
husband and with an "If you'll excuse me, I think I will," she
slipped away. A few minutes later she was back again, in a pretty
blue wool suit.

They were going to leave for Ise the next morning, where they
would formally report their marriage to the Imperial ancestors at
the Grand Shrine. From Ise they would go to the mausoleum of
the Emperor Jimmu at Umebi, on a mountain near Nara. The
Emperor Jimmu is officially considered to have been the founder
of the Japanese empire, and of the Imperial dynasty, in 660 B.C.
—but, the Crown Prince had said to me the night I dined with
him, "We don't really know whether the Emperor Jimmu existed
or not."

The three-day trip to Ise and Umebi would be a taxing one. All
along the way—and it was a six- or seven-hour train journey—
at railroad stations and along the railroad tracks as well, loyal
Japanese would be standing to greet their Crown Prince and get
a first glimpse of their new Crown Princess. At Ise itself the ceremonial would be carried out in every detail according to ancient
ritual, which involved the changing of clothes at different stages

and a complicated order of approach to the shrines with bows and prayers. It was considered important that all who might be concerned for the ancient prestige of the Imperial Family should see that Princess Michiko, though born a commoner, could carry out the prescribed ritual as perfectly as any noble's daughter.

After they returned from Ise I was to see them once again and to hear about the trip. Though they had been tired when they reached Tokyo they revived after a night's rest and told about their experiences with zest and humor.

"The tunnels and the bridges were the best part of it," said the Crown Prince, "though on one bridge we passed near a boat full of people and had to wave and bow even on the bridge."

I asked the Princess if she had been able to enjoy the beauty of the setting at Ise, the great trees and the crystal pure river rushing over its stones.

"All I saw of Ise," she sighed, "was the back of His Highness's collar!"

Later in the month there would be a party at Tokiwamatsu for all the classmates of both the Crown Prince and Crown Princess, a gathering of Gakushuin and Seishin together; Mr. and Mrs. Shoda would dine at Tokiwamatsu one evening and another evening Princess Michiko would take her husband home with her to dinner with her parents—another precedent shattered in a heart-warming way. Early in May, after various other affairs, they would go to Hayama for a week of relaxation at the seashore—though whether they escaped public interest enough to be really free there I never heard.

From Tokiwamatsu on the sixteenth I went on to have tea with Princess Chichibu. Mrs. Koizumi, Tané and Mrs. Matsumoto, wife of the director of International House, were also there. Since the death of Prince Chichibu in 1952, Princess Chichibu has spent most of the year in Tokyo, returning to Gotemba just for the summers. Her house in the Akasaka Palace grounds has been restored—or part of it. It was a curious thing that the big brick and timber Tudor mansion in which she and Prince Chichibu once lived, was completely demolished in the bombing, but the small Japanese end of it, wood and tile and paper, survived. It is in this part, with a new entrance, and a drawing room and dining room added, that Princess Chichibu now lives. The garden with a lawn stretching away to trees is lovely; roses bloom in beds near the house, and at the edge of the woods pheasants can be seen stepping through the grass.

The Dolls' Festival, which normally comes the third of March, is celebrated by the lunar calendar in the court and so comes later. Princess Chichibu's gorgeous array of dolls and all their fascinating appointments, chests of clothes, lamps, dishes, and the like, were still in place on the red-baize-covered tiers of shelves set up in a room opening into the living room. At the top were the Emperor and Empress dolls, seated, wearing costumes similar to those the Crown Prince and Princess had worn for their wedding, and below them arranged in an unalterable order were the ministers of the Right and of the Left (the former in vermilion robes, the latter in black, like the chamberlains attending the Crown Prince at the wedding), the ladies-in-waiting, the musicians—in short, the whole Japanese court in miniature. Because she was an Imperial princess, her set must be accurate in every detail, and it was interesting to hear Princess Chichibu explain the significance of small differences that the uninitiated do not even notice. In the traditional way we had tea in front of the dolls, with suitable delicacies passed in lacquer boxes.

Bob Togasaki's wedding took place on Sunday, the nineteenth, at the I.C.U. church—an appropriate place, since his father was president of the board of trustees of the university and his bride, Fumiko Tomoyama, had for the past five years been secretary to the Humanities Department. By that time I had moved from International House to I.C.U. and was again enjoying a vacant apartment in the Maple Grove House.

It was another glorious spring day. Earlier in the day some of the faculty ladies had decorated the church with knots of white carnations and ferns at the ends of the pews, a great burst of scarlet anthuriums on the console of the organ below the chancel, and on the altar, under the gold cross, dazzling white calla lilies. The most daring and effective bit of decoration, on either side of the calla lilies, was a pair of spread fans, gold and silver.

A few days earlier I had seen a wedding in the Imperial court, now I was to see a Japanese Christian wedding.

The bridegroom, best man and an usher came in from the vestry and stood solemnly waiting. The bridesmaids in pink dresses carrying orchids walked slowly down the aisle, and then the bride, a lovely, slender girl with a dimple in her right cheek, wearing a long-sleeved, high-necked white gown with a short veil over her face, came in on her father's arm, carrying a white prayer book with a spray of white orchids.

The service began with a hymn sung by the congregation and a Bible reading. After the double-ring ceremony, when the two had been pronounced man and wife, Bob introduced an innovation startling in Japan. Gently he lifted his bride's veil, arranged it carefully, and reverently kissed her brow. Nobody (except Fumiko) knew beforehand that he was going to do it; everyone was surprised and I think most were charmed; if some of the elders were shocked they did not show it.

After another hymn and the benediction, the guests, exclaiming over the impressiveness of the service and the beauty of the bride, walked across the campus under the trees to the dining hall, which has a handsome room for special functions.

Along both sides tables were spread with fruit punch, grape juice (it is one of the marks of Japanese Christians that they do not drink or serve alcoholic beverages), sandwiches and cakes. At one end of the room the wedding cake towered on a table with a gold screen behind it; at the other end another table held the register for the guests to sign and a flock of decorative gold and silver paper cranes.

After the usual slow motion of the receiving line, the serious work of the reception began. Standing together against the gold screen the bride and groom heard speeches by Dr. Yuasa and Dr. Abe, a prayer by Mr. Iino, the minister who had married them, and the proposal of a toast by another distinguished friend. Their health was drunk in grape juice, and Fumiko with Bob's help cut the first piece of cake. While the guests were eating cake, milling about and talking—I was delighted to have a chance to talk to many of my friends whom otherwise I could not have seen in so short a visit—Fumiko disappeared to change her dress.

She returned very soon in a salmon-pink kimono patterned with flowers and birds, and she and Bob sat down behind the table at the other end of the room, the microphone was moved near them, and the speeches continued for at least an hour and a half. Dr. Kanda, the chairman of the Humanities Department, a charming gentleman who has an Oxford accent famous throughout English-speaking circles in Japan, gracefully bewailed the loss to the Humanities Department in the marriage of its secretary; Dean Hinoto of I.C.U., the editor of the *Japan Times*, a colleague from Mr. Tomoyama's business, two or three family friends on both sides, a classmate of Fumiko's, a classmate of Bob's, all delivered congratulations, the personal histories of bride and groom, reminiscences of the past and advice for the future in an affectionate mixture of humor and seriousness. I was called on last and could afford to be brief, for the best thing that I had to say was to deliver the good wishes that the Crown Prince and Princess Michiko had entrusted to me when I had seen them three days before.

The young Togasakis rose and bowed punctiliously both at the beginning and at the end of each speech, and throughout the entire ordeal by oratory Fumiko remained attentive and responsive, her dimple in evidence. Bob, manlike, began to look fagged near the end.

At last the bride's father thanked everybody briefly and the young couple were free to depart. We all crowded around the car and waved them off—no rice, no old shoes.

They had a honeymoon before them and three months in Japan, then they would return to Cornell, where a research assistantship was waiting for Bob. "The number-one luxury for a graduate student," he told me, smiling broadly, "is a wife. Number two is a car." I should be seeing them both in the United States, and I was glad.

Now the two weddings for which I had come a long distance had been beautifully accomplished under sunny skies. I was deeply happy about both young men, the choices they had made, the new strength and fresh purpose with which they faced their lives.

The next day I would leave for home.

25

Farewell

ON the day I left Japan the Koizumis gave a last luncheon for me. It was a very distinguished group of older men, and the wives of some of them, who gathered in the lovely room that Mrs. Koizumi had designed. The conversation was warm, light and sparkling, still in the mood of happiness evoked by the wedding, but any one of those men could have talked profoundly and brilliantly about Japan, her history, her problems and her relationship to the modern world.

The oldest among them was my dear old friend, Mr. Yamanashi, gentle and a little removed from the world, deeply happy about the marriage of his Prince and rejoicing that I had been able to be there for it.

Dr. and Mrs. Yoshishige Abe, like so many husbands and wives, had come to look a little alike; both were generously built but not heavy, both calm, open, with a look of perpetual youth. Dr. Abe, with his unruly white hair and short white moustache, reminds one a little of Sir Wilfred Grenfell. A philosopher and an authority on Spinoza, he has been a college professor all his adult life, with a brief excursion into government: in 1946 he was minister of education, and he was a member of the House of Peers at the time of the adoption of the new Constitution and was chairman of the Constitution Revision Committee. Since 1948 he has been president of the Gakushuin School and University. He is a man of strong and independent opinions, which he is outspoken and fearless in expressing. As a middle-school student he memorized all of Patrick Henry's "Give me liberty or give me death" speech and in 1952 he told an audience at Columbia University that "Man's very essence is freedom."

Mr. Michiji Tajima, a banker, became director of the Imperial Household Agency in 1948. Five years later he retired, exhausted, having seen the Imperial Family through two weddings, two funerals, the Crown Prince's Coming of Age ceremony and his trip abroad. Since his retirement he has resumed his hobby, the study of the Chinese classics, and he became the director of a new and then struggling firm making transistor radios—those tiny Sony radios that are now sold widely in Japan and the United States. In his youth he was one of "Dr. Nitobe's boys," that happy band of disciples of Dr. Inazo Nitobe, most of whom have become liberal or religious leaders in Japan. He is a man of uncompromising integrity and high standards of behavior, candid and sincere. To some people, I am told, his austerity is frightening, but I have found him always most lovable, though he has not hesitated to scold me—kindly—on occasion.

Judge Kotaro Tanaka, whose charming wife is Dr. Koizumi's niece, is the chief justice of the Supreme Court. He was the youngest of the men there that day. Slender and sensitive, penetrating and flexible in his thinking, a Christian, widely traveled in Europe and America, he is one of the men most likely to exert a lasting influence in the Japan of the future. He also has lectured on the new Constitution both to the Crown Prince and to Princess Michiko.

In the days when I used to go to diplomatic and Occupation dinner parties in Tokyo, someone was sure to have said by the time dessert came on, "The Japanese women are wonderful but I don't like the men," or "The men are another race altogether." Much as I endorse the first half of that cliché, I could never agree

with the second part of it. When I think of the older Japanese
men whom I have known, the Emperor, Dr. Koizumi, those who
were there at lunch that day and many others besides, and of the
young men whom I have watched grow up and mature, I can
never generalize about "Japanese men": I can only see them as
individuals for whom I entertain respect and friendship. Some of
them may be a bit tyrannical in their homes—but who would
ever consider an American woman an unprejudiced judge of that?

Early the next morning I was twenty-four thousand feet above
the Pacific Ocean in a plane hurried along by the jet stream, wide
awake and thinking about Japan.

The most striking change I had seen in 1957 was the prosperity
everywhere evident, the new buildings, cars, restaurants, theaters,
stores, the well-dressed confident people. In 1959 it was that
there were fewer babies: fewer toddlers in the streets, fewer
babies on their mothers' backs, fewer pregnant women. Japan
had gone vigorously to work on her population problem—at a
price, for I am told that the number of abortions is extremely
high. In spite of the lowered birthrate, however, Japan's population continues to rise. The efficient Public Health and Welfare
section of the Occupation, which stopped typhus dead in its
tracks and greatly decreased the incidence of tuberculosis, and the
Japanese health agencies since then, have lowered the death rate
in proportion. Tokyo is now the largest city in the world. The
population of all Japan, dangerously high before the war at
70,000,000, is now 93,000,000 and rising.

The land on which those people must live is not stretchable.
Former overseas outlets in Korea, Manchuria, the islands of the
Pacific, are now closed. The four islands of Japan still consist
chiefly of mountains, beautiful but unproductive; only fifteen per
cent of the land is arable. To feed her people she must import
food. To pay for the food she must export manufactured goods.

To manufacture goods she must import raw materials. To pay for the raw materials . . . So the inexorable spiral goes.

Japan is the most highly industrialized nation in the Orient. Her trades union movement is growing. She is making for export now not paper novelties and celluloid trifles but heavy machinery, cameras, field glasses, radios, fine silks and porcelains; she is the greatest ship-building country in the world. She must have markets if she is to live.

Other countries, which also must have markets to live, or if not to live, to prosper, are increasingly uneasy. They complain that Japanese competition is unfair, that she can undersell them because of her low standard of living, her low wages.

The Japanese standard of living is the highest in the Orient. It is not comparable to ours because it is different. The Japanese do not, as many Western writers have said, "live on a handful or two of rice a day," but they do arrange their houses so that they can live in an ordered way in half the space that we require; they do not have central heating; they do not waste.

I thought of the dormitories for workers in industry about which I had read indignant articles in American periodicals before the war. In 1950 I had an opportunity to see some of those dormitories, and the reality was not as I had imagined it, not because it was better or worse but because it represented a wholly different way of living and of looking at things.

Dining one evening at the British Embassy, I had sat beside Mr. Robert Amis, who had been for three years head of the Labor Affairs Division of the Occupation. We talked about Japan and the gaps in my knowledge of her people, and he suggested that I learn something about the working people by accompanying his assistant, Miss Golda Stander, on an inspection trip to Kansai. Accordingly when the spring vacation rolled round in March, off we went.

Visiting the Sumitomo Rolling Mills, in Osaka, which employed a few hundred women, mostly in minor clerical positions,

I asked to see the women's dormitory. Young girls were recruited in country villages, I had read, their families were paid a lump sum for their work for a period of several years; until that sum was worked out they were not free to leave their jobs but must live in company-provided dormitories, sometimes so crowded that shifts of girls slept in the same beds.

The new labor laws after the war, I was now informed, had set up safeguards against the return of such conditions. The recruiting system had been abolished. Girls must come from the general region of the factories. Wages must be paid to the girls themselves as they earned them, not to their families in advance. Dormitories must meet certain conditions: for example, a minimum of one and a half *tatami* in the bedrooms must be allotted each girl. That is, no more than six girls could occupy a ten-mat room (twelve by fifteen feet).

Our request to see the dormitory was not expected and met with some consternation. Miss Stander quietly insisted, however, and we were taken to it with apologies for the conditions which in their present difficulties they had not had time to improve. It was about half a mile away and the entrance was through a badly bombed building which was still not cleared up. Holes in the floor were loosely covered with planks and on both sides of the passageway the windowless shells of rooms were filled with twisted wires and piles of rubble. What had the building been used for, before? I asked.

It had been a hospital, they told me. I was silent, remembering the outrage I had felt when I read of hospitals and schools in Europe destroyed by Nazi bombs.

When we reached the part where some two hundred girls were living, we found conditions very much better than the approach suggested. The dining room was stark and grim, with plain bare tables and chairs, stained walls and a cold and clammy atmosphere, but it was clean. There was a living room, also bare and dark and cold. The bedrooms for the girls had little wooden tablets on the door jambs bearing the names of the occupants, so that we could tell how many were in each room and see that there was no overcrowding. The *tatami* was clean. There was a cupboard for each girl, and each room had its *tokonoma* with an arrangement of fresh flowers. In some rooms there was a charcoal brazier. I saw a sewing machine. The bathrooms were primitive but well kept and clean. The kitchen, dark like all Japanese kitchens, had a well-scrubbed look, and fresh spinach was being prepared for supper.

The girls paid nothing for their room rent and only a thousand yen a month for their three daily meals, which provided 2,300 calories; the management contributed twice what the girls paid.

The next day, when we visited two printing and dyeing works, where cotton was printed for India, the South Sea Islands and Africa, we saw a model dormitory that had come undamaged through the war.

There was an attractive social room with bookcases and a piano and chairs upholstered with bright materials made in the factory. The bedrooms were fifteen-mat rooms (fifteen by eighteen feet) occupied by from six to nine girls. Each room had a charcoal brazier. The bathrooms were big and modern and there was a sewing room. There was also a well-equipped infirmary.

Food for the workers was served in a large central dining room which we saw just at lunchtime. The room was decorated with an artificial cherry tree at one end and a little shrine at the other. Lunch consisted of a large bowl of very substantial soup thick with meat and vegetables, and two big rolls. Rice was provided for breakfast and dinner.

They worked from eight to five, with an hour for lunch and a fifteen minute rest period in the morning.

For room, food, medical care and lessons, such as sewing, flower arrangement and tea ceremony, the girls paid 3,000 yen a month, out of a basic salary of about 7,000 yen (about $20). Most of them stayed two or three years and then went home to be married. The experience of working in the factory and living in the dormitory was a sort of substitute for boarding school, and the accommodations in the dormitory which we saw were almost certainly better than what they had at home.

It is a system that would be intolerable to us, but in an entirely different frame it is reasonably satisfactory to the workers. It fits, moreover, into the larger pattern of life in Japan where all salaries are low—the young banker whom Princess Takako is to marry is reported to have a salary of $36 a month—and a rate of pay in industry to equal that of workers in competing countries would throw the entire economic machinery of Japan out of gear.

I don't know what the solution is. Or rather, I do know, and I know too that it will be immediately branded as impractical and utopian. The only workable answer is generosity, self-restraint, understanding and cooperative planning on the part of all the countries as a group working for the good of all, not as separate nations working for selfish advantage.

Japan has an army now. It is very little in evidence, however; I saw more of the new German army in four days in Germany in 1957 than I did of the Japanese "Defense Force" in six weeks.

According to the Constitution it does not exist. Article Nine states that Japan renounces war and the implements of war as an instrument of national policy. There is much discussion as to whether that article was imposed by the Occupation or whether it was originally suggested by the former prime minister, Mr. Shidehara. The first is certainly true and the second may very well be true also. At any rate the Constitution was accepted by the Japanese and is now basic law.

It was a great shock to the nation when the United States suddenly veered around and demanded that the Japanese develop an army. It was disguised at first as a police force, but the disguise could not be long maintained.

Circumstances had radically changed: the Cold War had begun, the Korean War cost many American lives, it seemed to Americans inevitable that the Japanese should have the means of defending themselves.

To many Japanese, however, it seemed glaringly evident that the United States had been acting throughout in self-interest and not, as she had insisted, in the interests of peace and democracy. First she had disarmed Japan to get rid of a competing power in the Pacific; then, frightened by the menace of Russia, she had whirled around, "with an eye on Japan's manpower," and insisted upon Japan's rearming in order to have a military ally whose troops could be used if war should spread in Asia.

The new Japanese army is opposed by many Japanese for a variety of reasons. Some believe, with Dr. Abe, "that to be armed is to anticipate war, and to anticipate war is to be led into war." Some think that the rearming of Japan will awaken fear in other countries of Asia and bring about attacks upon her. Some argue that rearmament would undermine Japan's shaky economy and lower the standard of living, thus making her vulnerable to Communism. The Communists, however, greatly prefer an unarmed Japan, possibly because they think her capitulation to Communism would be quicker.

Meanwhile there are American military bases in Japan for the defense of the Pacific. These are popular with some for the revenue they bring in and the work they provide; not long ago the Japanese workers on one base actually went on strike as a protest against the reported imminent removal of the base.

The bases are disliked by others because of the agricultural land that they absorb and the promiscuous relationships that follow any army. The presence of a large group of better-fed and better-paid aliens in any country provides endless occasions for friction. But most of all, I think, it is felt that the American forces are there not as equals but as a remnant of the Occupation and its attitudes.

The Japanese, it seems to me, live not so much by rigid standards of right and wrong, justice and injustice, as by concepts of what is appropriate in given situations. In war they fight like demons; in defeat and occupation, they keep quiet and cooperate; in peace, they expect to behave in a manner appropriate to sovereign nations, to make their own decisions in conferences of equals. It is of the greatest importance that we respect this self-respect; that we do not regard Japan as a satellite and that we give her no grounds for supposing that we do.

There are many in Japan who, sincerely deploring the militarism that swept Japan into a disastrous war, believe that she should develop an army of her own, not merely in response to our proddings but because as an independent nation she must be responsible for her own defense. Dr. Koizumi in a letter to me in 1951 wrote:

"I am no pessimist. I don't think it impossible that the present state of an armed peace of the world can be kept on indefinitely, till mankind is a bit wiser and knows how to understand each other better. . . . Still there is the danger of small local fires to spread to a world conflagration, of which the Korean incident threatened to be an example. The North Korean aggression was not provoked by the strengthening of armament on the part of South Korea (or of America) but invited by their careless-and-defenselessness. This object lesson should be most carefully studied not only by Japanese but by the whole free world. . . . In my opinion (you may disagree with me) no independent nation on the whole globe has or should have the right to ask for the defense of her territory at the sacrifice of other nations' blood without shedding a single drop of her own."

I find what Dr. Koizumi said comforting and intellectually reasonable, and yet my own deepest conviction is that the possession of arms brings war closer, and that we can avoid war only by an overwhelming vision of the power of love, and by a drastic doing-away with all nuclear and bacterial weapons before someone who is temporarily insane through drunkenness, jealousy or some other passion presses the button that will set in motion total destruction. But I am profoundly thankful that neither political nor economic decisions are in my hands, and I have the greatest sympathy for the hard-pressed and devoted men in positions of overburdening responsibility who are trying to steer their countries and the world through the rocks and shoals of today's crises.

Depressed, I turned my thoughts to a happier subject—as many Japanese, who know far better than I the vise in which they are gripped, must also be doing. I thought of the Crown Prince and of his marriage.

It is always moving to see two young people pledge their faith to each other and begin to build a new home. It is deeply satisfying to see a young man who is dear to one win the girl of his heart and to know that she is the right girl for him, worthy of his devotion, who will be a help to him. But there was still more to this marriage.

As the Emperor is the symbol of the State, the Crown Prince is the symbol of the young people of Japan. In choosing a wife who is herself "one of them," he brings the throne close to the people as it has never been before in all its history. In themselves, the handsome, intelligent young Prince and his lovely warm-hearted wife represent the best of the old and the best of the new in Japanese life. They stand for the future and, perhaps, a new era.